I THINK
I'LL MAKE IT

A TRUE STORY OF LOST
AND FOUND

KAT HURLEY

Manor Park Press
BROOKLYN, NY

Manor Park Press
1497 Carroll Street #37
Brooklyn, NY 11213
www.kathurley.com

Printed in the United States of America
Designed by Joel Friedlander & partners

Ordering Information:
Quantity sales. Special discounts are available on quantity purchases by
corporations, associations, and others. For details, contact the "Special
Sales Department" at the address above.

I Think I'll Make It/ Kat Hurley. -- 1st ed.
ISBN 978-0-9897939-1-9
ISBN 978-0-9897939-0-2 (ebook)

CONTENTS

For My Two Catherines

I learned this, at least, by my experiment: that if one advances confidently in the direction of his dreams, and endeavors to live the life which he has imagined, he will meet with a success unexpected in common hours.

—Henry David Thoreau, Walden: Or, Life in the Woods

AUTHOR'S NOTE

To write this book, I relied heavily on archived emails and journals, researched facts when I thought necessary, consulted with some of the people who appear in the book, and called upon my own memory, which has a habitual tendency to embellish, but as it turns out, there wasn't much need for that here. Events in this book may be out of sequence, a handful of locations were changed to protect privacy, many conversations and emails were re-created, and a few names and identifying characteristics have been changed.

PREFACE

It was hardly a secret growing up that psychologists predicted I would never lead a truly happy and normal life. Whether those words were intended for my ears or not seemed of little concern, given the lack of disclaimer to follow. There was no telling what exceedingly honest bits of information would slip through the cracks of our family's filtration system of poor Roman Catholic communication. I mean, we spoke all the time but rarely *talked*. On the issues at least, silence seemed to suit us best, yet surprising morsels of un-sugarcoated facts would either fly straight out of the horse's mouth or trickle their way down through the boys until they hit me, the baby.

I was five when I went to therapy. Twice. On the second visit, the dumb lady asked me to draw what I felt on a piece of plain construction paper. I stared at the few crayons next to the page when I told her politely that I'd rather not. We made small talk instead, until the end of the hour when she finally stood up, walked to the door and invited my grandma in. They whispered some before she smiled at me and waved. I smiled back, even if she was still dumb. I'm sure it had been *suggested* that I go see her anyway, because truth be known, psychologists were a "bunch of quacks," according to my grandma. When I said I didn't want to go back, nobody so much as batted an eye.

And that was the end of that.

∞

When I draw up some of my earliest most vivid memories, what I see reminds me of an old slide projector, screening crooked, fuzzy images at random. In the earliest scenes, I am lopsidedly pigtailed, grass stained, clothes painfully clashing. In one frame I am ready for my first day of preschool in my bright red, pill-bottomed bathing suit, standing at the bottom of the stairs where my mom has met me to explain, through her contained laughter, that a carpool isn't anything near as fun as it sounds. In another, I am in the living room, turning down the volume on my mom's Richard Simmons tape so I can show her that, all on my own yet only with a side-puckered face, I'd learned how to snap. In one scene, I'm crouched down in the closet playing hide-and-seek, recycling my own hot Cheerio breath, patiently waiting to be found, picking my toes. Soon Mom would come home and together we'd realize that the boys weren't *seeking* (babysitting) me at all, they'd simply gone down the street to play with friends.

I replay footage of the boys (Ben and Jack), pushing me in the driveway, albeit *unintentionally*, toward the busy road on my first day with no training wheels, and (don't worry, I tattled) *intentionally* using me as the crash-test dummy when they sent me flying down the stairs in a laundry basket. I have the scene of us playing ice hockey in the driveway after a big ice storm hit, me proudly dropping the puck while my brothers—Stanley Cup serious—faced off.

I call up the image of me cross-legged on my parents' bed, and my mom's horrified face when she found me—scissors in hand—thrilled with what she referred to as my new "hacked" do. That same bed, in another scene, gets hauled into my room when it was no longer my parents', and my mom, I presume, couldn't stand to look at it any longer. I can still see the worry on her face in those days and the disgust on his. I see the aftermaths of the few fights they couldn't help but have us witness.

Most of the scenes are of our house at the top of the hill on McClintock Drive, but a few are of Dad's townhouse in Rockville, near the roller rink. I remember his girlfriend, Amy, and how stupid I thought she was. I remember our Atari set and all our cool new stuff over there. And, of course, I remember Dad's really annoying crack-of-dawn routine of "Rise and Shine!"

I was my daddy's darling, and my mommy's little angel—

Then—without warning—I wasn't.

Had I known I should have been squirreling away memories as precious keepsakes, I would have scavenged for more smiles, clung to each note of contagious laughter and lingered steadfast in every embrace. Memory is funny like that: futile facts and infinitesimal details are fixed in time, yet things you miss, things you wish you paid fuller attention to, you may never see again.

I was just a regular kid before I was ever *really* asked to "remember." Up until then, I'd been safe in my own little world: every boo-boo kissed, every bogeyman chased away. And for a small voice that had never been cool enough, clever enough, or captivating enough, it was finally my turn. There was no other choice; I was the only witness.

"Tell us everything you know, Katie. It is very important that you try to remember everything you saw."

∞

August 11, 1983

I am five. I'll be in kindergarten this year, Ben is going to third grade, Jack will be in seventh. I'm not sure where the boys are today; all I know is that I'm glad it's just me and Mom. We're in the car, driving in our Ford wagon, me bouncing unbuckled in the way back. We sing over the radio like we always do. We're on our way to my dad's office, for the five-hundredth time. Not sure why, again, except that "they have to talk." They always *have to talk*. Ever since Dad left and got his new townhouse with his new girl-friend, all they do is *talk*.

Mom pulls into a space in front of the office. The parking lot for some reason is practically empty. His cleaning business is all the way in the back of this long, lonely stretch of warehouse offic-es, all boring beige and ugly brown, with big garage doors and small window fronts.

"You can stay here, sweetie pie—I won't be long."

I have some of my favorite coloring books and a giant box of crayons; I'll be fine.

Time passes in terms of works of art. Goofy, Mickey, and Don-ald are all colored to perfection before I even think to look up. I am very fond of my artistic abilities; my paint by numbers are exquis-ite, and my papier-mâché, as far as I'm concerned, has real prom-ise for five. All of my works are fridge-worthy; even my mom thinks so. My special notes and handmade cards litter her nightstand, dresser, and bathroom counter.

I hear a scream. Like one I'd never heard before, except on TV. *Was that her?* I sit still for a second, wait for another clue. *That wasn't her.* But something tells me to check anyway—just in case.

I scramble out from the way back, over the seat, and try to open the door, but I'm locked in—*why would she lock me in?* I tug at the lock and let myself out. With the car door still open, I scurry to the front window of my dad's shop, and on my tiptoes, ten fingers to the ledge, I can see inside. The cage with the snakes is there, the desk and chairs are there, the cabinets and files are there, everything looks normal like the last time I was inside. *Where are they?*

Then through the window, I see my mom. At the end of the hall, I can see her through the doorway. But just her feet. Well, her feet and part of her legs. They are there, on the floor—her sandals still on. I can make out the tip of his shoe too, at her thigh, like he's sitting on top of her. She is still. I don't get it. *Why are they on the floor?* I try to open the door, but it's locked. I don't recall knocking; maybe I did. I do know that I didn't yell to be let in, call for help, or demand that I know what was going on—

It wasn't her. It sounded like it came from down the street, I tell myself. Maybe it wasn't a *scream* scream, anyway. Someone was probably just playing, I convince myself. I get back in the car. I close the door behind me and color some more.

Only two pages are colored in this time. Not Mickey and friends, Snow White now. Fairy tales. My dad knocks on the window, startling me, smiling. "Hey, princess. Your mom is on the phone with Aunt Jeannie, so you'll just see her Monday. You're coming with me, kiddo. We have to go get your brother."

Everything I've seen is forgotten. My dad's convincing smile, tender voice, and earnest eyes make all my fright disappear. He told me she was on the phone, and I believed him. How was I supposed to know that dads could lie?

∞

Two days later, my brothers and I were at the beach on a job with Dad when our grandparents surprised us with the news. "Your mother is missing." And it was only then, when I sensed the fear they tried so intently to wash from their faces, that the realization struck me as stark panic, that I was brought back to the scene for the first time and heard the scream I understood *was* really her.

My testimony would later become the turning point in the case—reason enough to convict my father, who in his cowardice had covered all his traces. Even after his conviction, it would be three more years until he fully confessed to the crime. I was eight when I stood, uncomfortable, in a stiff dress at her grave for the second time—more flowers, same priest, same prayers.

To say I grew up quickly, though, as people have always suspected, would be a stretch. Certainly, I was more aware, but the shades of darkness were graced with laughter and lullabies and being a kid and building forts, and later, learning about my period from my crazy grandma.

I honestly don't remember being treated any differently, from Grandma Kate at least. If I got any special attention, I didn't know it. Life went on. Time was supposed to heal all wounds. My few memories of mom, despite my every attempt, faded with each passing holiday.

I was in Mrs. Dunne's third grade class when my dad finally confessed. We faced a whole 'nother wave of reporters, news crews, and commotion. They replayed the footage on every channel: me, five years old again, clad in overalls, with my Care Bear, walking into the courtroom. And just like before, my grandpa taped all the news reels. "So we never forget," he said.

I Think I'll Make It

For our final TV interview, my grandparents, the boys, and I sat in our church clothes in the front room to answer the reporter's questions. I shifted around on Grandma Kate's lap in my neatly pressed striped Easter dress. Everybody had a turn to talk. I was last. "Katie, now that the case is closed, do you think you will be able to move on?"

I'm not sure how I knew it then, especially when so many years of uncertainty were still to come, but I was confident: "Yeah." I grinned. "I think I'll make it."

ONE

TEACHING MOMENT

"Well, I just called to tell you I've made up my mind." *Silence* … "I will not be returning to school next year." *Silence* … "I don't know where I'm going or what I'm going to do—I just know I cannot come back."

Barbara, my faculty chair, on the other end of the line, fumed. I could hear it in each syllable of Catholic guilt she spat back at me. We'd ended a face-to-face meeting the day before with, "I'll call you tomorrow with my decision," as we agreed to disagree on the fact that the students were more important than my mental health and well-being.

"What will they do without you? You know how much they love you. We created this new position for you, and now you're just going to leave? Who will teach the class? It's August!" she agonized.

God, she was good. She had this guilt thing down pat. An ex-nun, obviously an expert, and this was the first I'd been on her bad side, a whole year's worth of smiles, waves and high-fives in the hallways seemed to get clapped out with the erasers.

It was true; I loved the kids and didn't want to do this so abruptly, like this—in August. This was not my idea of a resume builder. Nevertheless, as each bit of honesty rose from my lips, I felt freer and freer and more true to myself than I'd felt in, well, *a long frickin' time*. A sense of relief washed through me in a kind of cathartic baptism, cleansing me of the guilt. I stopped pacing. A warm breeze swept over the grass on the hill in front of our condo then over me. I stood on the sidewalk still nervous, sweating, smiling, teary-eyed. *I can't believe I just did that.*

∞

St. Anne's was a very liberal Catholic school, which ironically, had given me a new faith in the close-minded. The building housed a great energy of love and family. I felt right at home walking through its doors even at new-teacher orientation, despite it having been a while since I needed to be shown the ropes. I'd already been teaching for six years in a position where I'd been mentoring, writing curriculum and leading administrative teams. I normally didn't do very well on the bottom rung of the totem pole, but more pay with less responsibility had its merit.

It was definitely different, but a good different. I felt newly challenged in a bigger school, looked forward to the many programs already in place and the diversity of the staff and student body. The ceremonies performed in the religion-based setting seemed foreign at first, yet witnessing the conviction of our resident nuns and tenured faculty restored a respect I had lost over the years. They were the hymns that I recognized, the verses I used to recite, the prayers I was surprised I still remembered, the responses I thought I'd never say again.

The first time we had Mass together as an entire school, I was nearly brought to tears. I got goose bumps when the notes from the piano reverberated off the backboards on the court—the gym-turned-place-of-worship hardly seemed the place to recommit. Yet, hearing the harmony of our award-winning gospel choir and witnessing the level of participation from the students, faculty, and administration, I was taken aback. The maturity of devotion in the room was something I had never experienced in any of my churches growing up. Students, lip-synching their words, distracted and bored, still displayed more enthusiasm than the lumps hunched at my old parishes.

It was during that first Mass that I realized there was only one person who could have gotten me there—to a place she would have been so proud to tell her bridge club I was working. She would have been thrilled for me to find God here. The God she knew, her Catholic God—the one who had listened to her rosary, day after day, her pleas for her family's health and well-being, her pleas for her own peace and forgiveness. Gma had orchestrated it all. I was certain.

As that realization unfolded, I saw a glimpse of her endearing eyes, her tender smile before me, and with that my body got hot, my lashes heavy, soaked with a teary mist. Although it would be months till I stumbled upon a glimpse of what some might call God, it was here, at St. Anne's, where I gained a tradition I had lost, a perspective I had thought impossible, a familiarity that let me feel a part of something, and a trust that may have ultimately led me straight out the door.

∞

Our kitchen, growing up, reeked of canned beans and burnt edges. Grandma Kate knew of only one way to cook meat—crispy. On most nights, the fire alarm let us know that dinner was ready. The table was always set before I'd come running in, at the sound of her call, breathless from playing, to scrub the dirt from my fingernails. She was a diligent housewife, though at times she played the part of something far more independent. The matriarch, we called her—the gel to the whole damn bunch of us: her six, or five rather, and us three.

She responded to Grandma Kate, or just Kate, or Kitty, as her friends from St. Cecelia's called her, or Catherine, as she generally introduced herself, or Gma, as I later deemed her—all names necessary to do and be everything that she was to all of us.

She and I had our moments through my adolescence where the chasm of generations between us was more evident than we'd bother to address. They'd sold their five-bedroom home in Manor Club when it was just she and Grandpa left alone inside the walls baring all their memories. The house had character worn into its beams by years of raising six children and consequently taking the abuse of the (then) eleven grandchildren like a docile Golden Retriever. It wasn't long after my grandpa died that I moved back in with Gma. At fifteen, it was just she and I in their new two-bedroom condo like college roommates, bickering at each other's annoying habits, ridiculing each other's guests, and sharing intimate details about each other's lives when all guards were off and each other was all we had.

Despite our differences, her narratives always fascinated me. I had grown up on Gma's tales and adventures of her youth. In most of her stories, she depicted the trials of the Depression and conversely, the joys of simplicity. She encouraged any craft that didn't involve sitting in front of the television. She believed in hard work, and despite her dyslexia, was the first woman to graduate from Catholic University's Architectural School in the mid-1940s. "Of course," she said. "There was no such thing as dyslexia in my day. Those nuns damn near had me convinced I was just plain dumb."

She was a trained painter and teacher, a fine quilter, gardener, and proud lefty. She had more sides to her than a rainbow-scattering prism. When we were young and curious, flooding her with questions, we'd "look it up" together. When we had ideas, no matter how silly, she'd figure out a plan to somehow help us make it happen. All of us grandkids had ongoing special projects at any given time: whether it was building in the garage, sewing in the living room, painting in the basement, or taking long, often lost, "adventures" that brought us closer to her past.

She was from Washington DC, so subway rides from Silver Spring into the city were a regular episode. We spent so many hours in the Museum of Natural History I might attribute one of my cavities to its famous astronaut ice cream. We also went to see the cherry blossoms when they were in bloom each year, visited the National Zoo and toured the Washington Monument as well as several of the surviving parks and canal trails from her childhood.

It was on these journeys that she and I would discuss life, politics, war, religion, and whatever else came to mind. She was a woman of many words, so silences were few and far between. I got to know her opinion on just about everything because nothing was typically left unsaid—nothing.

By the time I was in high school and college, the only music we could agree on in the car was the *Sister Act* soundtrack. On our longer jaunts when conversation dripped to a minimum, I would toss in the tape before the banter went sour, which was a given with our opposite views on nearly everything. I'd slide back the sunroof, and we'd sing till our hearts were content.

"Hail mother of mercy and of love. Oh, Maria!"

She played the grouchy old nun, while I was Whoopi, trying to change her stubborn ways.

Gma and I both loved musicals, but while I was off scalping tickets to see *Rent* on Broadway, which she would have found too loud and too crude (God knows she would have had a thing or two to say about the "fairy" drag queen), she was content with her video of *Fiddler on the Roof*.

As I sat in the theater recently for the Broadway performance of *Lion King*, I couldn't help but picture her sitting there beside me, her big, brown eyes shifted right with her good ear turned to the stage; it was a show we would have both agreed on.

For the theater, she would have wetted down her short gray wispy hair and parted it to the side and then patted it down just so with both hands. A blouse and a skirt would have already been picked out, lying on the bed. The blouse would get tucked in and the belt fastened not too far below her bra line. Then she'd unroll her knee highs from the toes and slip on some open toe sandals, depending on the season; she didn't mind if the hose showed. Some clip-on earrings might have made their way to her virgin lobes, if she remembered, and she would have puckered up in the hallway mirror with a tube of Clairol's light pink lipstick from her pocketbook before announcing that she was ready.

Gma would have loved the costumes, the music, the precision in each detail. And in the car ride home, I can hear her now, yelling over the drone of the car's engine because her hearing aid had remained in the dresser drawer since the day she brought it home. "There wasn't but one white fella' in the whole gosh dern show. Every last one of 'em was black as the day is long, but boy could they sing. God, what beautiful voices they had, and even as deaf as I am I could understand what they were saying. They were all so well spoken."

Rarely does a day go by that I don't smile at one of her idioms or imagine one of her crazy shenanigans, her backward lessons, or silly songs. I used to feel guilty about the proportion I spent missing her over the amount I did my own mother. I guess it makes sense, though, to miss what I knew for far longer, and I suppose I had been swimming laps in the gaping void I housed for my mom.

Over the years, I often thought if I truly searched for my mom she would give me a sign, but where would I even look? Or would I even dare? Gma believed in those kinds of things, and despite having long lost my religion, she made me believe.

She told me a story once, without even looking up from the quilt she mended, about a dark angel who sat in a chair by the window in the corner of the room, accompanying her in the hospital as her mother lay on her deathbed gripped by cancer. She said the angel's presence alone had been enough to give her peace. I had watched her get misty-eyed while she brought herself back to the scene, still pushing the thimble to the fabric. Another time, she continued, she sat on the front step of their first house on Pine Hill in hysterics as she'd just gotten word of her three-year-old daughter's cancer diagnosis; she'd felt a hand on her shoulder—enough to calm her. She knew then she wasn't alone.

These conversations became typical when it was just us. When she cried, so did I. We wore each other's pain like thick costume makeup, nothing a good cry and some heavy cold cream couldn't take off. She shared with me her brinks of meltdowns after losing my mother, and I grew up knowing that she had far more depth than her overt simplicity echoed.

It wasn't until my latter college years, though, when we had become so close we were able to overlook *most* of our differences. By then, I wanted all the time I spent running away back; I wanted my high school bad attitude and disrespect erased; I wanted the smell of my cigarette smoke in her station wagon to finally go away. She was my history. She was my companion. She was home to me.

In the last few years, we shared our haunts, our fears, our regrets. Yet, we laughed a lot. She never minded being the butt of any good joke. She got crazier and goofier in her old age, shedding more of her crossbred New England proper and Southern Belle style. One of my favorite memories was of the time my college roommate, Kathleen, and I taught her how to play "Asshole" at our Bethany, Delaware, beach house.

Gma had said, "The kids were all down here whoopin' it up the other night playing a game, havin' a good ol' time, hootin' and hollerin'. I would like to learn that game. They kept shouting some curse word—what's it called again?"

"Asshole?" I had said.

"Yup, that must be it. Asshole sounds right. Think you can teach this old bird?"

Kathleen and I nearly fell over at the request but were obliged to widen Gma's eyes to the awesome college beer-drinking game full of presidents, assholes, and beer bitches. And she loved it— quite possibly a little tipsy after a few rounds. We didn't typically play Asshole with Jacob's Creek chardonnay.

Throughout the course of several conversations, Gma assured me that she'd had a good life and when the time came, she'd be ready. In those last few years, if I stood in her condo and so much as mentioned the slightest gesture of admiration toward anything she owned, she'd say, "Write your name on the back." She'd have the Scotch tape and a Sharpie out before I could even reconsider.

It was 2003, a year into my teaching career, when Gma finally expressed how proud she was of me. She said that my mom had always wanted to be a teacher, that she was surely proud of me, too. I'll never forget waking up to my brother's phone call, his voice solemn. I was devastated.

∞

It was my mom and Gma who helped Brooke and I get our house, I always said. I had signed a contract to start at St. Anne's in the fall, so we needed a home outside the city that would make my new commute toward DC more bearable. Three years after Gma died, since I wasn't speaking to God much in those days, I asked Mom and Gma to help us out if they could. Brooke, who only knew Gma through my incessant stories, was just as kooky as I was when it came to talking to the dead—so she never batted an eye at the references I made to the china cabinet.

Gma's old antique china cabinet—green until she stripped, sanded and painted it maroon the year she moved to her condo—sat in the dining room of our rented row house in Baltimore. (The smell of turpentine will always remind me of her leathered hands.) Sometimes, for no good reason, the door would fall slightly ajar, and each time it did, I swore she was trying to tell me something. While dating a girl I imagine Gma was not particularly fond of, I eventually had to put a matchbook in the door just to keep the damn thing closed—it creeped me out in the mornings when I'd wake up to the glass door gaping.

The exact night Brooke and I put the contract in on our house, we mentioned something to Gma before going to bed, kissing our hands and casually patting the side of the paint-chipped cabinet. The next morning—wide open. Two days later—contract accepted. I was elated; I'd never had such a good feeling about anything.

I felt so close to my team of guardian angels then. Everything seemed to be in its delightfully divine order, and I thanked them immensely from the moment we began the purchasing process until the time we moved in, displaying my gratitude thereafter with each stroke of my paintbrush and each rock pulled from the garden. I adored the home we were blessed with, our cute little cobblestone accented condo, our very first house. Even though we knew it wasn't a forever home, it was ours to make our own for now. And we did—or we started to.

So when the fairy tale began to fall apart, just a little over a year later, I couldn't help but question everything—intentions, meaning. There was no sign from the china cabinet. None of it made sense, the reason behind it all, I mean. Sure, I had always known growing up that everything has its reason. I have lived by that motto, but I could make no sense of this. It's one thing for a relationship to fall apart, but to have gone all this way, with the house to tie us even further? I was beside myself.

Needless to say, my bits of gratitude tapered off as I felt like I had less and less to be thankful for. I still talked to Mom and Gma, but not without first asking, "Why?" And something—quite possibly the silence that made the question seem rhetorical—told me I was going to have to get through this on my own. Perhaps it was a test of independence or a sudden stroke of bad karma for all the years spent being an obnoxious teenager, ungrateful, untrustworthy. Either way I was screwed; that much I was certain.

∞

I had always wanted to leave. To go away, I mean. Study abroad or go live in another state and explore. I had traveled a little in college but nowhere extensively. So, as all the boxes moved into our brand new house were unpacked and making their way into storage, the reality of being bound started creeping into my dreams through suffocation. I was faintly torn. Not enough to dampen the mood, because I imagined that somehow all that other stuff, my writing, my passions, would come later. It would all fall into place somehow. I guess I trusted even in the slightest possibility, although I knew that with each year of teaching, the job that was supposed to give me time off to be creative, I felt more and more comfortable and lackadaisical about pursuing my dreams.

I took a writing course online that drove in some discipline, only to drop it midway when things got complicated. Brooke often entertained the idea of moving to California, which kept me content, although I knew with the look of things that was only getting further and further from practical. But since being honest with myself wasn't my strong suit, I ignored my intuition, and looking back, ignored a lot of signs that might have politely escorted me out the door rather than having it slammed in my face.

TWO

SEX IN A PLURALISTIC
SOCIETY

I took a course, Sex in a Pluralistic Society, in my last semester of college. Somehow I thought it was going to be a lecture on the sociology of gender. Keep in mind this was the same semester I tried to cram in all my last requirements, registering for other such gems as Plagues and People; Death, Dying and Bereavement; and History of Theology. Yes, the sex class was the lighter side to my schedule, but my prude Catholic upbringing made a sex journal, "Or, if you don't have a partner, make it a self-love journal," a really difficult assignment. Plus, the guy who taught the class just creeped me out. The videos he made us watch—I'm still traumatized. A classmate and I thought to complain, on several occasions, but it was both of our last semesters so it's fair to say that, like me, she left that sort of tenacity to the underclassmen.

Despite the dildos, the pornography, and the daylong discussion on G-spots, I did take away one valuable lesson from that loony old perv. It was toward the end of the semester when the concept of *love* was finally introduced. By then, I had done my fair share of heart breaking and had tasted the bitter side of breakup a few times myself. I was sure I knew everything he had to say.

Instead, I was surprised to find myself taking notes when he broke down the Greeks' take on the four different kinds of love: *agape, eros, philia, storge*. We discussed unconditional love versus conditional love. *Yeah, yeah*; I knew all that. He went on to describe eros as manic love, obsessive love, desperate love.

"This is the kind of love movies are based on. It's high energy, high drama, requires no sleep, is built on attraction, jealousy runs rampant; it comes in like a storm and subsides often as quickly as it came in." I cringed when he said, "It's immature love."

And here I thought this is what it was all about. All lesbian love, at least—all those wonderful, electrifying things!

Eros—it even sounds erroneous.

It was when I was dating the most confident and beautiful, twinkly-eyed woman I'd ever laid my hands on, some four years later, that I was brought back to that lecture. Despite our good intentions and valiant attempts at maturity, Brooke and I had a relationship built on many of those very erroneous virtues. It *was* movie-worthy high passion infused with depths that felt like coming down from a rock star kind of party.

Perhaps it's because it began all wrong. She was fresh out of college. I was already teaching, working weekends at a chick bar in Baltimore at the time, Coconuts—our very own *Coyote Ugly*. One night, a friend of hers (she admitted later) noticed me, in my finest wicker cowboy hat and cut-off shirt, slinging beers and lining up shots between stolen, flirtatious moments on the dance floor. A week later, Brooke and I were fixed up at a party. We were both in other relationships that we needed excuses to get out of, so why not? She was beautiful (did I say that already?), tall, caramel skin and hazel eyes, tomboy cute when she was feeling sporty, simply stunning when dressed to the nines. She even fell into her dad's Brazilian accent after a few cocktails, which sealed it for me; I was enamored. Plus, she was a bona fide lesbian (a first for me), and we wore the same size shoe. What more do you need?

We did everything together: tennis, basketball, squash. She'd patiently sit on the beach while I surfed. I always said yes to her shopping trips. We even peed with the door open so as to not interrupt conversation. And I'm almost certain I slept right on top of her for at least a solid year—I'd never been considered a "peanut" before. In fact, I don't think we separated at all for the first couple of years we dated, now that I think about it. Maybe for an odd trip, but it didn't go without feeling like we'd lost a limb, I swear. We'd always say, "No more than five days," as if we wouldn't have been able to breathe on day six.

When we first started dating, I went to Japan for nine days to visit my brother Jack who had been stationed at Atsugi. I was pretty pathetic. It was my first time traveling alone, so when I stepped off the plane on foreign soil and my family wasn't at the gate ready to collect me, I quickly reverted to my inner child, the sweeping panic stretched from my tippy toes to my fingertips.

(It was the same feeling I used to get in Kmart when I'd look up from the shelf to tug at the skirt of the lady standing beside me, only to be both mortified and petrified when I realized that face and body didn't belong to my Gma. I'm not sure who was supposed to be keeping track of whom, but whoever it was did so poorly. Hence the reason why I developed a system: I'd go sit in the back of our station wagon where I knew it would be impossible for me to be forgotten among the dusty racks of stiff clothes. The first time I put this *system* into place, unbeknownst to anyone, I resurfaced from the car when the two police cars arrived, to see what all the hubbub was about. Boy, were they glad to see me when I strolled back through the automatic sliding doors, unaware of all the excitement I had started.)

Thank God my sister-in-law found me in Tokyo *after* I'd already figured out how to work the phones and had dialed home. Brooke had calmed me down by talking me through the basics: I wasn't lost; I was just on the brink of being found, she assured me. I'd hung up and collected myself by the time Jill and the kids arrived.

Every evening in Japan, I slid away from the family and hid in my room where I clumsily punched hundreds of calling card numbers into the phone just so I could hear Brooke's voice before bed. And like me, she was dying inside at the distance between us.

Sure, there were some caution signs, some red flags being waved, but all the good seemed to outweigh the bad, and who's perfect, really? I thought some of my ideologies about love were too lofty and maybe—just maybe—I had to accept that I would never have *all* that I desired from a relationship, like say, *trust*. Plus, people grow, they mature, relationships mature; surely we'd be the *growing kind*. We liked self-help books. We had a shelf where they sat, most of them at least half-read.

Her family loved me, and I adored them. Yes, it took a while for them to get used to the idea of me being more than just Brooke's "roommate." Thankfully, the week Brooke came out to her family, a close family friend, battling breast cancer, took a turn for the worse. Brooke came back at her parents' retorts with, "Well, at least I don't have cancer." And to that, well—they had to agree.

Brooke and I traveled together. We loved the beach. We loved food and cute, quaint little restaurants. We loved playing house and raising a puppy. We loved talking about our future and a big fat gay wedding, and most of all we loved being loved. We bought each other flowers and little presents and surprised each other with dinner and trips and concert tickets. I'll never forget the anniversary when she had me get all dressed up just to trick me into a beautiful candlelit dinner at home. I could have sat at that table forever, staring into her shimmering, smiling eyes, or let her hold me for just as long as we danced among the rose petals she'd scattered at our feet.

It was for all those reasons that the darkness never outweighed the light—the screaming matches, the silent treatments, the distrust, the jealousy. All those things seemed part of our short past when we began shopping for our first home. It was a blank slate, a new beginning—signing the paperwork, picking out furniture, remodeling our kitchen.

God, we danced so much in that kitchen.

We laughed at our goofy dog, Porter. We cried on our couch, watching movies. We supported each other in our few separate endeavors. We shared chores and "mom" duty and bills and credit cards. And I think it was under the weight of all the things of which we were once so proud that it all began to crumble. "Do you have to slam the cabinets like that?" as if I were picking up new habits to purposefully push her away. "I hate fighting like this in front of him!" she'd say, pointing at Porter. "Look, we're making him nervous."

She sobbed and sobbed, and her big beautiful eyes remained bloodshot for at least six months as I watched her slip away from me. I begged her to tell me what she needed, and even *that* she couldn't do.

∞

Brooke finally had a social life that I supported wholeheartedly, but that social life seemed to echo more and more of what was wrong with us. During the day things appeared fine and good and normal, but at night her cold shoulder sent me shivering further and further to the opposite side of the bed until I eventually moved into the spare bedroom.

I didn't get it. I said that I did, that I understood, but I didn't.

She spent an awful lot of time with a "friend." Julie, a mutual friend, or so I thought. We all hung out together, thus I didn't think to question anything until it became more and more blatant. I would beg, "Just tell me what's going on with the two of you. I'm a big girl. I'll just walk away. But I can't just sit around here feeling batty while you deny what I can see with my own two eyes!"

She wouldn't admit to it. "Nothing is going on." She said she just needed time to figure herself out.

In the meantime, I was still her home. I was still her best friend and even at the furthest distance she'd pushed me to, I was the one who calmed her when the weight of it all made her come unhinged. I was the one who rubbed her back and kissed her forehead.

She wanted me to be an asshole, so she'd have an excuse. She wanted me to get pissed to lessen her compounding guilt. I'm not sure if it was that I couldn't or that I wouldn't do either of those things. I still hung onto what I'd promised with that sparkly little ring I'd given her, not the real thing, but a *big* promise. I had taken it all very seriously. "In sickness and in health." And here she was before me, as far as I could see it, sick.

Well, sick was the only diagnosis that wouldn't allow me to hate her as she inhabited our home with me, a platonic roommate, sometimes cold and aloof and other times recognizable and warm. I felt like we had somehow been dragged into the drama of a bad after-school special—without the happy commercials of sugary cereals and toys that will never break or end up like the Velveteen Rabbit, who ironically, I was really starting to resemble—in the confines of our condo with its walls caving in.

While the final days of summer strode past in their lengthy hour, the honest words, "I want to take a break," were inescapably spoken. I felt sick—stunned by the syllables as they fell from her lips. We'd been at the beach for the weekend where I naively thought we might be able to spend some time all to ourselves, mending the stacks of broken things between us. I knew this had to do with Julie, but still nobody had the guts to admit it. I was infuriated. So much so, that I reduced myself to checking cell phone logs and sleuthing around my own home. I hated myself for the lengths I allowed her to push me.

There was no way I could return to school as my signed contract promised. I couldn't imagine focusing on my students while I was so busy focusing on my failing relationship. Although the last thing I wanted to do was uproot myself, I had finally begun to gather the pebbles of self-respect that would eventually become its new foundation. I had to go.

And with the phone call to my faculty chair, I did exactly what I never imagined I would do. I resigned. I had never been so excited to throw in the towel … well, except for that one awful restaurant where I was too much of a coward to quit so I faxed in my resignation an hour before my shift—that time felt good too. But this was different. I didn't chicken out. I stood up to Barbara's crucifix-firing cannon and prevailed.

When Brooke and I weren't fighting or walking on eggshells around each other, she dove into my arms expressing her undying love for me, and I held the stranger I no longer connected with, consoling her. I didn't know what to make of all the mixed emotions. I had taken my accusations to Julie herself to try to get some answers, but she laughed at my arguments, claiming Brooke was "too confused" to be dating anyone right now. Julie was older, with graying wisps, loafers and pleated pants. To look at her anymore made me sick. And, after all, Brooke still wore the ring I'd given her. Still, after nine months, none of it made any sense.

The night she woke me, cross-legged on the floor at my bed because she couldn't sleep and it was driving her crazy, she looked desperate. I held her and stroked her hair, calming her with my patient voice, exuding every ounce of love that could look past my own pain to reduce hers. Healthy? Probably not. But that was the only way I knew how to love her. To put everything of me aside. Everything.

∞

I have always wanted a family. From the time I was little I knew I would be a mom. At eight, I thought marrying a rich man and becoming a housewife was the golden ticket to true happiness, along with becoming the president, a monkey trainer, and a marine biologist. My pending future changed with the weather, but rich was almost always a constant. A valid measure of success at eight, I suppose. A family, and its entire construct, was very important to me: the house, the dog, the hus—or now the wife, all of it.

And that's what Brooke and I had, or we talked like we did. Raising our puppy from ten weeks to his "man"hood and buying household goods on joint credit cards. We were all grown up like a real family. With our names linked on more than just the dog's birth certificate, "taking a break" was really a separation and anything beyond that was really a *divorce*. I hadn't reached that logic in my head, perhaps because I still refused to believe that all I imagined was disintegrating before me, where I stood, clenching fistfuls of hopeless dust.

THREE

ON THE GOOD FOOT

I toyed with the idea of California, as I had always talked about. No reason to stay here. Seriously, with no excuses holding me back, I searched tirelessly for jobs on craigslist day in and day out. And there was an edge of excitement in taking control, or that's what I convinced myself was going on. I applied for a few teaching jobs in California, Colorado, British Columbia, and even New York. I was intrigued by the schools that touted their outdoor education programs and offered classes like rock climbing and snowboarding. I reasoned with myself: teaching can't be all that bad with a mountain backdrop and class cancelations for white-water rafting.

My other option was Hawaii, to stay with my brother for a while, an awesome Plan B, indeed, but—I had already planted the seed of the fantasy: me showing up, a stranger in a town, a place where I wouldn't have a crutch. Because, Lord knows, I'd use it. The only problem was that each time I sent off a teaching resume, I'd see myself in the classroom again, masquerading as a math teacher, and I'd feel flat and uninspired. It became obvious that all the *other* aspects of the deal were the real draw—not so much the teaching. I didn't want to play "teacher" anymore—even if it did mean free housing, and even more tempting, a free meal plan. I'd been bartending all summer, teaching spin classes and kickboxing on the side, which equated to about three days a week and triple my teaching salary—I could do that anywhere, right?

With a mortgage still hanging over my head, "free housing" was key to any move, seeing that I'd essentially already be paying rent. I couldn't put Brooke out on the street (although it was tempting), and she didn't want to live with a stranger—I'd lost that battle.

Let's be honest, by the time we even got to that battle, I had stopped counting my losses.

When I didn't hear back from the boarding schools, I applied for jobs like "live-in personal assistant" and "live-in nanny," weeding out the creepy ones, which were plenty, from what seemed like the normal few. I was really only looking for a cool place to live, and I figured those who needed "live-in" anything had far more resources than what I'd grown accustomed to on my meager wage. Even if the job was horrible, which I imagined it would be, I could live in and travel to really cool places and network with people who would certainly see me for all I'm worth and reward my talents with a high-paying awesome position somewhere far away from all this nonsense.

Well, that was the plan at least.

Brooke seemed less than thrilled with all my hopeful horizons, which I'm sure only added deeper fault lines between our two states as she saw me falling further and further from the social norm she dutifully clung to. I was the reflection of the starving artist she fell in love with, was enamored by, and adored, the same one she now had an aversion to as she made new friends in a different age group and clearly a higher tax bracket.

My brother was so excited to have me out to Hawaii that he called often. It broke my heart each time I talked to him and skirted around the invitation, making it sound like it was out of my hands as fate would soon knock, sending me off to somewhere remote and exotically independent. It was almost October. I'd quit my job in August. Things at home were only getting more awkward by the moment. His idea was simple: "Buy a ticket to Hawaii. If you're supposed to get a job in California, it will happen more quickly that way. Murphy's law."

He was right; no sense sitting around, waiting on the world to change. I bought a ticket to Honolulu—Murphy had two weeks.

∞

I had been so focused on *her* that I never really let myself go, but when I did, I dove headfirst into the bleakness I immediately recognized as my own—a familiar I should have never forgotten. The smell, the taste, the skewed vision, the aching of a depression I remembered from years past. This held a higher rank than just a broken heart. Here I was, in all my glory, back onstage in my leading role as *victim* yet again—of my environment, of circumstances, of life. It felt like only a cruel harsh world would push me down and let the thousands of feet from the herd trample over my weakened body, forgotten, for yet another time.

Hadn't I already paid my dues? Wasn't I a good person? I enjoy doing all sorts of good, selfless things: I pick up trash at the beach, I always offer a hand when I see a needy person in trouble, I would leave a note if I backed into a parked car—I swear, and I always return my shopping cart to its proper place even when in a desperate hurry.

Certainly this wasn't my winning ticket. Who, goddamn it, had tricked me into thinking I had a chance? And why? Because I was nowhere near the right place at the right time. I just couldn't decide whether it was the right place at the wrong time or the wrong place at the right time. It was all a joke, I swore. A ploy to get me to step out of my comfort zone—

I get it.

The only difference between this ghost and that of depressions past was in the moments between the lows, or that there were in fact those moments. The times when I knew I was going to be just fine, when I knew oddly that it was all happening for a reason, and that maybe my five-year plan had been doomed all along. And besides, the girl I left in the airport, sniveling with my dog in my brand-new truck as I hauled away my surfboard and as much of my life as I could muster to take with me, wasn't the girl I cried over. I didn't know her, and frankly, I didn't much like her anyway. I mourned almost as if she had died. It wasn't like *The Godfather*, "You're dead to me." It was the blatant truth that *my* Brooke was, in fact, gone. By now, she already talked like Julie, she wore—of all teams—a Steelers jersey, and I'll be damned if she didn't start voting Republican that year.

∞

The worst part was that false feeling like I'd already come a long way only to realize I was just at the beginning—a swift, refreshing smack in the face. After a grueling fifteen hours of travel, I stepped off the plane having reached my destination and perfect Honolulu seven o'clock weather; the island breeze had a "welcome back" offering in its cool sweet undertones. I was still wearing the jacket I'd grabbed before leaving Baltimore at 5:00 a.m. It was a long, now familiar trip I'd made several times before, yet surreal this time, holding a one-way ticket.

With little idea of what my entire agenda was here on island, I moseyed down to baggage claim, excited, anxious, confused, all over the place. In between glimpses of hopeful spirit, I was numb.

I watched the bags twirl by like sushi-go-round, drifting off, half-awake in the wrong time zone. I almost missed my ginormous suit-case and golf clubs swinging around the belt. As the last bags be-came sparse and the passengers began to dwindle, I realized my surfboard was in a special baggage graveyard unattended and sym-bolically destitute. Now, with everything in tow, I headed out the door, stumbling awkwardly, a Japanese tourist outweighed by camera gear.

There was no big welcome sign, no family standing there with open arms to greet me with smiles big enough to hold orange wedges. Not like the ones I watched other passengers receive. Even the hula girls looked for perhaps more excited, less exhausted looking people to adorn with their fresh, invigorating leis. I wad-dled out to the curb, fighting with different methods to carry and roll my eight-and-a-half-foot surfboard in conjunction with my other bags. I thought at any moment my brother would drive up, witness this sad display and rescue me.

Out on the curb, my frustration turned to sadness as I watched each car go by with families strapped inside that didn't belong to me. I looked longingly into the windows only to be disappointed with each passing car. I called my brother, hoping he'd pick up with anticipation, stating he was just around the corner. Instead, after two calls I reached him at home where I knew full well, given the distance and traffic, he was at least a half hour away.

There is really no better place in the world to feel sorry for yourself than an airport.

In many ways I felt like I had just been here, yet, deep down, it seemed like several seasons had passed before the dawning of this episode. I had made the same trip out to Honolulu only a few months back, alone, joining my family for my brother's big wed-ding. Brooke had been planning to attend, but with all that was going on, she opted out at the last minute. I had stayed three weeks or so and kept myself pretty well distracted. My mind had not been willing to admit that things with us were over and was still hopeful that when I returned it would have been enough time for her heart to have grown fonder. Brooke and I had spoken daily, and the "I miss you's" were just as sincere as they'd ever been.

I was just as uncertain now, sitting on the lowly bench, as I was then. Nonetheless, I was giving myself six months this time—six months for me, and six months for her to figure things out. Try as I might, there was no denying that I still loved Brooke, and if she needed six months, I would give it to her. Shit, I'd give her the moon if I thought it would help. We were on a "break," I guess, although I hated that expression. Had I not used it so often in high school as I ping-ponged from one relationship smothered in teen angst to another, it might have still carried some weight. We were *separated*, as in, almost *divorced*, but neither she nor I had the guts to call it what it was.

∞

All was forgiven when my brother rolled up with his two eager children. Even though he was an asshole and should have been there when I arrived, I melted like I always do when I see him. My big brother of three years, Ben, the best manipulator I have ever encountered, knew that bringing his two sweet children, whom I adore, would lessen any and all frustration as soon as I heard them yell, "Auntie!"

I let him rearrange the trunk and strap the board to the roof. I was busy attacking Hilton and Gavin with kisses whilst expending great effort to focus on each of their stories they couldn't wait to get out, speaking over each other, scrambling their words.

Thankfully, Ben isn't one for intimate conversation, so small talk about my travel was plenty to occupy us between spurts of singing and yelling from the back seat. When we were about five minutes from their newly remodeled single-family home in the western suburbs of Honolulu, Ben dove in for the kicker. "So she's fucking the old lady?"

"It appears so," I said, choking on my own laughter, equally embarrassed and relieved by the poetic phrasing.

He handed me a beer from the fridge in the garage on the way into the house after grabbing my bags in penance for not picking me up on time. I knew he was excited. He just had a funny way of showing it. He never believed I would take him up on his offer. He had offered for me to stay each time I'd come out for the past ten years. Only before, I had important things to consider: work, relationship, life; and now, conveniently, all three were under deep, very deep, scrutiny.

I stepped over the toys, the clothes and the shoes that littered the path all the way from the driveway into the garage to the door, just as they had when I left this summer. I could never tell if it was the motorcycle holding up the three golf bags or the golf bags holding up the motorcycle. The tennis rackets and bicycles were all tangled, leaning in the same direction, too. It dawned on me that I could have left my golf clubs here, but then again, I suppose I didn't realize I'd be back so soon. (And of course, I would have missed out on all of those stress-releasing swings at the driving range.) The surfboards hung as we'd left them, dangling from the ceiling in Ben's jury-rigged racks. He didn't surf much anymore. He said it was because the beaches had gotten too sharky and he had small children to consider now. He was full of shit. He had just gotten sidetracked with one of his eight hundred hobbies and hadn't had a consistent surf buddy to prompt him, or he'd just gotten a little chubby and a little lazy—take your pick.

Lea walked toward the door right when Hilton flung it open to yell, "Auntie Kathy's here!" She had probably heard Gavin screaming up the driveway. We met each other at the door, her arms extended from her petite Korean frame. She smiled as we hugged.

"You have no idea how thrilled we are to have you," she said over my bent shoulder into my ear. Much more convincing than my brother's lousy welcome. I squeezed her, my big haole (white) self, engulfing her tiny typical for Hawaii, Asian body, holding on for an extra second too long, making a point of it.

"Thank you," I uttered as sincerely as I was greeted. "Thank you."

We stood around the island in the kitchen with our drinks as the kids sped around with their toys, their papers and their things, trying to distract us. Gavin had big brown almond-shaped eyes and a head full of light brown curls. He resembled his mom only in complexion and the fact that he remained in the twenty-third percentile for both height and weight. He tugged at his mom every couple of minutes to see if she would pay him any attention.

Hilton had big brown eyes too, cropped shoulder-length dark brown hair, her mother's killer complexion, but our Hurley athletic build that she disliked because, according to Hilton, her butt was too big. (Ben insisted, in his eloquent fatherly manner, that she not compare herself to her mother who, like most Asians, has no ass.) Hilton desperately tried to catch me up on the past three months of her life by performing a fashion show with her latest wardrobe additions as well as *show and tell* with all her newest, absolutely random, belongings. She uncovered a Dooney & Bourke purse and held it up proudly. To which I gave Lea a scornful look as Hilton shouted, "It's real, see the tag sewn inside."

Lea laughed. "I know," she said. "She kept stealing my nice new ones, so I thought this might keep her grubby hands off mine."

"You're creating a monster," I said.

"I know." She laughed. "I know."

In our focused (despite the interruptions) adult conversation, Lea was hesitant but understandably curious. "Do you feel like talking about any of it?"

She knew most of the story. I had already unloaded it all this summer. I caught her up on all the latest details, enough for her to put the pieces together.

"So," she said, sipping her wine, pausing too for effect. "She's fucking the old lady?"

"So it seems." I laughed, puffy-eyed but refused to shed another tear. "So it fucking seems."

F O U R

THERAPY WITH ALOHA

I called it my "study abroad," but in my heart, I knew I had run for the hills. My life at almost thirty had been dumped into the lyrics of a familiar country song. Sure, I'd always been intrigued by moving out West, or somewhere distant, I just never imagined everything would have to turn upside down in order to get there. It went from something I'd always imagined as liberating, to something I felt I had no choice in. I liken it to the day I worked to muster up enough courage on the diving board, where I stood, toes to the edge—and in the same fashion that I acquired other life lessons, my brother got bored and pushed me off.

Turns out that push was all I needed. Hawaii was an amazing place to recover. The natural therapy the island offered gave drowning my pathetic sorrows a glamorous tropical touch. The surf, the sun, the beaches, the vast greenery, and backcountry trails allowed me to connect to a greater space that felt bigger than my life, my story, my pain. Loneliness dissipated in the water or in the lush mountains. The island hums with a natural spiritual energy, a poetry that plows right through you when you let it, allowing you to let go. And let go again. Until you trust that the tide will continue to come back in. In its own time. On its own cycle. In perfect stride with the moon and the stars, effortlessly.

The whole not crying thing did involve some strategy. All country music was completely out of the question. In fact, anything but Island Rhythm 98.5 FM was risky, and therefore, out of the question. I will admit that I fought back tears my very first night. Even with my brother, his wife, and kids in the house, standing in my new room with crayon-graffitied walls, a musty smell, and a hodgepodge of furniture—all things I hadn't noticed when I was just visiting—I was alone, vacant-alone, desperate.

The room he swore was "all set up for you!" had toys littered on top of the bed and electronic equipment strewn about. He'd done nothing to it since I'd left this summer except physically re-move the child, whom I'm not sure actually slept in his own bed. I teetered steadily on the brink of annoyed and thankful; Ben was awesome at keeping me one foot over that fence. I just kept re-minding myself that I was grateful I had a room and even more grateful that said room happened to be located in Hawaii, where even hand-me-down rooms are considered paradise. I opened my suitcase and the waft of my condo hit me like I was caught in a chase—my flag captured. I picked up a T-shirt and brought it fold-ed to my face. I breathed it all in, one last time, and with a forced sigh of uncomfortable relief, I snapped it out from its shoulders and hung it on the hanger.

Pictures of my mom and Gma on the dresser made me feel even more a stranger to my own past. I'd been so busy trying to relocate my life that I hadn't much spoken to either of them in months. I picked up my mom's picture and held it in my hands. I have always looked deep into her eyes, wishing just once they would reflect back to me a little more of what she was like. She always seems so innocent, so unencumbered. I have my mom's gleaming smile, her perfect teeth; my Gma always said I should be a teeth model, to which I never thought to take offense until Brooke once asked, jokingly, "What's wrong with the rest of you?"

Over the years I've had family members approach me at a funeral, or a wedding, or a party, and comment in a low voice, "You're really growing up to look more and more like your mother, you know." I'd recognize that soft voice, or change of tone, reserved for conversations about my mom, from several steps away. I was used to it. She was thirty-five when she was killed, and as I crept closer to thirty that number hounded like a blatant stalker, shadowing my every step.

In a new setting with the freedom of an open road, or in my case, a vast ocean, I no longer felt a part of my personal history; it meant nothing to anyone here. No one knew who I was, or where I'd come from, except for Ben and Lea's close circle of friends. It was as if I'd changed schools mid-high school career and could reinvent myself in any way imaginable. Like a bratty teen, though, I didn't want a reinvention. I was still kicking and screaming, in some respect, on the inside. Honestly, I just wanted to know who I was—that is, who I was without *her*.

∞

It all seemed like another well-deserved vacation until Monday morning when the two carpools wrestled each other out the door and the house hollowed out. The walls echoed back to me my own lonely heartbeat, and my anxious short breaths reverberated in the stillness. The percussion dissipated in the breeze passing through the open windows, bringing with it a taunting whisper and the potent, bitter scent of reality. Something I hadn't checked in with in a while.

What next? (Open laptop. c-r-a-i-g-s-l-i-s-t-.-c-o-m. Select state: Hawaii.) And the search began—for jobs of any kind, preferably the ones that "start tomorrow." *Hmm, let's see, surf all day and work all night.* (Job category: Bartending.)

The tourist industry is huge in Hawaii, obviously. I quickly found several hotels and restaurants in Waikiki with available positions. As I started to fill out the lengthy corporate applications, I thought about my last few trips to Waikiki, and it dawned on me—all the wahine (female) employees wear muumuus. *Yikes!* Plus, I doubted a tall, short-haired haole was exactly the cover girl they were looking for, anyway.

(Broaden search: Desperate.)

Two days later, I was a valet. Day One: $8 an hour plus tips. Day Two: *Supervisor*, $15 an hour plus tips. Among many of my random jobs in college, I valeted cars in Baltimore's Little Italy one summer—me and a bunch of guys. So, as it turned out here, I was the only one who actually knew what I was doing. The irony being, of course, that my whole M.O. here in Hawaii, shouted *I HAVE NO IDEA WHAT I'M DOING!* But I just kept *doing*—one foot in front of the other. And that in itself, my friend, said more than I ever could have imagined.

∞

My job was from 7:00 a.m. to 3:00 p.m. with terrible traffic both ways, so I had a lot of time in Lea's car to fester. Fester with small flashes of surprising all-rightness, then back to festering some more. Traffic with palm trees and spontaneous whimsical rainbows was hardly the DC traffic I was used to. I felt like I should be miserable given my circumstances, so I made a point to tirelessly plead my case of victim when my friends back home called to check in. I'd be sure to tell them how much money I was sending for bills and mortgage payments and God knows what else, just so they could get a Swarovski-clear picture of the saint I was becoming. They would tell me how cold and shitty it was back home, and I would complain about how dreadfully stunning Hawaii was, and then they'd remind me, "Girl, if you got the short end of the stick, then I'd say you made out. Just enjoy this time; you deserve it." I would admit that I'd been feeling okay, then they'd pump me with compliments about how I made the right decision and how proud they were of me.

Thank God for my friends, really. I might have jumped off a cliff long ago if I hadn't deep down firmly believed that one of them would have found me, picked me up, dusted me off, and when she realized I was still alive, grabbed my face from under my chin, with that cheek-dimpling, fish-lipped face pinch. She would purposely bring my face so close to hers that I could feel the emanating threat of her hot, wicked breath. And then, through her teeth, she would read me the riot act with spit-splashing fury—with some surefire, open-hand slapping and heavy shaking to punctuate. Afterward, she'd inevitably console me over drinks until we were good and shit-canned, all stupid and reckless suicide attempts forgotten.

And any one of 'em would do it, just like that, I swear.

∞

I was on top of the hill at Tripler Army Base, in front of the unsightly massive Pepto-Bismol-pink building that is the Army hospital, in a blue polo shirt and cargo shorts, holding valet tickets, smiling from ear to ear. The warm Hawaii ocean breeze tickled the trunks and shook the leaves of the tall palms above me as I stood in the unlikeliest of uniforms grinning at life and its unexpected turns. I had every reason, according to my long list of things, to be unhappy and just as many to feel sorry for myself, but I couldn't. Not here. Not where I was being paid *well* to perform an effortless task, where I could work outside and stare out into the horizon and gasp at the stunning Oahu coastline. Where my senses were heightened and my heart was wide open to discover anything I was intended to learn. With the excitement of a kindergartner on the way to greet the bus, I stood there unashamed of my craigslist valet job, without regret of my decisions, tasting hope in the salty air, breathing in possibility and the prospect that I'd finally begun the quest I was destined to conquer all along—whatever it was.

It was also on top of that mountain, in my little supervisor beach chair, under my much needed umbrella that I finished the book *Eat, Pray, Love*. I resisted reading it. I really did for a long time. I had seen the author, Elizabeth Gilbert, on *Oprah* and decided she was too God-y for me. I imagined I could steep cliché from its pages like potent hot tea. So with every concerted effort, I passed it by. And I would have succeeded if its cover hadn't taunted me wherever I turned, reminding me that I had absolutely no control over this ship and things would likely continue to unravel exactly as they had been intended to all along.

To my surprise, I enjoyed every word of *Italy* and *India* and only thought the *Love* part was a little drawn out but in the end wrapped things up rather beautifully—perhaps because I was also celebrating single-hood and celibacy. But when she dove right into the deal breaker with her hot little man and their hot little encounters, I felt slightly betrayed. I just wanted to hold hands with someone, that's all. No baggage, no drama, not even first base, just hold hands. I missed that more than anything.

The temporary psychosis Gilbert described in the beginning of the book spoke so clearly to me. Well, to be honest, it reminded me a lot of Brooke. I made sure to call home to have her pick up a copy. And, surprisingly, she did. Although I'm not sure she saw it all quite the same way, some of the parallels were uncanny. Surely that's the reason the book continues to be so successful; there is definitely something universal about love, especially the part that makes you batshit crazy.

Oh, look at that, right here, Brooke to a T, page 65:

If I love you, you can have everything. You can have my time, my devotion, my ass, my money, my family, my dog, my dog's money, my dog's time—everything. If I love you, I will carry for you all your pain, I will assume all your debts, I will protect you from your own insecurity, I will project upon you all sorts of good qualities that you have never actually cultivated in yourself and I will buy Christmas presents for your entire family. I will give you the sun and the rain, and if they are not available, I will give you a sun check and a rain check. I will give you all this and more, until I get so exhausted and depleted that the only way I can recover my energy is by becoming infatuated with someone else.

But *Eat, Pray, Love* had a happy ending. Not so much the *happy* or the *ending* I was capable of wishing for, but a little clarity would be nice. Might I add that this was the first book I'd read for pleasure in a long time. I laughed out loud, unashamedly. I fell for it—all of it. My life was clearly unraveling into its own memoir so how could I not—although I wasn't being paid handsomely to travel to the exotic ends of the earth and write about it, a slight disparity. I thought if given the assignment, like for a writing course or something, I'd title mine *Blink, Surf, Breathe.*

Blink because my eyes were wide for so many months upon arriving in Hawaii. Having lost everything, your perspective changes quite a bit; you see the whole world through a different lens. Not wanting to miss out on anything, the beauty, the experience, the moment, I didn't blink—ever. I took everything in like a thunderstruck tourist, snapping mental photographs and taking visual notes of my new habitat. I suppose I did blink when my eyes dried enough to make it necessary. And they were dry, because for some reason I didn't cry. Not much anyway, not like the current I had trod through before I'd left. Something told me I'd cried enough. Besides, wasting time on tears would only hinder my momentum. So I kept on truckin', one foot in front of the other, often not knowing where I was going but going just the same.

Surf because it was my therapy. The ocean cleanses, rejuvenates, exhilarates, all while reminding you just how small you are. You and your skyscraping stacks of insidious problems. Tiny. Itsy bitsy. Under the wrath of a crumbling wave, or even in the face of the changing tide, it all washes away. All of it. I charged at surf far larger than my capabilities warranted. I wanted to Go Big, or Go Home! Nearly drowning a few times, rolling around in pounding surf, gripping my board anxiously not knowing which way was up, then I'd pop up like a buoy. And there I was, often to my own surprise, still breathing. Heart pounding, sucking air, I'd get right back on my board and paddle out beyond the break where peace and solace are served for breakfast, lunch and dinner. Where your feet could be dangling in shark-infested water, and you just don't care. Because it's worth it. The picturesque beauty. The immense energy. The yearning to score the ride of your life and maybe, just maybe, have one person catch it and throw you a shaka (Hawaii's famous "hang loose").

Breathe for the months when I finally found my breath and recognized its connection to everything. A breath of awareness that brought tears to my eyes when I greeted it—trusting for the first time my own inhalation and all that it offered. In every capillary of my body, I felt its warm honest embrace, and I knew immediately I'd found home. The structure I'd left months prior, the family I'd kissed off, the life I'd led was all superficial now. Serenity in my own presence, here it was, home sweet home. *Welcome.*

FIVE

NATURAL MYSTIC

During the week, I'd try to time my departure from work just right so I could get home with reasonable light to score a happy hour surf session. I'd surf until dusk with great effort spent disregarding the dark shadows I'd swear I caught out of the corner of my eye, swimming past. On the weekends, I was sandwiched between Hilton and Gavin in the backseat. We'd do a Costco run, or pack the car for a big day at the beach. I'd never spent so much time with family. I had to admit, even in the midst of the organized dysfunction, it was rather nice.

Lea is a great buffer between Ben and me. She huffs and rolls her eyes at his boyish nonsense as much as I do, so a lot of our bonding is spent commiserating. I have never loved to hate and hated to love someone as much as I do my own brother. He is gentle and sweet and kind and compassionate, but terribly annoying and childish and immature. And just when you think you're dealing with one side of him, he throws out the other. *Aha, I fooled you*—every time.

I've gotten used to it over the years, and it appears Lea has too, God bless her. I think she is more forgiving though because he has given her such precious children. In fact I know this to be true because she often threatens with, "You're lucky you make beautiful babies." She's a spitfire; I love her immensely.

But poor Hilton, growing up quite the candid diva, couldn't seem to understand the tug of war of love and hate she has reserved for "Be-en!" (with two syllables, when she's pissed). She'd never articulated it in those exact words, but I could see it in the frustration her face contorted into when they fought or could hear it in the stomping of her feet on her way to the door before slamming it behind her. He stooped down to her level, and the two of them bickered: *uh-uh, I told you so, no you didn't, you smell. All night long.*

"What does he think he's accomplishing?" I asked Lea this first time (of several) while she stood at the dryer, feet buried in laundry.

"I don't know exactly, but I've learned to just not get involved. That's their deal, and as annoying as it is to listen to, they always seem to work it out. I mean she adores him, and he adores her; I just think they're way too much alike."

She was right. I watched more squabbling than I thought I could stand, even tossing in my own two cents when I couldn't tolerate it anymore, and sure enough, each night they'd be snuggled together on the couch—two birds of a feather.

I preferred Lea's parenting strategy instead. "Ai-yaaaa!" which I think is Korean for "Holy Shit!"

"Not okay, Gavin, not okay. Do you hear me when I tell you this is not okay?" For Hilton, who was older and therefore more malleable, Lea just so happened to leave her alone with *Mommy*

Dearest one cheery Saturday afternoon as she caught it near the beginning while flipping through the channels. "A little perspective never hurt," she said to me and Ben, through an evil snicker, later that evening.

Gavin, a.k.a., Boy Boy, ran around in his diaper screaming most of the time because he begged for far more attention than his two-year-old vocabulary would credit him. For such a little boy, he had a mammoth personality with command of more comical facial expressions than I'd ever seen on a child his age. It was as if there was a tiny manipulative man hidden inside his brain. Now that I mention it, for both Sister and Boy Boy, the manipulation apple didn't fall far from the tree; each of them would have us eating out of their hands at intermittent intervals.

In fact, it didn't take long to discern who typically ran this Hurley household. The first Saturday morning after I'd arrived, I listened to an hour's worth of screaming and yelling over *SpongeBob* before I woke up to see what was going on. I crept my way down the stairs, not sure if I was ready to be seen and therefore *commit*. I folded at the waist to peek from my perch at midstairwell. The living room looked like a frat house during rush week. And I was caught just as I turned on my heels in retreat—I swear they had some crazy stealth powers that must have sensed the warmth in the room change—"AUNTIE!"

Shit.

∞

Hilton's seventh birthday was in early November. Lea asked, *like I might have other plans*, if I wanted to join them on a family camping trip to celebrate. Of course I would join them, I said. "Although I'm no camper. Don't go mistaking me for one of those firewood-collecting, Swiss Army Knife lesbians."

"Do I look like a camper to you?" she asked, holding up her arm, Burberry bag dangling from the crook. "I rented us yurts," she said and laughed. "Whatever they are. They say they're a more permanent tent like structure, already set up for you."

"Perfect. I'm down with that."

Lea, as always, had the car packed with bags of stackable Pampered Chef Tupperware. For this trip, she had filled it with soba noodle salad, marinated beef to cook on the grill, ramen for her, s'mores for the campfire, and all kinds of other camping goodies that Walmart had easily sold her on. We had three of Hilton's friends with us, the food, toys, and prizes, and off we went—Ben and Gavin in the other car, following.

For all that packing, I might have thought we would have driven more than ten minutes before we started the trek up the side of Mt. Makakilo to Camp Timberline. It hardly felt like the expedition we had suited up for, but what the hell. We crawled at a startling incline, winding farther and farther up until we reached the oddly flat peak. "There are the yurts." Lea pointed. "This must be it," she said, laughing at the sight of the yurts sitting all by their lonesome on top of the hill.

The yurts were bigger than I had imagined, tall enough for a grown man to stand up inside, each housing two bunk beds on opposing sides. We rented two: one for the girls and one for us. While Lea got us checked in, the girls jumped out to run around the great open space on what seemed like the top of the whole island. Once Boy Boy unbuckled himself, and Ben opened the door, he practically fell out of the truck in a haste to chase after the girls, screaming at the top of his lungs, trying desperately to get their attention.

I trailed the kids; we ran around like drunken fools, like we'd been cooped up in the car all day. Then we set up our stuff inside the yurts. And it wasn't long before the girls got in some sort of spat and the outcast had to tattle, so Lea refereed. Then we ate a late lunch. The girls retreated to their yurt to tell stories, and do hair, and watch movies, and eat candy, and all the other stuff girls do at sleepovers. Finally, Boy Boy dropped like a fly, exhausted from trying to keep up with the girls all day.

Only a handful of other campers were there with us. They brought their own tents and had set up, thankfully, on the far side of the yard. By the early part of the evening, several cars had trekked their way up the hill, definitely more cars than tents. A meeting seemed to be going on in the wooden cabin at the end of the drive, a group of hippy-looking haoles. We didn't take much notice of the meeting until the drums started, and then—the chanting.

"Um …" My eyebrows started in on Lea before I did. "How in the hell did you find this place, anyway?"

"Hilton's summer school took a day trip here; she chose it," she said, laughing in defense.

Spooky comes with the territory of camping, certainly, but add chanting and drums and the isolation of the tippy-top of this mountain and the black of the night, and you get a stiff cocktail of hesitant curiosity. Ben, Lea, and I sat in our beach chairs in front of the skimpy blue flame of the starter log looking at each other, all at a loss. *Okay, who brought the booze?* Either each of us thought the other one had, or maybe it was that we felt guilty for secretly wanting to get wasted at Hilton's birthday party. I'm not sure what happened exactly; all I know is that I took charge. First of all, we were freezing. Nobody mentioned it was going to feel like Antarctica up in this piece; it *is* Hawaii for shit's sake. So, I would need a sweatshirt or more blankets or both. Plus, we needed pizza. We had finished most of our food for lunch, and the girls were still hungry. And, let's be real, if I was gonna make it through this cold, lonely-ass night, listening to some not-a-care-in-the-world Hare Krishnas whoop it up, I needed booze—strong, stinky booze.

With that, Ben and I unwound our way back down the mountain. And, like a supermarket sweep, we ran through the house, grabbed every sweatshirt we owned and a few more blankets. On the way back to Camp *Freaky* Timberline, we stopped at the nearby shopping center for Pizza Bob's pizza and at Long's for a hefty bottle of whiskey. The serious stuff.

While we climbed back up to camp, Ben broke our momentary silence. "Uh … I hope they're still up there," he said through a nervous laugh.

I played along, even though I was thinking the exact same thing. "Nah, they've probably been sacrificed by now."

When we arrived, the music had taken on a Beatles "I'm So Tired" kind of eerie. We found Lea hiding in the yurt with the girls, watching the tiny portable DVD player, singing along, perhaps to drown out what we were now referring to as the séance. She had retreated inside, she said, after getting creeped out when it was just her and the inescapable sound of the ghostly drones.

We ate pizza under a canopy of confident stars, each one trying to outshine the other. It was beautiful, I had to admit. I was glad I came. The girls seemed happy—so far, a birthday party success. And with crispy pepperoni, greasy cheese and doughy, crust-filled, warm bellies, they danced and cheered their way back to the yurt. Funny, it hadn't occurred to me to move, much less dance—seriously, to have the metabolism of a seven-year-old again.

With the girls out of sight, I was proud in presenting Lea with the big brown-bagged bottle of bourbon. I was right, red wine wouldn't have cut it. The wind began to whip up the hill and shoot through the threads of our sweatshirts. And the harder the wind came, the louder the chanting resounded. The three of us gave in; we got into our own rhythm, taking one drag off the bottle, *crack-le*, pass.

We talked story, as they say in Hawaii, mostly about all the dumb stuff Ben does—our favorite topic—especially since Ben exudes little effort in his own defense, often throwing himself under the bus for the sake of a good story.

Between our own howling laughter, not entirely at Ben's expense, and other stories we dredged up for shits and giggles, the chanting would rise, the drums and guitar would crescendo and we'd look at one another for a second in angst before we burst into laughter all over again. Because we weren't at all convinced whose party, for real, we were crashing. They seemed too happy to be Satan worshippers, but we weren't entirely certain. How can you tell? None of us were willing to get a closer peek, that's for damn sure. I *do* know that they chanted and sang and beat that frickin' drum until the wee hours of the morning. We could see silhouettes of sweaty bodies dancing while we sat huddled under blankets and piles of sweatshirts sipping *crackly* fire down our throats.

Even though we finished that giant bottle before calling it quits, somehow it wasn't enough, for me at least. I didn't pass out like everyone else did. Instead, I lay there with one eye open curled up in a tight ball, fighting to stay warm, worrying about the construct of the yurt and it withstanding the wrath of God that was being thrashed upon it. The sound of wind and rain and chanting and drums ricocheted off my temporal lobe like nails falling on a glass table, and all I could do was lie there and feel sorry for myself— clearly, not a happy camper. The yurt moaned and creaked and buckled in the wind. I felt sorry for it, too—but who knows, unlike me, maybe it was built for such testimonial beatings.

It was as if I was being shaken from my dream. Like I had all these fantasy characters bustling around me throughout the day, distracting me into such illusions as laughter and joy until I put myself to bed at night where no matter how much I drank, reality still haunted me. I was convinced I might not make it out of that damn yurt alive. The whole setting, and the way the scenes unfolded, felt too bizarre, too ambiguous, too raw; like even though we were all here in the same place, the shadows were only cast on me, like *I'd* gotten the bad mushroom and was lost inside my own shitty trip.

I don't remember falling asleep, but I must have because I woke up to the sound of laughter and shrieks. Sunshine was thawing the canvas of our yurt that I couldn't believe was still intact. I opened the door to a clear blue Hawaiian Pacific morning, expecting, at least, for those tiny little tents they'd staked to the ground to be littered like newspapers all over the grass. Surprisingly, they were still standing. In fact, there was no evidence of a storm or the wild dance party that had ensued at the cabin, no added cars left over to prove that anyone but us survivors had been here at all.

If it wasn't for the mother of all headaches, I might have thought I'd lost my mind entirely. I felt like a sponge left out on the kitchen counter, all curled up at the edges. I guess a bottle of straight bourbon will do that to you. In college, times like this would call for forty-four ounces of fountain Diet Coke, crushed ice preferably, and a Veggie Whopper with cheese, or something of equal or greater greasiness before I'd smoke my first cigarette of the day. Here—now, I would give anything for some coconut water and a soy latte.

Before Ben and Lea woke up (and before I could be ridiculed for such a senseless act), I laced up my running shoes and headed down the hill. It was an undeniably beautiful morning that I didn't want to waste on a hangover, and apparently after last night's episode, I needed some fresh air. Plus, I thought, sweating out some whiskey might do me some good. That is, *if* I could sweat.

Working out was the only meditation I knew: "mind over matter," "no pain, no gain," and all those other goodies I had taken away from a life of athletics. I coasted down the road to the gate, which at the time still seemed like a good idea, until I turned around and assessed the absurdity, nearly throwing up at the sight of the hill. But I did it. I ran, if you could call it that. Fighting back legitimate vomit the whole way up, three miles, I think; I about crawled to the top. When I reached camp, Lea took one look at me and asked, "What the hell is wrong with you?"

I sighed hard, trying to catch my breath and keep down my own saliva.

"Good question."

SIX

WHEN IT POURS

November through March is rainy season. My valet job was all "right on!" until sheets of tropical rain and wind attacked from every angle. We set up one of those big event tents, but it stood no chance in the wind. We had umbrellas that just seemed silly in their lack of all-around protection. And I would rather get wet than wear the sticky plastic ponchos that still smelled like China when we pulled them out of the packs. So, more often than not, we crammed inside our little booth only to have people drive up and beep their horns, expecting us to ignore the momentary monsoon and take their "I'm late for an appointment" attitude.

It was me, three rotating local boys and a haole military guy named Andrew from Virginia. We had a crazy supervisor, Auntie Maureen, who would show up unannounced every so often to tell us her latest and greatest ideas for how we might best run the place. With my guys rolling their eyes behind her, I would kindly explain how terrible her silly plan was, my hand on her shoulder in reassurance that I had everything under control, while escorting her back to her truck. I'd get her into her SUV, close the door, smile and wave as she drove off down the hill.

I have no problem taking charge. I can be a little apprehensive day one, but by day two, I got it—you might as well move over. So I was grateful I was the boss, because these boys needed a boss. Not a bitch, which I wasn't; they just needed a sturdy guide to keep them in line. I covered for them when they'd nick a car. We'd jump start a truck when one of the boys left the lights on, trade off fighting with a remote when an alarm wouldn't stop wailing, heave and push when we got a car stuck in the thick of mud. I'd break up the petty battles over the keys to the monster trucks and the gleaming sports cars the military guys proudly stepped out of (their housing allowances, clearly, making payments on expensive penis enlargements dressed in shiny wheels). And to make the three long lunch hours pass less painfully, we played walkie-talkie tricks on each other, talked story or told jokes. They'd forget I was a chick and be crude, which unfortunately I was used to.

I had grown up with two boys; I played sports with boys; I don't really know how it happened, especially since I'm not particularly all that fond of them (like *that* anyway), but it seems it was often just me and the boys. And here I was in a butchy phase with short, blonde, spiky hair and a polo shirt and cargo shorts, playing the girl card just wasn't happening. When I met drivers at their car to take their keys, they'd often call me "sir." I'd look at them with my mascara-painted lashes and my Chapstick shimmered lips, and then they'd quickly apologize. I was used to it, but I can't say it didn't bother me.

I always hated being called a tomboy as a kid. And, it wasn't long after I moved in with Hilton that she had me pegged. One day I was working out in the garage, wearing a tank top and backward hat, listening to Justin Timberlake or The Black Eyed Peas or whomever else seemed to be dominating the airwaves at the time.

"Auntie, are you a tomboy?" she yelled over the music as if it had just dawned on her when she was running out the door.

"What?" I said like I hadn't heard, knowing full well I had.

"You know; are you a tomboy?" she repeated, suddenly worried she might be the first to break the news. She was using her toes to turn over her slippers (flip-flops) so she could slide her feet in properly, looking at them then back at me.

"Yeah, I guess I am," I said, adjusting my weights. "Why, do you have a problem with tomboys?"

"No, I was just wondering." And with that she went running off to her friend's house, leaving me with dumbbells in hand feeling mildly humiliated.

Such was life with Hilton Hurley.

∞

I was convinced a door to my bedroom was not necessary because neither Hilton nor Boy Boy ever knocked. My showers were just as much of a free-for-all. Hilton, at least, knew as much to merely poke her head in the door, where Boy Boy would just run up and rip back the curtain.

The first time his curiosity got the best of him, I was taken completely by surprise. Nobody had given me the Auntie Handbook, and it was clear I still had a lot to learn. As the curtain flew, I instinctively covered all my parts as to not frighten the poor child. As I stood there, chicken-skinned from the blast of cool air, speaking sternly through my teeth like Gma used to, I wondered what the appropriate reaction was. Some families are really liberal about nudity. I hadn't a clue what my family's take was on all that business. Without the know-how, I barked at him enough that he backed up, slammed the toilet seat shut to climb on top so he could finish what he swore he was just trying to tell me.

"Um, Auntie? ... Uhhh, Auntie?" He stammered along, fishing to come up with something important only for me to see beady little eyeballs peeking around the curtain every couple of minutes until I'd bark at him again. He was bored and gone by the time I got out of the shower but not without having touched everything I owned on the counter and unwinding all the toilet paper. Let's just say that I learned to let go of a lot during that time.

∞

Brooke and I spoke off and on all through November, mostly about the bills that were being sent to me and the ones that kept showing up at home. I was thrilled to report that the fam and I had spent Thanksgiving on the beach, a major plus to living in the tropics, and she seemed pleased to tell me that her family had missed me but everyone was doing really well. I hadn't spoken much to her family in over six months. At the time, they were just as confused as I was about what was going on. They, like me, were hoping this was all just a spell and in no time we would be right back where we left off, with only a speed bump behind us. I will admit that I took long delight in hearing that they missed me. It made me sick to think about how much I missed our holidays together, vacations and weekend jaunts.

November rolled into December in a fashion like you've suddenly realized you haven't peeled the days off the desk calendar and you have to catch up, ripping a week and a half's worth off at a time, letting all the jokes fall into the rubbish with their corresponding days. To break up the monotony, I had been given cat duty at Lea's boss's house in Kailua, the east side of the island. She had a nice home where I was to stay for five days, with peace and quiet and two cats with herpes. My sole job was to administer the meds, and of course, keep them company. I had a cat, but I'm not terribly fond of cats, especially really furry cats, and even more especially, really furry cats with eye herpes. I took the gig for the vacation. I needed a break from *Auntie*. Plus, I wanted to explore the other side of the island. I couldn't wait for some time to myself.

On my drive over from the house, on H3, I called Brooke to check in. I hadn't talked to her since Thanksgiving. It had been gray for days, which coerced me to come down from my tourist high. We spoke for a few minutes when I finally admitted, "I'm having a tough time."

"What'ya mean?" She sounded concerned.

"I mean, it's hard, and even with my family here it's lonely, and I just wish I knew what was going on with you—or us."

"Well—a lot has happened." She exhaled heavily; there was a long silence. I waited. "I think it's time, Kath," she paused again, "that maybe you should move on."

I was quiet, taking it in, my mind and heart racing to get out of this moment unscathed.

"Kath?"

"What'ya mean move on?" I paused, half waiting for a response. "I mean, is that what you're doing, moving on?" I said, choking up.

"Well, yeah. Y-yeah, I am."

I could tell she was trying to be hard.

"You mean with Julie you're moving on!" I switched gears, holding back tears with sheer rage.

"No, I told you already; I'm really working on myself, and I'm spending a lot of time alone."

"You mean alone with her! In my house!" I was pissed.

She was defensive. "We're not together, Kath! I'm serious. I am finally happy alone!" She paused. "But—"

"But what?" There was more silence. "But what, Brooke!"

"Well, I mean, I guess I'd be lying if I said I didn't have feelings for her."

"Awesome, Brooke. That's perfect. Really. And when were you planning on telling me?"

"I thought you knew, Kath. I thought it was obvious."

"It's BEEN obvious, Brooke! You just never had the BALLS to tell me when I BEGGED you to. And I think it's RATHER CONVENIENT, now that I'm FUCKING GONE, you're all FUCKING BETTER, and now you guys can have FUN, playing HOUSE, in MY FUCKING CONDO!"

I hung up. I would have slammed the damn thing if it would've done much good on a cell phone. (I think they should install that feature; *end call* just doesn't suffice in times like these.) She'd said all I needed to hear. I was furious. So furious that I bawled my eyes out. (I hate when I do that.) I was so ashamed. I knew that some of my friends back home must have known before I did, which made it worse, the sting more potent. I knew that Brooke and Julie were *together*, "feelings for her" *my ass*.

I thought by *not* prying these past couple of months on the phone with friends, all those times, just showed how mature I was and how over her I was, but now it seemed overtly naïve—sad even. Like all the while they'd been feeling sorry for me when I was bragging to them about how great I was doing. My closest friends didn't know what was going on. Brooke knew better than to tread through that neighborhood, down those tracks, but everyone else, I imagined, had long since accepted her and Julie as a couple. It made me nauseous.

When I arrived at the cats' house I wasn't certain who was more nervous: me of them, or them of me. And here I was all alone, just like I'd wanted—miserable. I had never needed more of a distraction from screaming Boy Boy or loquacious Hilton. Of all the days to be by myself, on the even grayer side of the island, with clouds following me like Eeyore—

"It isn't much of a house. Just right for not much of a donkey."

I even called my brother, all at a loss. "Ben—it's true."

"What's true?"

"She *is* fucking the old lady."

"I thought we knew that already."

"Well, we did, but we weren't certain."

"No, see, I was certain." He chuckled to my silence. "There was no doubt in my ... " he continued until he picked up the echoing sniffles. "I'm sorry."

"It just sucks, Ben. It really sucks."

"Well, there are lots of hot chicks out here. That's cool, right?"

"Sure, Ben, thanks."

"You comin' back home?"

"No, I got the cats. I'll call you later."

"Okay—don't come home with herpes!"

I had to go surfing. I hadn't even unpacked my board before I was back in the car with puffy eyes and a runny nose in search of a good break. I'd never been to this side of the island, so I drove aimlessly until I saw the crystal blue-green of the ocean. I'd heard of a good break at Kaneohe Marine base, but the part about climbing over, or was it under, a fence and paddling out across two or three breaks seemed a little ambitious at the moment. Instead, I pulled into a neighborhood with beach access and almost ran over the dude from *Lost*, Matthew Fox, on his bicycle while I was wiping my tears. *That woulda sucked.* According to a friend, most of the cast lived on this side of the island. I smiled for a second until I remembered that I was, *right*—destroyed.

I huffed and puffed all the way to the water, just bikini and board. I would've stomped if I thought it would've done any good in the sand. I passed a guy sitting half lotus on the beach back by the palm trees, meditating. He looked kinda hippie, way too happy to be normal, just sitting there. I had him pegged as one of those *simple* breeds, not a care in the world. I stormed by—*get over yourself!*

The conversation with Brooke played on repeat until I paddled out where it slipped through my ears and into the water. There's a focus that lets you forget, even when the waves aren't all that good. This was really my meditation. You can sit with your soul when no other surfers are around, listen to your own breath, drop your hand into the sun where its reflection on the water is pointing directly at you. And the ocean always embraces you in a way that you feel like you've missed. I plugged into the energy that is unattainable anywhere else, and I let it go. Not forever, but long enough.

I didn't think of it then, but now it's apparent: the Greeks would call this passion between us—me and this majestic, bountiful, blue source—agape love, true love, unconditional.

∞

That same night, because life has a wicked sense of humor, I got stuck with two nasty cats with no power in—what we call them on the mainland—a *fucking* hurricane. I had been online chat-fighting with Brooke, and I remember thinking to myself, at least it's my favorite night of the year in television. What better way to bring in the holidays than with the Victoria's Secret Angels? Their runway show was to air at 9:00 p.m. Pacific, and I already had the channel tuned in. That was, of course, before the sideways rain and the howling winds. The house was completely open, windows that looked like they had never been shut, a slider that was rusted open. I wrestled with each point of vulnerability with no luck in my godforsaken favor. I grabbed armfuls of towels to soak up all the water seeping in. Long, white, wiry cat hairs were whirling around in the wind and then sticking to whomever (namely me) and whatever they landed on.

We lost power twenty minutes before the Angels were supposed to prance their way into my living room. If I hadn't been forlorn before, I'd now reached a pivotal rock bottom. While I stood near the TV, pushing every button on the remote, just in case God, if there was such a being, was handing out pity, the cats looked up at me from the couch with that stupid look, "We'll be your friend."

"Oh, go fuck your furry selves!"

Ugh, I bet we have power at home.

I was certain that a tree would fall on the house or the whole house would just lift up and twirl around like Dorothy's had and drop me deep in Kansas somewhere, a place where they, more than likely, hate gays. The phone lines were down so I couldn't even call Ben if I wanted to. *Is this a typhoon? Do I need a kit of some sort? Will they sound a warning?* My anxiety escalated with thoughts of impending doom while I lit candles, hiding them from the gale force winds that continually invited themselves in.

I finally gave up and went to bed—surely, a nightmare would be less tormenting than this. I couldn't sleep. Tree branches taunted me at the windows—*We're coming in after you, muhahaha.* I buried my head first under one pillow, then two—*of all the places to die, and of all the varmints to die with.* This made all the other times I felt sorry for myself seem juvenile—I'd reached a more mature *pitiful* with this, indeed.

I woke up to drool at the corner of my mouth and cat hair in my teeth. *Awesome.* I heard birds, a good sign; no broken glass anywhere, another good sign; still no power; everything had a solid layer of moisture on it; the towels at the windows and doors were soaked through and through. My phone was still out, so I couldn't call work to see if I was to come in or not. For all I knew the storm might've picked up and taken that putrid pink Army hospital with it. I sure hoped so.

Since I could easily calculate my sleep in minutes, rather than hours, I determined a snow day was in order, no question. The only problem was that you can't surf when it has rained this hard. Well, you *can*, but it's not recommended. The runoff into the ocean brings with it all sorts of debris, not to mention other pollutants. Although I couldn't think of a better way to spend a snow day, I'm not a fan of things touching me in the water. I scream like a schoolgirl when seaweed gets me, so surfing was absolutely out for the day.

I stood at the fridge, holding the door open longer than I should have without power, with that fridge-induced blank stare, wishing the stupid appliance could do more than just lazily display chilled, dismantled food. It was too hard. Was I even hungry? I was, damn it. Why couldn't I just be one of those depressed girls who loses her appetite so I could at least get *skinny* out of all this? I cleaned up the house and went outside to sweep off the car, operating in that familiar autopilot. Small branches and big leaves were down all over the street. I hate to say it, but it was nice to see that I hadn't been the only plagued target.

Soon, I would go for a drive and find a place to order a massive, wildly expensive soy latte, and maybe a bagel with an exorbitant amount of schmeared cheese that I will debate scraping off all the way till my last bite. But in the meantime, I sat on the couch with the two damp fur balls, accepting my day's fate. I took hold of the brush lying near the futile remote and began working through the kinky naps of my only two friends in the world.

The next day I received an e-mail response from Brooke. Apparently she had read the long, well-versed, accompaniment to my hot-winded *fuck off*:

> *Kath,*
>
> *My intention has never been to hurt you, and I hope you know that. I think about you all the time and honestly want nothing but the world for you. I'm taking responsibility for this. It doesn't get much worse than you saying get out of my life and fuck you.*
>
> *I suspect I won't hear from you for a long time. I will respect that. You made it clear that's what you want, which kills me, but I understand.*
>
> *Please take care of yourself. Just know that I miss you.*
>
> *My hope is that you will never lose sight of the love we once had. Because there was a time, if you remember, that we were good for each other.*
>
> *I'm happy for you that you have moved on. You deserve that.*

WAIT—DON'T LEAVE! I HAVEN'T MOVED ON! The truth was I hadn't gone anywhere, that fuck off was just a reflex, in fact, *I take it back*. Don't fuck off, because then what would I do? I cried through every syllable of her e-mail, blurry letters scattered all over the screen, tears fell to the keyboard. I read it two or three times, processing it the same each time—I read: "I love you. I want to be with you; I just can't right now. But soon, when I get this Julie thing out of my system, I'll realize that you were the best thing that ever happened to me. Wait for me."

SEVEN

SAVE THE TATAS

My brother and I surfed a lot my first few months on island. It was nice bonding with him in the way that we bond. We'd listen to music, mostly me listening to his music. "Wait, have you heard this song? It has the best line, wait for it … wait for it …" He'd be singing and air drumming and driving, turning it up and shushing me when the good parts came. "Seriously, this song is amazing; please tell me you know this one?"

"No, Ben, just like the last four songs, I don't know it."

"It's embarrassing to me how little music culture you have; this is classic!"

And if there was any time in between all this *bonding*, we tended to fill the gaps with talking shit about our impending surf session or making fun of each other for, say a weird smell, a shiny zit, or lack of sex—which was about the extent of it, for conversation that is.

So big-wave season in Hawaii coincides with rainy season, starts about November and goes till March, roughly. All except one of my visits to Hawaii had conveniently been during small-wave season. I say this only because I had begun counting surf sessions that ended in revelations of how frickin' close I came to being gobbled up by the wrath of Mother Nature, imagining falling prey to the boundless blue of the mighty mouth-foaming sea. Flashes of my body floating up as shark bait flew by in quick darts and dashes. Or more embarrassing, living only because I'd been dragged to the sympathetic shore, spitting up salt water and seaweed, by a waterman bred with greater skill and know-how, or just plain common sense.

It just so happened that on this day a whole string of those kinds of moments befell me. In fact, this was the first all-inclusive ordeal of those to come. For the record, though, I never had to be saved. Instead, I suffered several mild panic attacks and swallowed gaping mouthfuls of the Pacific, making sure I didn't have to be.

The problem was that I grew up in the water. We had a beach house from the time I was born, so I surfed or body boarded as I've been told, starting right at or around age three. I had a confidence in East Coast surf, from Rhode Island to North Carolina, which I exuded through my slick mahogany tan lines. I saved countless children when they rolled topsy-turvy into the whitewater, finding the surface with those panic-stricken eyes, and even a few grown-ass men who didn't know a lick or two about undertow. Yet surfing in Hawaii reminded me of shooting hoops on the neighbor's court, where the boundaries were set wider and the basket, crooked and several notches higher, just to keep your game honest. I likened my experience to being the MVP on JV and now riding the pine, waiting for one solitary minute of varsity playing time.

So we didn't go looking for the biggest. We usually set out toward forecasts that would coddle our ego, not demoralize it, which I appreciated given the current status of mine. In fact, my brother had a rule, "You go where there's a smaller differential between the wave heights." You wanted it to be about a two-foot differential but no more than four. So if they were calling for six to eight you were good, but six to twelve could get dicey, quickly. You'd be sitting too far inside to catch the six-ers, and when you least expected it, a twelve-er would rise out of the distance, driving you to paddle frantically, praying to make it over the thick wall of water before it came crashing down on you *and* your hurt feelings. Keep in mind, Hawaiian six to twelve is almost twelve to twenty-four foot faces, so this is no bullshit, folks, in case you were wondering.

This particular day started with my brother standing in the doorway of my room in just his boxers, belly hiding the waistband, hands on his hips giving me that *are we gonna do this or what?* attitude. This was his favorite way to guilt me into getting up in the morning on a day we had planned to surf. He'd be sure to keep me to my word that I'd spouted off, after a few beers the night before, about waking up with the sun to surf.

On this day, like so many others, I rubbed my eyes to get the sleep out and stretched noisily to iron through the kinks and buy some time while I battled out in my head the quick pros and cons of getting another hour or so of sleep. But then looking up at that stupid face puckered into a question mark, I moaned myself vertical and shuffled around in search of my suit.

Most of the time after I'd risen, that jackass would crawl back into bed, assuming my morning routine of, I don't know, breakfast and hygiene would give him plenty of time to snooze out fifteen more minutes. Except, this particular day came before that habit dawned. I must have still been new enough to the island, and he, still enamored with having me because he diligently waxed the boards and got them strapped to the roof before I'd even made it down the stairs.

I'm not sure all "real" surfers stop at Starbucks on their way to charge monsters, but we always did. Then again, I'm not sure *real surfers* would call the waves we were hoping to score *monsters*, or for that matter, that *real surfers* would even call us "real surfers." But, we were okay with that. Our typical morning routine would have me comfortably sipping a latte in the passenger seat, buckled, before he'd even make it out the door, balancing some sort of birthday cake-looking breakfast on top of his Americano, fiddling with the keys or his wallet, rattling off the standard joke about carbo-loading.

I'm not sure of the exact forecast, but I imagine it was six to ten and rising on this gray December morning. I remember thinking the report was definitely greater than the two-foot differential we preferred. We went west side, looking for swells following the Surfline report (brought to us by our good friends at Cholos, brah!). We passed Tracks, Shorebreak, Maili Point before we found our spot, Green Lanterns. It was my first time surfing this break, and I have to say I was a little nervous when we found it empty.

The nice thing about "empty" is that you have the waves all to yourself; crowded surf spots often leave you watching more than riding, but there are definitely benefits to having other riders nearby. One, it's nice to cheat off their spot or follow their line so you know where the waves are breaking most consistently. (For instance, it wouldn't be weird if you were all alone and someone paddled out to a spot right near yours. You wouldn't say, "Dude, there's a whole effin ocean here!" because if you were smart you'd do the same thing, depending on the break.) Two, you can easily learn about the current and conditions by watching a rider for just a few sets. Three, it's only the natural order of things to stay inside of said rider(s) just in case there's a belly-grumbling visitor beneath you looking for a quick snack.

The sets were far enough apart that it wasn't too much of a struggle to get outside and wait. Sitting up on our boards, we rose and fell with each massive heap culminating beneath us. Occasionally we'd paddle like two kooks (posers) when we'd fallen too close inside and a wave was rising to its mammoth face before us. At first, the ocean felt like it had a welcome mat laid out for us, but the wind picked up in clips, seeming feverish to stir things up, mess with the morning's mood somehow.

Not having a board I could duck dive (submerge under an oncoming wave), I fought to paddle far enough out beyond the break to avoid being tossed back twenty feet or so by each oncoming avalanche. The timing was all wrong; the sets were inconsistent, and the swell continued to rise. Both of us had looked down the face of at least four waves without taking the plunge. Ben warned, knowing its evil stepsister would be right on its tail, "Don't take the first wave of the set." It turned into one of those days, too, where if you actually dropped in on a wave, you'd cut out early to make the paddle back out slightly less painful. My brother caught one wave doing just that.

Thankfully, other riders had joined us, making things seem a little less daunting. And the sun became a halo behind the thick of clouds working to push its way through.

I was out of position again. A huge set came in from the outside that was far too distant to paddle out for. I was in the middle of the channel, so I thought I'd be fine, dragging my hands deep to stall, waiting till it broke to see what was to follow. Turns out, my safe spot was no more out of sight than a toddler wearing a pot on his head. The two sides of the waves joined hands and peaked to massive heights directly in front of me. Again, not having a board I could duck dive, and trying to avoid a quick snap of my leash, I did what all paranoid haole girls new to the island would do—I gripped my board, sucked in a mouthful of air, and took a deep Hail Mary plunge.

After being tossed like a ragdoll for about fifteen seconds, not knowing which end was up, I felt a pop and then an unnecessary freedom over my top half that brought on larger panic than the petulant ocean itself. My chest was cold, wetter than usual, and spring-break topless as I bobbed to the surface. My bikini top dangled from my neck like a flirty flower lei. I didn't hesitate. I untangled my straps as fast as I could, fighting to fasten everything back together. I knew I had only seconds, thanks to the wave that had knocked me into even more dangerous territory. My board floated along about six feet from where I treaded, attached to my ankle with only a thin, black rubber strap. The fate of my $600 board never occurred to me as I repeatedly plunged and surfaced like a stupid bobber near the end of a seaweed-dragging fishing line, losing a frustrating battle with my bikini straps. It was as if I'd been dangled from a crane in a straightjacket with the rope aflame as I fought desperately to untangle myself—a total parallel as I saw it. White water continually rolled in, tossing me about. In a heightening panic, I barked commands at the skimpy pieces of string under my short, distant breaths.

I grew closer and closer to shore, and the tangible threat of the thick, bone crushing shore break emanated. Still, determined to save myself the embarrassment, I scuffled with my suit, embracing that it was indeed broken and all my efforts had been lost on a cheap plastic clasp. Too tight to tie in a knot and be done with, I recognized I had no choice. The audience on the beach, who I'm sure by this point, had already seen my boobs and was probably bored by the spectacle, only watched—I swear—because you simply can't turn away from a good train wreck. I'm certain they were thinking, "This chick is toast." As I imagine it pained them to witness, I could almost hear them say, "Just give up, lady."

And, for the first time in my surfing career, that's exactly what I did. I gave up. With two huge waves cresting just inches behind me, I unleashed my board, grabbed my suit and bailed. And in the last seconds of the super wash before the spin cycle, I felt the sweet abrasiveness of sand beneath my toes. I looked back only to see the arms and grin of another huge wave shadowing over me like a jerk face monster straight out of Scooby Doo. Only this wasn't the professor, the shop owner, or the innkeeper; it was the real thing. And like Scooby, Shaggy and all their gang, I ran like hell out of there, feet and legs scrambling faster than the ground beneath me.

In my hustle, I tucked and tugged as a model on a runway with a wardrobe malfunction would try so discreetly. With rubber legs and a pounding heart, I made it to shore. I had enough sand in my suit and hair for a decent-sized drip castle. My board had washed up safe. I tied my suit finally. My tatas were safe. But my pride had been raked well across the coral—good thing there wasn't much of that to sift through.

I looked out toward the water and caught my brother paddling in. He had been watching me, I suppose, and was now doing a shit job hiding his concern. As any little sister can imagine, his fear always heightens mine. For a guy who can hide any emotion under the moon, fear is the exception. His face turns a shade of egg whites, and his eyes send out smoke signals, spelling the word h-e-l-p. I learned to recognize that face from very young when it turned up taking me by surprise because he was usually at fault for what sent him into such despair.

Perhaps it was one of those Spock pinching episodes where I didn't wake from my short slumber quickly enough. I remember him leaning over me, face stark white, shaking me awake, terrified because he had been the one doing the pinching. Or there was the time he let me tag along with the boys. He had been bragging to his friends about how well I could skateboard, except when he got me all perched up on my first real skateboard ramp, I missed the drop in, sending myself over the side of the homemade ramp's skinny platform onto my back where I knocked all the hot wind out of my body. I saw that same face of his when I got the breath back into my lungs and the tears fell away from my lashes.

I strapped my board back on, lifting it to my side. I didn't want to leave the beach in such awful defeat. I yelled to him that I was coming back out, but he pretended not to hear. He had probably already made up his mind. Who knows, maybe he was happy I had beached myself like Shamu. It's not like he was doing much surfing, anyway. I think he may have caught only that one wave. A wimpy one as I recall it, but one more than me, unfortunately. I'd be sure to hear about that for days.

We rinsed off at the spigot, me dumping half the beach into the drain. We got our boards rigged up and wet like two rats retreated back to the house. Big-wave season had only just begun. I sat in the car deflated, hoping this wasn't a forecast for the rest of the winter.

With my window down, peering out at the clipped images of coastline flying by, I pondered the lessons learned in case I should ever be in this situation again. One, leave lei-like suit to dangle from neck. Two, remount board, pressing naked chest firmly to surface. Three, paddle back out beyond break, far away and in the opposite direction of oglers on beach. Four, when to safety, dismount board and bob like a buoy as originally displayed. Five, if instructions one, two, and three are not viable options, for some unforeseen circumstance, I'm thinking … go out like a shameless party girl—save yourself first, then the tatas.

EIGHT

MELE KALIKIMAKA

Mele Kalikimaka is the thing to say
On a bright Hawaiian Christmas Day
That's the island greeting that we send to you
From the land where palm trees sway
Here we know that Christmas will be green and bright
The sun to shine by day and all the stars at night
Mele Kalikimaka is Hawaii's way
To say "Merry Christmas to you."

My ego was bruised, yet nothing in my life had changed otherwise. I was still all the way over here; she was still all the way over there. I still woke up, and went to work, and did all my chores, and smiled and laughed when it was appropriate, but my ego just dragged behind me like a pair of unzipped footie pajamas that I wasn't willing to step out of. I was depressed all through Christmas, because for single people, let's be honest, the holidays blow. I tried to hold it together while we strung lights to the nice tree our neighbor, Charlie, had given us. (He had a few.) We were pretty sure they had "fallen off the truck," as they say, but it was a tree nonetheless. Regardless,

Christmas just doesn't feel like *Christmas* in Hawaii no matter which way you cut it, even *with* all their Mele Kalikimaka. So I was incredibly grateful for the lingering scent of pine in the house, black market or not.

We unraveled the plastic web and revealed the most glorious, expensive Douglas Fir. Lea huffed at the mess as the needles fell in clumps to the floor like hair strewn in a salon, but I was thrilled to have at least one piece of home here with us. I'd gladly sweep up the sticky mess. Especially since my trees back home were typically Charlie Browns. I'd woken up one year to the sound of my very large, heavily ornamented, thirty-dollar job crashing to the floor. Lucky Badass, my other four-legged dependent, all sappy and tangled inside, meowing like someone else was to blame for the chaos. So, every year thereafter I'd roll up to the seediest lookin' roadside lot, asking, "What's the cheapest one you've got?" And $10 later, I'd be shoving the squatty, prickly thing into the hatch of my little white Honda.

We listened to carols, and I'll be damned if I didn't get in the mood, singing along with Dolly Parton's "Hard Candy Christmas." I even made it all the way through Kenny Loggins's "Celebrate Me Home." I guess it was rather masochistic to be listening to the mix I'd made for Brooke and me when we'd hosted our first Christmas party in the new house, but somehow I was able to ignore the drama and just enjoy the kids. Christmas was all about the kids this year, anyway. Besides, I didn't need a thing—well, except maybe a new pair of footie pajamas.

Ben spent his evenings and weekends around Christmas rotating shifts at the mall. He had been volunteering for the railroad society and had been asked to drive the kids' train for the second year in a row. I have to admit it was hard to remain mad at him for anything when I saw him propped patiently on top of a miniature train, waiting for the screaming kids to be loaded on so he could take his 150th lap of the day—wearing a red handkerchief, an engineer hat, and that dimpled *dad* smile he makes. (The one that goes with that weird high-pitched voice that he uses when he talks to other people's kids in front of their parents). He got away with a lot in those weeks.

I can't say it didn't get me in the spirit of giving though. While he was at work one Saturday afternoon, I decided to tackle the garage disaster at home. I made a pile of giveaways, a pile of throwaways, and tried to organize the rest by category: kids' stuff, shoes, tools, sports equipment, random. When Ben got home, we took the loads to the dump before the rest of the crew woke up from their nap and could assess what they'd be missing.

∞

We spent Christmas Eve at my favorite beach, Makapu'u. Ben and I body boarded all day, acting like kids in the shore break. The waves were consistent, and other riders only speckled the surface, bobbing in the tides, so we dropped in on everything we lined up for until the sun dipped behind the cliffs, casting a cool shadow over the beach, and the chill that came with it chased us out of the water.

It never fails that if Ben's nearby when I line up for a wave, he will invariably grab my flipper, pull me out of position and take off right in front of me. I had to laugh at his typical boyish antics only because all the other waves I caught I knew he was watching me, and after spending so much time in the water, I'd gotten to be pretty damn good.

As the baby of two talented older brothers, there was never anything I could do better. And *everything* was a competition. I remember in fifth grade, after moving in with my aunt and uncle, when I'd gotten my new saxophone. I thought that since Ben played trumpet, perhaps there'd finally be one thing I could do better. I took it out of its case to show him my new, shiny brass awesomeness, and within five minutes he had mastered the four pieces I had just begun honking my way through. This is also the same guy who later taught himself to play guitar by ear, and for that reason among others, it justifies why I'm still keeping tally on all the things I can do better.

∞

Christmas was good. The kids had a blast. Gavin got a train (which took us over an hour to build) and played with it for a half hour, at most, before he crashed it all down. In fact, he played with all of his toys for just about forty-five minutes before he was back to slamming cabinets and banging pots with a wooden spoon. Lea gave her best effort putting together what she joked was a "haole Christmas dinner": her famous soba noodle salad, of course, spicy green beans, mashed potatoes and some marinated meat grilled on the hibachi. (I was still on the Brooke-induced hiatus from vegetarianism and was really taking to Lea's flavor-filled fatty meats.)

Lea did this little kim-chi squat, we called it, when she'd cook on the hibachi. She'd fold her petite frame in half and sit about three inches from the driveway with her little feet firmly on the ground, flipping meat in one hand, holding a fat glass of red in the other. The poor thing doesn't even eat meat. Noodles and veggies, and if it's not too much trouble, a shrimp or two sometimes; or if she gets crazy, fish, but all those extras are seen less as essential and more as a bonus because she'd be happy to sustain on those square, ten cent, salty packs of Top Ramen if we'd let her. If I ate just one of those packs, the sodium alone would blow me up like a

Macy's balloon, not to mention what the carbs would do to my ass, but she never seems to outgrow her size two, and for that, I incessantly remind her that she's a bitch.

∞

I love my family, but boy was I thrilled to find out that just after Christmas some friends from home were flying out. I used to work with Kristen at Coconuts; she was bringing her girlfriend, Kim, and two of their other friends from New York. And they were all coming to stay with Kristen's sister, Kathy, who lived on island at the time. Although they never said boo about it, they knew I was going through some shit, and therefore, were kind and gracious to invite me on every excursion they fit into their weeklong itinerary. I did more with them in that week than I had done by myself the entire two and a half months I'd lived on island.

I drove up with some beers for an impromptu beach bonfire they put together on one of their first nights. We smoked a joint and shot the shit like old times, except not in a dumpy bar in Baltimore. Kristen and Kim both said how jealous they were that I lived here. And I admitted how surreal life had become waking up to paradise every morning, but really I was jealous of them holding hands, sharing cute glances and wrapping their arms around each other when the night brought in the cold.

I met them at beaches I had never been to. One time we took a boat out to the Sandbar where, knee deep in water, we all drank like fish, and I knocked back some top shelf tequila like nobody's business. Another day we climbed Stairway to Heaven where, thank God, I was out in front so the girls didn't have to see me all blurry eyed and wet cheeked through the whole last section to the top. I don't typically do heights. It was really windy, and while I clung to the ladder, white knuckled, climbing as fast as I could just to get it over with, we burst straight up into the clouds. I have to admit it was awesome, painfully so.

∞

The ladies invited me to join them on a New Year's Eve booze cruise. Since my other option was popping cut-rate, smoky fireworks in the cul-de-sac with the fam, feeling sorry for myself and the environment, which also has to suffer through this cheap thrill of a holiday, I said yes. It was nice having the week off, but by the time we got to the cruise, I had boozed my whole way through vacation. I drank a little on the boat, enough to help me ignore the three cuddling couples. There were a few of us bitter singles on deck (which padded the wound a bit), but it was impossible to avoid the couples being all cutesy every time I turned around to say something. I tried to focus on the fair-weathered night, the nice-enough boat, the moonlit water, the simple pu-pu (appetizer) spread they had set up inside the deck.

The houses along Diamond Head were all lit up beautifully. I thought, *smart people to stay home, rather than get all fancied up for a fussy party, making a big deal out of nothing*. I tried to sound enthusiastic as we counted down the seconds to midnight. And I was even *more* thrilled to watch the glorious explosions raining pollution, one right after the other, over Waikiki beach.

I brought '08 in with a bang all right. I got home late, and there was still shit all over the cul-de-sac. Stiff, smelly smoke hung in the humidity. I climbed the stairs to my bedroom alone and defeated, feet heavier with each step, and crawled into bed. Not that I wanted anyone to join me, my mojo had long since eloped—I imagined it had bolted at the first sight of sticker stars on the ceiling and superhero sheets. I had only wanted, maybe, just one person to hold hands with, and if things went well, perhaps a playful lil' peck at midnight to bring in the stupid New Year.

NINE

WILL YOU BE MY FRIEND?

I had dated someone from the time I was thirteen, hopping from one relationship right into another—a perpetual monogamist of sorts. I liked having an avid listener of my show, a single fan of my daily news feed. I had grown rather used to it.

On the sidelines, Gma was always more than willing to offer some coaching (for the rotation of boys at least). "Mix 'em around; dangle a few a time," was her suggestion. In high school, I argued, advice like that would be sure to secure me a *killer* reputation, but in college it may have been wise to play the field a little, I suppose.

Instead, I dove into one love story after another, writing my own drawn-out, love-sick script. Two years, then eight months, then three years, then eighteen months, then Brooke; and that's just counting those since I could vote. Sure, there were some make-out sessions in between, some unfaithful moments that I'd swear karma's kickin' me in the ass for now, but that was it.

In fact, Brooke was the first person I'd ever been completely faithful to. (Well, besides Brooke, there is my unconditional loyalty to Britney Spears I should mention. Even through her worst days, careening off the deep end, bald headed, I've stuck by her. Through thick and thin, literally, I have never denied her my faithfulness and compassion, defending her even. In fact the worse off she got, I imagined, my chances only got better, so I not only supported her meltdowns, I welcomed them. That's gotta earn me points in some system, right?)

I wouldn't describe myself as a cheater, but cheating often *happened* to me. I mean that in the sense that I didn't go looking for it, it just found me; which, as I saw it, made me totally less of a player in it. Plus, when you're *exploring your sexuality* you get all sorts of freebies because you're, well, *exploring*—there's like a separate badge and everything. So, here I was celibate, and I was planning to stay that way for a while—a long while. I was going to have a nice, extended, endearing relationship with myself, except for not really *that* kind of relationship. In fact, *that* part was either broken, or completely distracted by *SpongeBob* and screaming children, or maybe the two pictures of my matron saints on the dresser staring at me constantly. And for all those reasons there would be no relations with myself.

∞

Prior to my friends coming to town, I had been out without the family once or twice if you count the Ziggy Marley concert with Lea's friend, but only once *out*-out by myself. And, it shouldn't even count because Lea had told me about the party through her friend G, who was the DJ at his lesbian friend Roobe's (Ruby) ladies party that she threw in town every first Saturday of the month. I felt like a shy, nerdy kid whose mom was trying to help make friends by dropping her off at a YMCA mixer. In fact, Lea had originally planned to go with me, but at the last minute bailed. I debated going right back upstairs in a tizzy to change. Instead, I did the quick math, calculating the obvious: I had nothing to lose. I was on the *list*; I knew G; I could do this.

I'd never been to a bar by myself, unless I was on my way to meet someone, *or* if I knew there'd be the likely familiar faces bent up on the bar stools when I arrived. Here, I only hoped that perhaps one of the three lesbos I knew on island might show up.

It's great to know the DJ, *I guess*, but it's not like you can hang out with him. I screamed over the music into his ear, which he kindly lifted one side of his mega-earphones for. "How are you?"

He yelled back, "Where's Lea?" He was gracious enough to give me drink tickets and introduce me to Roobe, but since she was managing the event, she too couldn't save me from my station as wallflower.

The bar was nice, at least the nicest ladies' bar I'd ever been to. Coconuts made this place look like the Ritz Carlton. It was chic and modern, black and white décor with huge glass windows overlooking the harbor. There was even a lady in the bathroom who gave out towels and gum and deodorant and all kinds of other interesting accoutrements. By night's end, I had spent more money with her than I had on the bartender. I see it a total injustice when you shi-shi as much as I do. I should only have to tip every *other* time, because really—I can get my own paper towel.

The big square bar in the middle of the restaurant made doing laps seem like a perfect way to scope the scene. I made it look like I was trying to find someone, which in a sense you could say that I was, and those seated on the couches or the far side of the bar had no idea whether I ever found that *someone* on the other side or not. So every few minutes, rather brazenly, I'd look again.

Thankfully, I found my swagger hidden in the bottom of my first cocktail. Sometimes there just can't be enough said for a dose of some liquid courage. I walked more upright, shoulders back, chin lifted with each sip.

So the bar was nice, the music was good, and the ladies, well, let's just say things were looking up. In my experience, not just at

Coconuts, but ladies' bars in general, you have to weed out a lot of the scary ones to see the smattering of cute ones. This place was a diamond in the rough, or perhaps it had just been a while. Even with no one to talk to, I smiled at all the possibilities. As for my evening, I was either on the dance floor, in the bathroom, or doing laps, and before I knew it, I had closed the bar down. I might have had fun, even. I had talked to four whole people. I knew G and Roobe, and I met two other haole women from Texas who were leaving to go back to their God-lovin' Lonestar state in the morning (which was a good thing because Texas was totally out of my jurisdiction). It wasn't a total fail.

The entire bar spilled out front into the long open hallway, where the ladies all stood around waiting for friends or just hanging out, cooling off from the steamy dance floor. Chicks handed out flyers for upcoming events. I grabbed a few as I walked through the line by myself, with no one to go to the after party with. Could I even stay up for an after party? At 2:00 a.m., I was already pushing it. This was going to be a little more difficult than I'd imagined.

On my way to the parking lot, it dawned on me that I would inevitably drive past all those ladies in Lea's mom-mobile. Don't get me wrong, I was very grateful she let me drive her little black Honda box. For *her*, it was an adorable car, and in fact, she loved it, so I should have been even *more* grateful. I just really happened to *adore* my truck, the one that was sitting at home with no one to wash it like I used to, religiously. It was my first brand new car, and I swear it made me feel like Michael J. Fox in *Back to the Future*—you know, in the end, with the hot black truck—every time I hoisted myself up into the seat.

Mine was storm gray, not jacked up on wheels or anything, but sleek and sexy—a *chick truck*. I had bought it as the "family car." I'd originally wanted something smaller, with better gas mileage and had toyed with a Mini Cooper, but when Brooke sat inside of that little Matchbox of a thing in the showroom, she said, "No way." Plus, Porter was tipping near a hundred pounds by then— point taken. But now, here I was with a family car that just sat at home collecting dead leaves and dusty pollen while I was out here driving a mom-mobile.

Yes, this is my ego. *Pleased to meet you.*

What should have been my clue is that NOBODY has an ego about cars in Hawaii. They rust, they get sun spots. Unless you are one of those people who can afford to replace your car every two years, you drive whatever you can get your hands on for as long as it will go. (Plus, when I did finally make friends, my mom-mobile turned out to be the nicest ride in the bunch.) But, on this night, when I was trying to impress whomever I thought might be im- pressionable, I wanted my truck. Since getting what I wanted wasn't really how things were plotting out around here, I drove by the emptying bar full of chick prospects with my seat tilted back to the door seam.

∞

I couldn't wait another month till the next party to hook up with people. I had solid evidence now that hanging out with folks out- side my immediate family was good for the psyche. I just needed friends who weren't going back to New York or Texas for that matter. I went to the Internet, *there's got to be another ladies night.* Yet, most of the gay scene I found online was for men. *Isn't this the Rainbow State? Where are all the frickin' lesbians?* It was only just as I was about to give up that I found the flyers that had been passed out at the party. I had put them on my dresser when I'd emptied my pockets that night. I went through each of them, searching for information, but they all seemed to point to their Myspace pages.

Shit. Myspace.

And that's how I, at almost thirty years old, after teasing my students all along for their online obsession, created a Myspace account.

At first it was fun, I have to admit. Design template: done. General interests: I went through the list, making it punchy and creative (with probably more guilty pleasure than necessary). I must say—thank you, Jesus—how grateful I am that Myspace was not yet conceived when I was in high school. I can only imagine the great shame I would have branded on my character, not to mention my family. Without sufficient documentation (like, say, an online database), I bank on the poor memory of those who witnessed those formidable years of mine. That and the fact that I haven't forgotten the mess of themselves they made right along with me.

Now what? Upload profile pic. *Great, I have like four pictures of myself.* I was about a decade behind and had only just gone digital. I had bought a new camera for my move, but for as many laps as I'd made around the island by myself, I'd never asked anyone to take a picture of just me. I had a few of me and the kids, I suppose I could crop.

Oh great. I needed a song too, or an anthem, really. (Hmm— what song says: independent, not one lick o' lonely, confident, hella awesome, looking for a damn good time, no drama?)

Right ... that's what I was thinking ... skip that one for now.

Next, I needed friends. When you sign up, everyone gets the same friend, Tom. So far, Tom was my only friend. I searched for people I knew and was relieved to find that I was one of the last to join this crowd-pleasing bandwagon. None of my really close friends at home had a page. They were all mature and/or married and certainly didn't need a frickin' "network." This was all so ridiculous. The last time I was single the Internet wasn't even invented!

Okay, so how do I make friends? Wait—I have to *ask* people to be my friend? For real? This goes against every ounce of coolness I had collected and bottled over the years. I was immediately sixteen again and popular with an attitude. The idea of asking someone to "be my friend," and to have those exact words spelled out in an e-mail horrified me.

Please welcome back my ego to the stage.

I got over it, because really, what's worse: having one friend, Tom, or asking people *to be my friend*, many of whom were already my friends in real life, anyway?

Jesus, this is dumb.

I knew Brooke was going to have a field day with my Myspace page, but I didn't care. I needed this to figure out the scene over here and to figure out me in this scene over here. I saw it as a fabulous research tool. Plus, it was great for mindless entertainment. I'd often spend hours flipping through pages, *researching* of course, and then bam, one night I ended up on this chick's, Steph's, page.

She had sort of the same fauxhawk as me, and when I was out at the party that night, a couple of people had called me Steph before apologizing for their mistake. In her *work* section, she mentioned Gold's Gym. (This is where the island gets really small.) I had an interview lined up with Gold's for a spin instructor position the following week. And, as fate would have it, I met Crazy Steph the very first day I went down to the gym. I think she recognized me from the bar that one night, and we became fast friends, laughing about our "twin" status.

We had a lot in common, but where I was docile and poised, she was aggressive and outspoken. She was shorter than me. I'm five foot eight, so I nearly towered over her and (what felt like) the whole damn state. She was about five three, had a half-sleeve tattoo, an ex-military attitude, and a crooked smile. She had muscles to envy, no doubt, and she knew it, too. I caught her checking herself out in the mirror more times than not. Steph surfed, which was a big bonus; she'd been on island for more than a year, so she knew people, bonus; and she was reading a lot of the same books I had just begun to read—a seeker of sorts, as well.

The first time we met at the gym, she took me to her desk, sat me down, looked me straight in the eye and asked me what I knew about *The Secret*. I had no idea what she was talking about, but I lied and said that I'd heard of it. "You have to go home tonight and watch it," she said with every ounce of *I know I just met you but*...authority. "I have a copy; you can borrow mine if you can't find one." She wasn't done. "Dude, once you've lived here for a while, you'll start to notice that this island has sick energy. Things like this," she pointed at me, her piercing blue eyes still fixed, "me meeting you today, it's crazy, you'll start to see synchronicity everywhere." She was amped on secrets—she was always amped on something. I just looked at her and nodded, stoked on the wisdom she spilled into my brain: *secret, synchronicity*—on it!

I left Gold's thrilled, smiling from ear to ear, almost skipping to my mom-mobile. I had a friend; I had homework; I lived in a magical place of synchronicity; life was good—*chee hu.*

The next morning, on top of the hill at Tripler, I asked the guys about *The Secret*. "Ho, coz, dat stuff crazy kine." They always had the best responses in Pidgin English, full of emotion and, "ho, coz!"

Everyone in Hawaii is cousin, and to show respect, all your elders are your aunties and uncles. My guys called me "Auntie" once. They howled at the stink eye I threw back at them, but they never did say it again. In the meantime, I picked up their Pidgin like I always pick up accents. I spoke to them in Pidgin, and I spoke to Andrew, the haole guy, in his own dialect, Virginia Redneck.

I have a terrible habit of taking on accents. It started when I was young. My uncle always said that I sang country songs with the best twang he'd ever heard from a kindergartner, practically a Yankee. And then in fourth-grade Spanish class, I'd get the greatest compliments on my diction, even though I hadn't learned a lick. In fact, I sat next to *Pablo*, for obvious reasons, just to keep up. Then it was late middle school and high school, when I was finally in a classroom with more than one black kid I started to talk black—in deserving company, you know. In college, I noticed I sounded just like I was from Texas when I visited a friend in Dallas. And I was embarrassed to realize that I even laughed more like a lady when I hung out with my drag queen friends from work.

I always saw it as my innate sense of empathy, my way of making everyone feel welcome, assimilating with my surroundings, if you will. But when I questioned it as an inauthentic flaw, I'd remember how Gma used to call me a chameleon with that very connotation. In high school I had preppy flannels and rugby shirts I wore with one crew, bell bottoms and thrift store T-shirts with my folky pothead friends; I'd even rock the standard white-girl gangster wear on occasion. You name it, and I'll be damned if Gma didn't call me out on it.

I'll admit that my dialect dysfunction was dragged into the awkward spotlight one night at work when I waited tables, in my mid-teacher years, at the Metropolitan. This poor woman looked up from her menu and placed her order with an awful, unmistakable lisp. And, as God as my witness, when I repeated the order back to her, I too shared her very distinctive impediment. I was mortified. What if she thought I was making fun of her? I begged my co-worker to deliver their food and then to check on them, refill their waters, and give them the check to get them the hell out of there—so I didn't have to hide in the kitchen any longer. Total fail. And worse, Gma was right.

∞

Hawaiian Pidgin is a creole language originally used for the English-speaking residents to communicate with the non-English speaking immigrants. It was influenced by Portuguese, Hawaiian, Cantonese, and then later, Japanese, Korean, Spanish, and Filipino. There are a lot of word and sound omissions or replacements, and a rare falling intonation comes with any question. My guys would say, "How's it?" or "I went for da store," or "Where you stay?" or "Ho coz, gonna be plenty good kine surf ovah dare dis Sataday." They called all effeminate men "mahus," which I loved for some reason, and when they had to pee they'd say, "I gotta shi-shi."

Most of the time I caught on; it wasn't hard to figure out. It was just faster than the casual speed of the English I was used to. They talked more quickly and with much more emotion, reminding me of the Spanish that I never did pick up. Even in the kitchens of all those restaurants I worked where the language flew faster and in much greater repetition than the appetizers, I got hola, gracias, and de nada—das it.

Apparently there are Hispanics in Hawaii, but most would probably be confused for Hawaiian or many of the other cultures that once landed here. I don't think I heard any Spanish spoken my entire stay on island. There were also like seven black people, most of them military. I'll never forget when I got off the plane my first trip back home. I had been on island for a year and hadn't heard a Southern black woman's accent in all that time. I almost jumped into the arms of this poor woman when I walked through the gate in Houston. Let's be honest, everything about a Southern black woman makes you just wanna dive into her bosom.

∞

Steph finally gave me the DVD so I could see what this *Secret* was all about. I watched it. I was a believer, but I already swore by fate and good intentions and karma and the power of positive thinking. I just didn't use the positive part all that often. I'd gotten used to my habits of perpetual pessimism. I thought they suited me. I figured if you were a pessimist then whatever happened would either be what you expected, or a pleasant surprise. Much better than the cruel disappointment of fastidious optimism.

Steph took this whole law of attraction and power of positive thinking thing to a whole new level. I would say something like, "Oh great, now we're probably gonna hit traffic."

She would blow up, which I saw as a glaring inconsistency. "Well, great, now we will—thanks. Why would you say something like that?" she'd bark from the passenger seat. I was always skeptical of her criticism since she was a terrific example of a walking contradiction.

But she was right. I should've been more positive. She was also right about the synchronicity thing. Weird little happenings began poking up, their charming faces, flashing me winks as I went by. It was starting to become obvious; I *was* in the right place—and a magical place it was.

TEN

HOLY FATHER

It was right about the time when I started to feel settled that Ben dropped the bomb on me.

"Dad's coming in two weeks."

I immediately felt that thick warmth in my body rise up from the floor; then came the soundless, thwarted scream from a recurring nightmare. And with heart-gripping grief came suffocating panic. My mind raced, clawing at the hatch to escape. *What will I do? Where will I go? But I don't want to go!* Ben knew I wasn't speaking to Dad, and hadn't in years, which was why he'd waited until the very last minute. He was notorious for forever harboring lies of omission. He stood in my doorway, not knowing what to do as he watched my bottom lids fight back the flood, the dam buckling by sheer force. He assured me I could stay with Sheila and Michelle, two great family friends—but I wouldn't hear of it. I wanted my room, the complacency of my things, my new home that had just begun to feel comfortable.

He left without resolution, rightfully afraid. I slammed the door behind him, rolled my back to its thin wood and let go the resistance—murky, heavy tears rushed forth. I heaved and gasped and threw the greatest production of a pity party that even I didn't recognize. Banging things. Throwing things. Then—within minutes, I was standing at my dresser, with salty, soaked cheeks and that whooping, crying cough that you get, trying to pull myself together.

I couldn't even make sense of why I was so upset. I mean, I hadn't cried like this over *that* in ages. In fact, I couldn't remember the last time. It was just everything culminating all at once like it always had. (This is usually the part where we roll out the abandonment carpet, so I can clomp my way down the familiar empty corridor.) I felt badly for poor Lea, who knocked bravely before coming in to console me. I just spat leftover tears and snot all over her as I tried to explain. "It's just too much. After everything, it's just too much."

The truth of the matter was that I collected pain. I stuffed it onto the shelves whose brackets would tremble at the notion of one more thing. And I kept it all there to be dealt with later. I would tidy myself up, put my heart right back on my sleeve, and then when another bit of insult would hit, I'd toss it on up there until every once in a while the whole mess would come crashing down on my head. I'd melt down like a child because that's how old I was when some of the first haunts were boxed away.

And not only did I collect my own pain, I collected all that I could pick up for my loved ones as well. I'd clean their cabinets and stock mine, because maybe, just maybe, I thought if I could take their pain away then mine would go with it. They'd make friends somehow and skip off into the sunset. Plus I always wanted to be the hero. I wanted to dart around and save people: an old lady from an icy fall, a kid from the attack of a big jerk face bully, a mom from driving off with her coffee strapped in the car seat and the baby on the roof. I would just swoop in and save them all.

Do other people think this way? It's totally normal, right? It could be the sheets that got me thinking like this. I mean I know kids want to grow up to be superheroes, but deep down, I think I still do—hot pants and all. Perhaps it's because rock star hasn't quite panned out. Or maybe it runs far deeper—an unfulfilled prophecy of sorts.

Maybe it's because I always wondered whether I could've actually done something. Honestly, the thought may have never crossed my mind if it weren't for my brothers, who had asked why I didn't try to save her. We were all still so young then, yet I knew what they were saying—if either one of them had been there, perhaps she'd still be alive. But it was only me there that day. I was the only one who heard her scream. I was the only one who could have protected her.

I remember I was confused—that wasn't her, I thought—but something told me to get out, just in case. I scrambled out of the way back of the wagon, I would tell the courtroom later, leaving my crayon in the crease of the unfinished page. I would use Barbie and Ken dolls and a model of my dad's office to show the jurors where I stood on my tippy-toes to peer inside the window only to see my mom's and dad's feet through the doorway, lying on the floor. I struggled to open the front door to the office, I assured my brothers, but it was locked.

"Why didn't you break the window?" they wanted to know.

I guessed then—when I didn't know what to say—it was because I was dumb, or because I was small, or worse, because I was a girl, I didn't even think to try.

∞

I remember one time in college, when I lived in Ocean City, Maryland, with my five faves, it was ninety consecutive days of drinking, drugs, and Dave Matthews Band. I had one of my infamous meltdowns. I came running into the Twenty-First Street Phillips Crab House Carry-out where we all worked at the time, wiping tears with my tank top, to tell my best friend, Whitney, I had a flat tire.

And on that particular day, under those particular circumstances, a flat tire meant: "I don't have a mom, my dad just got out of jail, I don't get along with my family, I miss my brothers, I don't have any money, I smoked my last joint already, there's only one beer in the fridge, and I'm really sorry, but last night at 4:00 a.m., I ate your leftover nachos!"

Whitney grabbed me by the shoulders, looked me in the eye and said, "It's just a tire, Kath." She couldn't help but smile. "It's just a fucking tire."

And I both hated her and loved her for saying that.

If I had kept track of how many times since that day I've heard in my head, "It's just a tire, Kath," I'd have another book—each time hating her and loving her more and more.

That said, I packed my bags and moved in just down the street with Sheila and Michelle, their two dogs, a cat, and a talking parrot for the next two weeks. And by day two, I'd nearly forgotten I had a family to fuss over at all.

But that's how this sort of thing goes: life doesn't wait for us to pick up the pieces—we just do—or we don't, dragging on broken, incomplete. I always resented my father for having all that time withdrawn to get comfortable with what he had done. It's easier when there's no homework and chores, I suppose. Over the years, I had openly paraded between the poles of *effin pissed* and *it is what it is*. I think I frightened a whole class full of co-eds once with my strong arguments *for* the death penalty. Not revealing my reasoning, they were rightfully confused given it had been the only bit of right-wing politics to come flying out of my mouth (and with such fervor) all semester. In the years since, I had been hanging out more near the opposite pole. *It is what it is.*

Sheila and Michelle were innately hospitable. Michelle loves to cook, keeping me well fed every night. Sheila got me all set up, insisting that I make myself at home. Suki, the parrot, cracked me up when he yelled at the dogs, just like Sheila, or talked on the phone, just like Michelle. He'd laugh like the girls and sing along with Jack Johnson, just like Jack Johnson, but his head-bobbing moves were all Suki. In the garage, they had every big-kid toy imaginable, including a kayak, which I couldn't wait to get wet. They also had dinner parties that didn't involve sippy cups, tears, and temper tantrums. Their house was less than a block from the beach, so I fell asleep to the sound of the rolling waves. It was quiet, tranquil, a blessing really.

I never saw my father in those weeks that he visited, nor did I think about him much after my meltdown. The fact of the matter was that I couldn't exactly articulate why I wasn't speaking to him anyway. It's true, we had begun a relationship when he'd gotten out of jail. We had sought therapy together, and I honestly thought I was doing the mature thing. Hating him wasn't going to bring her back. I'd already spent years trying. I had forgiven him for what he'd done, or so I thought—fifteen years after the fact—I couldn't imagine my life any other way.

It wasn't long before the therapy teetered to a halt, only because the lady was weird and we never bothered to find another not so weird one. I had two more messy years of college that he willingly helped me through: picking me up from parties when I was too wasted to drive or forking over to get my car out of hock when I'd ignored the signs and parked there anyway. Pretty much anytime I felt too guilty to call Gma, I called him. It was nice having someone bat for me for a change, someone whom I wouldn't be compelled to resent later for the disproportionate weight of the inevitable guilt trip.

He was the first person in my family I came out to, because what was he going to do, judge me? He looked at me as if I had just told him I was a natural brunette—*nothin'*. Seems he was one of the few I hadn't fooled. Our relationship stumbled along through cracked sidewalks and inevitable potholes for almost six years when I came home crying one night, frustrated at his laxity in conversation, talking about his constant quest to find a girl-friend, which I didn't care to be clued in on, and Brooke finally asked, "Why do you do this to yourself?"

The truth was, at that point, our relationship had ebbed and flowed on guilt and gratification for some time. Because when I was with him, all I could do was pick him apart to tiny bits to kick around in the dirt and cloud up my unease. That was part of the problem with creating a dad in my head for all those years. When he came out looking like mine, I couldn't let go of all the things I wanted him to be. I'd come home fuming or frustrated, yet feeling badly because he'd lent me a hundred and fifty bucks. It was prob-ably '06, just before Brooke and I bought our new house and were getting ready to start our new life and create our own family that I took her advice.

I dropped him, and because she never wanted any part of him anyway, it was easy. Except for when I spoke to Ben, I barely thought about Dad in those days, or my unattended baggage for that matter. I only looked forward, walking on sunshine—well, at least until everything fell into the shitter again.

I was sad that my Grandma Mary, whom my dad had cared for, died during the time when I ignored him. She was kind, and her face always lit up like a bulb when I walked through the door. She had sent cards all those years and $25, but never knew what more to add to the generic wish than, "Love, Grandma Mary and Grand-pa Jack." My Gma always thought she could have done more and said so. She hated how Mary had defended her son till the day he finally confessed—three years after his first conviction.

Over the years, I came to Grandma Mary's defense. "You would have done the same for your son. How was she to know he was lying?" And Grandma Mary had stood by him looking past, or perhaps just ignoring, the shame—his hands—what they'd been capable of. I saw her pictured with Dad in all the holiday visits at the jail, smiling. He always sent photos along with his letters. I resented those smiles for years, yet for some reason I always wrote back—well, mostly.

In those last few months, Grandma Mary would have barely been able to recognize me, and it would have been hard to get to her without seeing him. So that's how I justified ignoring the fact that her time dwindled. My dad never bothered calling about her funeral. I guess it was just as well.

My brother Jack also put some effort into a relationship with Dad, after he watched me embark on the intriguing new territory. He was curious, had just as many questions, but when the time came, it was mostly beers and jokes and avoidance and brushing it all under the carpet, like always. There may have been some e-mail exchanges, some questions asked, and answers offered that never seemed quite good enough, I'm sure. Yet as a grown-ass man, after all these years, Jack felt he really didn't need a father—like he wasn't willing to hand over the title. Or, at least, that's what he said.

I imagined the relationship had opened too many wounds that he had already stitched himself, no anesthesia, just crooked scars and worn-out bandages. I understood. It was his decision, made easy with the help of his wife, who like Brooke, wanted nothing to do with Dad.

So Ben was the only one still speaking to him, and I had my opinions about that. We didn't talk about it much. I just hoped he wasn't holding on because he felt guilty like I used to. I hoped he was being genuine to himself. And through the mystery that is my brother, I may never know.

Regardless of all that, Dad stayed two weeks, and ironically, I was kind of sad to see him go. I felt like I was on vacation at Sheila and Michelle's. Sure, I helped them around the house a bit; doing the dishes and picking up dog poop was well worth the exchange.

Back at the house, Dad had fixed up the whole yard. He and Ben had worked around the property all week, mending and fixing things. He didn't really *have* to go. Plus, I had already decided that if I saw him at the supermarket or something I wasn't going to run the other way. I'd be cordial. I didn't hate him. I just didn't much like him. Well, in all fairness, it was *us* I didn't care for.

∞

My Gma fought tooth and nail with the concept of forgiveness. At Mass she'd get her britches all in a bunch when the presiding Father would pray for the convicts but forget to also say a prayer for the victims. Following Mass, she'd be sure to shake her fist and give him hell as she walked through the receiving line. Those last few years she expressed *that* as being one of her biggest regrets, not being able to forgive my father. She knew I had begun a relationship with him, and I credited her generous restraint. Yet she'd fold at unexpected times, revealing her disdain, and out would come every awful thing he ever did (before and after), including why she never liked him in the first place.

I would defend with, "It's different when you're the child. I don't know if I'd be able to forgive him either if I were you."

Which was true; we would never have been able to walk in each other's shoes.

She was a good Catholic and had doled out forgiveness beyond measure in all her years, with slight hang-ups on things like anything baring the label *Made in China*, or one of her other faves, the Democratic Party—Bill Clinton in particular. But even with him, she worked through her indignation. She wrote Mr. Clinton a letter damn near every week he was in office, expressing her sheer contempt. I would watch her at the dining room table diligently transcribe his address from the yellowing pages of her address book, huffing and puffing with each illegible word. Her return address proudly in bold and a patriotic stamp licked corner to corner to symbolically snub. And then she'd be hell bent for election to get that letter to his desk before her "bone to pick with him" lost its thunder.

But she never wrote my dad a letter. She talked about it once or twice, but never did. I always wondered what it might have said. She prayed to her Father instead—God the Father—and asked among other things to be given the forgiveness she couldn't find the strength to offer herself—

"And while you're at it, if you would be so kind, might you grant me some peace. I could sure use a little of that around here."

ELEVEN

AN EDUCATION

Steph and I surfed all the time. She was adamant about teaching me all the rules of the water, which I was pretty sure I *got* already, but she always knew more than me, according to her, so I let her. We complained about our broken hearts, where we'd try to outdo each other's devastation. She would inevitably tell me to get over it, and I'd do the same for her. She introduced me to friends and took me to yoga classes with those friends, who turned out to be strippers supporting their grad school pursuits, so we went to see them at work a few times to say "hey."

I'll admit I'm a lousy lesbian to take to a strip bar. I immediately get shy and stand in the corner—hands in pockets, no eye contact. I refuse to spend money on five minutes of entertainment (never mind the fact that I didn't find most of the women entertaining in the slightest). I especially didn't like being dragged all around the club by confident, aggressive Steph, who enjoyed talking to our friends (who were the hottest in the room by a long shot) while they awkwardly danced in front of us and we gave them money. Not my scene.

But since it was usually just the first stop before going out, I'd crumble in the face of conflict and get talked into it somehow. We went to clubs and parties often, each of us carrying out our own masked mission. Mine was to forget; my drug, dancing. I have never danced so much in my life.

We were the two haole twins, both good dancers and both having fun, so we stood out in a sea of hot Asian chicks. With Steph's energy and outgoing personality, we got a lot of attention. But because Steph's ego preceded her, and because she always had an air of aggression about her, we got into scuffles a lot. Big Samoan women, all nostrils flared, would chest bump Steph. And like a feisty, yappy Chihuahua, she'd get right in their face: *yap, yap, yap, yap*. I had to pull her out of a few clubs before those wo-*men* (emphasis on the *men*) tossed her onto a skewer and grilled her up for lunch.

Everywhere we went, she'd say someone stared at her or tried to talk shit. (See what I mean about her Zen?) Yet, if ever I had a mirror of a twin to remind me of how unbecoming an ego can be, she was it. And she *was* working on all those things; I had to give it to her.

Despite her moments, Steph was my closest friend on island then. And, like she did every so often, she surprised me by proving she wasn't entirely self-absorbed when she asked what I wanted to do for my birthday.

"Body boarding," I said. Nothing fancy, I just wanted to go body boarding. She had always talked smack about being a better surfer, which she was, but she had never seen me sponge, as they call it. I picked her up after work in the mom-mobile, and we sat through all the eastbound lights on our way to my favorite side of the island for some shore-pounding surf at Sandy's.

And it was on that long drive that she opened up about her family and asked me about mine. Her story explained all the aggression that I'd always imagined was left over from the Army; she told me that heavy story too. It wasn't the pissing contest that I might have imagined it would be, her story versus mine. She let down her guard that day, the thick armor shed with the tears. She *was* just a lost little puppy.

I started to realize that Hawaii was just that, the land of lost souls—our very own never-never land. So many people had come here and had never left. I heard that all the time, but deep down I knew I wanted to leave one day. I wanted to grow up eventually. As much as I adored all that the island offered, I still had a home, even if I didn't know where that was just yet.

We body boarded for a few hours. She body boarded like a surfer, and because I was wearing fins, which she scoffed at, I caught most of the waves for a change. We had been a little farther out when the tide was better, but when the section died, Steph was done. "I wanna watch you sponge," she said while paddling in, with a shot of sarcasm on the *sponge*. Spongers and surfers have the same smack-talkin' rivalry that skiers and snowboarders have; one side is always arguing that their sport is more technical.

I followed, paddling behind her till I got closer inside near the shore break, stoked to have my moment to shine. I rode about fifteen or twenty waves, *charging*, or so I thought. I didn't want to be selfish though, leaving Steph on the beach like that, so I spun out one last drop-knee 360 before heading to shore. When I walked up to her sitting on the beach, I looked for a high-five, a compliment—something—she'd been watching the entire time, *hadn't she?*

"What happened?" she said.

"What'ya mean, what happened? You didn't see me?"

"I didn't see you charge, dude. I expected you to go after it. Seriously, go back out there, you pussy. I wanna see you charge it."

This was my *awesome* friend, Steph. What she meant by *charge* was me sacrificing bikini, hair, ears, nose and throat because the waves she wanted me to rip were going to send me down the face of a cresting wave into the sand beneath it only to have that crest meet me at the bottom with a giant BOOOSH!

She's such an asshole.

She was right though, goddamn it. I was thirty now, and if I was going to claim to be a body boarder, next to all these hungry little groms (surf kids), I was gonna have to charge like one. Eight or ten poundings later, I crawled out of the water with sand in my suit, in my hair, and every orifice; she grinned wide.

I took that as a compliment.

∞

We drove just over the hill past Hanauma Bay into Hawaii Kai where we stopped to get a six-pack and watch the sunset over the bay. "That beer's what makes you fat, you know," she said. Nothing she hadn't said before but feeling more frank on my birthday. She'd rub her washboard abs and stretch or something right after, to punctuate. Steph had this thing where she insisted on staring at the sun as it went down. She swore it would give her *energy*; at least that's what she'd read. As I sat on the tailgate of the mom-mobile, I ignored her stern request to join her. I would watch intently at the last minute hoping for the green flash, yet in the meantime, I was content just soaking it all in.

It was such a simple birthday, so much more so than the fanfare I would have received at home. I allowed myself only a minute to be salty about being so far away from friends on such a milestone birthday, but all that dissolved with the sunset, the breeze, the mesmeric hum of life—all in accordance.

On the drive all the way back ("all the way back," in Hawaii, is anything over twenty minutes) to our house in Ewa Beach, I thought about how I was supposed to be getting married at thirty, planning a family. Yet, with my sturdy, spitfire of a guru, I was actually starting to learn to let go of all those misgivings. Crazy Steph could sniff out self-pity a mile away and karate chop it before you could crack a tear. She was good for that.

∞

Just before my birthday, I had typed out an e-mail to Brooke that, looking back on now, I could have very well addressed to myself. But it was intended for her, and without Steph there to smack me upside the head and slam the screen on my laptop closed, I sent it:

I can't hate you because I am where I know I should be. I can't blame you because it was only this that would have pushed me to come this far. I truly believe that forces higher than both you and I separated us for whatever the purpose. And I believe those same forces will keep us together in some realm for a very long time.

I thank you for being a friend when I didn't want to think I needed you. I thank you for being a good mom and taking care of our babies. I thank you for continually reminding me not to settle for less.

She replied on my birthday:

Kathy,

I am just so proud of you and how far you have come in the last few months. I truly feel like you are in the right place to explore things you have always just dreamed of. You mean a lot to me, Kathy. You are still one of the most important people in my life and that has never changed. I'm happy you spend time in the water (I know that's your meditation), I'm happy you are surrounded by a fun and loving family, I'm happy you are meeting friends ... even if they are strippers. I think about you all the time and wish you well. Have a beautiful day! Embrace it! You deserve that. This is the first day of a new beginning and wonderful future.

I love you, old lady:)

E-mails like this were what kept me holding onto the rope, running behind the car. I'd fall and get dragged with dust kicking up, rocks and debris pelting me from every angle, but then I'd find the footing, stagger back up, ragged, and start running again, never once thinking to just drop the ever-loving rope.

TWELVE

IF OPRAH CALLS, TELL HER
I'LL CALL HER RIGHT BACK

Steph discovered meditation, and although I saw her as further from enlightenment than Satan's bratty nephew, she *was*, indeed, doing more than me. She had just begun taking a class that she made sure to mention was "invite only," yet she'd be happy to teach me everything she learned. In those weeks, she invited me over to meditate, relentlessly, and it wasn't until she discerned a pattern in my no thank you's that she informed me how I could set it all up on my own, if I wanted to. She was determined, dropping hints about all the insight and clarity she gained. Yet I remained skeptical, staying tuned for any signs of the slightest outward improvement that seemed to only trickle in. She was well intended, but it all just seemed way too hokey, too woo woo. I wasn't interested.

It was around that time that I started searching for a new job. The drive to Tripler during rush hour was likely to kill me—that is if loneliness didn't beat him to it. I must say that traffic with aloha is a lot less aggressive than the horns and fingers of the East Coast, but it's still traffic, with zero redeeming qualities. Rather than jeopardize my good sense, I found audiobooks calmed my road rage. They made me feel productive, rather than trapped in a fish bowl, gulping stale air, wasting time.

As a teacher, I always felt like I never had time to read, so here I was, in front of a backdrop of palm trees and lush green, bumper-to-bumper, reading stickers like, "Slow down, Haole, this ain't the mainland!" smiling at my productivity. I was so hungry for books and what they had to offer I downloaded several a week. And it was really only by accident that I discovered a budget-friendly alternative. Thank the Lord for *free* podcasts.

Hot damn! Oprah's got a podcast. A *Soul Series*, of all things—I can hear the jingle now: "It's uplifting, enlightening, truly power-ful." Therapy couldn't get any cheaper and more convenient. (I should really do the ads.)

Besides, me and Oprah—we go way back.

∞

I was eight or so, on the corner of our scratchy plaid couch when I saw the episode air. Coveting the remote in hand, I sat attentive—alone. I had short hair that I parted in the middle like my oldest brother, Jack, wore sweatpants with shorts on top, copying my brother Ben. I was their most devout groupie. But much like a fly on a horse's back—a subtle nuisance at best—they barely even noticed me. Since the boys and I never talked about Mom and Dad, I remember the relief that episode had brought. I couldn't believe it, we weren't the only kids who'd gotten gypped.

As I watched, I imagined Oprah herself had tried to call me, to invite me to her stage. Instead, my grandparents had intervened, politely declined, and like many things, had never mentioned it. In an effort not to exploit the family, or me rather, after all the hype surrounding my controversial testimony, they would have seen no value in our case being any more televised. I was certain I'd missed the call. I squirmed in my seat as sparks of jealousy swept through and compounded with each commercial break. Rightfully disappointed, I considered the few perks you get out of your dad killing your mom, and I thought at the time, being on *Oprah* was one of them.

It was a blessing to have grown up with Oprah all those years. Her show gave me a sense of perspective that penetrated the canopy of our all-white, all-right, country club. Before the dawn of the Internet or the constant ticker tape of CNN, when the whole world's issues weren't broadcast 24/7, Oprah brought me glimpses of suffering that made my voids seem selfish and a little childish— even for a kid. Over the years, I watched *Oprah* sporadically. My schedule always interfered, or I'd forget, and by the time I remembered, I'd only catch a few minutes. Yet, in those few minutes, I'd be caught smiling wide or weeping sappily, even over an amazing giveaway or a fabulous makeover. It's not like she could ever give a makeover to a regular person; it was always a cancer patient, single mom who just lost her house in a fire, kinda person. There's nothing worse than fighting back tears in the gym watching *Oprah*.

I was grateful I had a roommate in college who, before TiVo, was a VCR fanatic and taped *Oprah* on the regular. We watched her in prime time with commercials on fast forward and microwaved Lean Cuisines in our laps. My roommates teased me about the tears, despite the fact that *their* corner of the throw saw its share of salty stains. Since I was a jock, people were always surprised to hear that I cried over commercials featuring anything sounding like Sarah McLachlan and almost every episode of *Oprah*.

After college, my time spent on the couch dwindled. My time available for *Oprah* was left to sick days and snow days. Even as a teacher, getting home for *Oprah* was nearly impossible, exam week or half days being the only exception. So, as far as a fan goes, I can hardly compare. Her "super fans" would scoff at my minimal viewing. Yet, this connection to "Auntie O" continually pops up for me, more so than one would deem normal.

Maybe it started back in third grade, that same bad haircut, shorts peeking out from under the stiff Catholic school jumper, butterfly collar more prominent (and ridiculous) over the plaid, socks pulled to the knees, and leather Top-Siders—that met school guidelines, but more importantly, matched my brothers'. It may have started then, with *her*, thinking all these years that things might have been different had *she* gotten the call—who knows? Either way, we're connected, me and O. *We're* sure of it.

∞

I combed the podcast library and every few days was introduced to a new topic or new author. It was during a *Soul Series* interview when I first heard about Eckhart Tolle's *A New Earth*. I listened to each episode diligently. He said something so simple, yet so profound: "If the only prayer you ever say is *Thank You*, that would be enough." And it was that notion—of genuine prayer—that actually seemed attainable. I'd been whispering thank you's under my breath since I stepped off the plane. Prayer still felt contrived, but "thank you" I could say till the cows came home.

I read his book and then listened to the accompanying podcasts, which reiterated all that I'd learned. It was simple; I had a huge ego, a ginormous pain body, and until I let go of my personal history, I was totally screwed. So, of course, I decided to start at the beginning, Ego for Dummies, or—instead, Tolle's first book, *The Power of Now*.

In it he described my mind to a T: "When the master is not present in the house, all kinds of shady characters will take up residence in there." I could only imagine what kind of shifty motel I ran. He said you must remain the "ever alert guardian of your inner space." Hmm, let's see, with my amount of self-medication, I suppose I was more like one of those guards—feet kicked up—snoring and drooling in his chair.

He spelled out the definition of such romantic relationships, like the one I was unavoidably still missing, as "ego attachment and addictive clinging." Not to worry; it was completely normal, in the sense that it was "deeply flawed and dysfunctional." He really drove the point home with some of the attributes that make up this sort of riveting relationship: "possessiveness, jealousy, control, withdrawal and unspoken resentment, the need to be right, insensitivity and self-absorption, emotional demands and manipulation." But it's typical to miss all those noteworthy aspects of a relationship.

And like most people, I had become addicted. I had brought it all on myself. I had taken all the bad with the good like a valiant crackhead. I had played the game right along with her—my dealer. It just seems as though I had lost, and I wasn't sure if, after reading his book, I felt better or worse for it. I knew in the long run I would benefit from cutting the cord, but I had to listen to that chapter at least four more times for everything to sink in.

It's true, I had abandonment issues, and I used her as a Band-Aid to cover up those gaping wounds. We had contorted ourselves into the perfect shape of each other's voids. And when she pulled the plug, my body blew around in the wind, waiting to be grounded by something, anything.

Well—my girl Oprah did it. She pulled me out of the tree where I'd gotten stuck like a dejected plastic bag floating around all full of itself, brought me back down to earth and said, "Why don't you pull up a chair, honey, 'cause you're gonna be here a while."

Or, at least, that's what I imagine she would have said. And boy, did I listen. Between the books and the podcasts, I was plugged in any chance I could get. I held on with a fierce grip to something Tolle said, something so simple, yet I can't tell you how many times I've repeated the phrase, "This too shall pass," believing it more each time I've said it—*this too shall pass*. And it was through these books that I began seeking the simple recommendation of obtaining four conscious breaths (a beginner's meditation), turning inward—finally.

∞

I didn't *always* drive the mom-mobile. There were days when Lea needed her own car, days when carpool could get tricky, or Ben played tennis after work and wouldn't be home in time. So I rode the motorcycle, which was cool with me. I had bought, or I should say my dad had bought me a little used Honda Magna my last year of college as a preventative to any more campus parking tickets. I'd ridden that bike for about six years before I put it on craigslist, following the decision to liquidate my meager assets for Hawaii. This one was slightly smaller than mine, a little black Buell, only 490 cc. I say this only because I rarely rode mine on the highway, and here I was driving an even smaller bike on H1, some mornings scared for my life. *Trust, trust, trust*, I would mutter from underneath my helmet—my first mantra. My only other complaint was that rain would often combat my every attempt to get to my destination. I'd perpetually show up soaked, water sloshing in my shoes.

Those wet months made working at Tripler difficult. Well, in all honesty, working at Tripler made Tripler difficult. I regret to report that the majority of people who came through my valet lot were miserable. They despised "the rock" as they referred to Hawaii. They were displeased with veterans' services, with army hospital services, with life's *disservices*. Let's just say they really vomited a mess of nasty negativity on my positive parade. That is after they'd already barfed all over the inside of their cars before handing over their keys.

And not only that but many other aspects of the job really started to wear on me. A good number of the people spilled out of their cars malevolent, often treating me worse than I'd been treated in those few short wretched weeks waiting tables at Applebee's (the most painful restaurant experience I ever had), and here I was only trying to make their lives a little easier, dare I say, even make them smile.

It was my *kind* ego that stood up for me for a change, reminding me that I had a master's degree and that I should tell those ignorant *fuckers* to do what they do best and "fuck off!" But each day my downloaded therapy helped to lessen a little more of that chip on my shoulder, and it felt good not being on the defense, playing victim all the time. I also didn't feel aligned in a job where I constantly hustled for a dollar. I didn't like to think about throwing out accusations of stealing, although I was almost certain it was going on. It was time.

I got back on craigslist.

∞

On the ride home from work one day, on the motorcycle mind you, I decided to find those four conscious breaths Eckhart Tolle suggests. Four mindful, attentive breaths, *pfff ... done a'ready,* I thought, naïvely over-confident. Slowly and calmly, I took in a breath and just as I headed to the next inhale I heard, "One." *Surely I can get to four without having to count!* I tried again. I brought in a beautiful, deep inhalation, and then quickly scrambled to the next, not giving my mind time for diversion. Then just as before, with lost focus, I heard, "Two." *Ahhhh!* Distracted, frustrated, and annoyed, I started again. With each irksome effort, over a stretch extending several trials, much of the same argument continued, never actually making it to four.

Thankfully around that time, Oprah gave me *The Last Lecture.* A friend told me she'd just finished the book, but not without mentioning she'd first seen the live lecture on *Oprah.* Eager for a distraction, I searched for the footage on YouTube. It was nice to take a break from heady Tolle and jump into a story about pursuing childhood dreams. Randy Pausch encouraged the dreamer in me, although reality kept me scrolling through craigslist each night. He quoted Walt Disney, "If you can dream it, you can do it."

I had always deep down believed that but how? I just wanted the manual. I'd cry when I'd think about my dreams of becoming a writer, and how they sat laden on a shelf. I wasn't even a *reader* until just yesterday it seemed; how could I be a writer?

And I'd been so caught up on Pausch's writing about the power of dreams that I was completely blindsided by the pages of beautiful dedications he left to his wife and children. I was two hands gripped on the wheel, sobbing in the car, listening to the letters he wrote to his children, especially his little girl, Chloe. I bit at the tears on my upper lip, thinking about what one of those letters would have looked like from my mom—the advice she would have given. To have been able to hold a tangible piece of her unconditional love in my hands all these years; would that have changed things?

I stayed up one night, staring at the glow-in-the-dark stars on the ceiling; maybe it was having just finished *The Alchemist* that got me buzzing with energy. I knew all that I wanted I had to create, but where to begin? I remember thinking: maybe Oprah will give me a grant? Since that souped-up, shiny Wildest Dreams Bus can't pick me up all the way out here, maybe she'd make an exception. That would probably require people writing letters on my behalf though, pumping my pitiful to the max. Besides, I was too proud to let anyone know I was thinking about calling on Oprah for a little *sugar*. It would be almost as embarrassing as telling people that I'd sent in an audition tape for *Survivor* even though I've never once sat through an entire episode. (I had no other strategy besides just being awesome, by the way. I thought it could work.) I came up with a fair enough figure that I imagined Oprah would find reasonable: $50,000 was all I'd need (after taxes). I just needed one year to write my book.

Hmmm—now how does one go about getting in touch with Oprah?

No, a grant for just me would be way too selfish. Plus, people ask O for money all the time. It's tacky. Then suddenly it hit me, a better plan, less selfish: I needed a grant to start a company that would help other artists—*children*—yes, amateur artists, by offering a space where they could express themselves, where they could develop their creativity and share their passions. It would be a website for artists, just like craigslist. Simple design, no pop-up ads—no ads period—easy to use: I could see it scrawled across the ceiling amongst the dim green blur of the glow-in-the-dark stars. And it would help me make a little money on the side so I could take some time to start writing my book. Perfect.

The only problem: I wasn't a web developer. I could barely work MySpace. Nor, for that matter, was I an actual business person. But people with little education start businesses every day.

Immigrants even, new to the country with only two licks of English, have thriving businesses all the time. I could figure it out, right? *It can't be that difficult.*

I stayed up for most of the night, buzzing with ideas, poking into every mental nook and cranny, dripping with fervor like a generously buttered muffin. And in the end, I decided I wouldn't ask Oprah for a grant after all. I would wait. If a genie might grant me only one wish, I suppose I should know exactly what it is that I'm asking for first. All I had to do was get help developing the space. I could design it. I just needed it to function like craigslist, which shouldn't be that difficult, compared to all the fancy alternatives. I could hardly wait till morning to share my idea with Ben. He was a computer guy; he'd know where to start.

The next morning, Lea coddled my enthusiasm while we searched for a clever name on GoDaddy. After several failed attempts to lock in a domain name—we couldn't believe what people have already purchased. ("everythingbutthekitchensink.com?" Really?) We finally came up with the winner: Freeterrain.com.

∞

In the midst of all the entrepreneurial excitement, I got another job. An ad had finally come up for a personal training position at The Hatch, and I leaped for it. I have to say, there was not one glamorous thing about this gym in downtown Honolulu, but when I went in for the interview, there was just something about the place. Sure, it was less pay and even farther away from the house, but my hours would be noon to 7:00 p.m., so I'd be going against the traffic. I'd work Saturday, as well, for five hours, but I'd be out by 1:00 p.m., which was earlier, unfortunately, than I got out the door on most Saturdays. So, in the pros versus cons debate that played in my head on the way home from the interview, it was the sheer fact that it *wasn't* Tripler that tipped the scale rather plainly for the pros.

Working in gyms over the years, I had always toyed with the idea of becoming a full-time personal trainer. I liked people. I liked health and fitness. I was healthy and fit. Everyone seemed encouraging that I'd be good at it—but that was my problem. I'm *good* at a lot of things. I have always acknowledged that I was the jack-of-all-trades but master of none. I am a genuine product of the American well-rounded school of thought.

I excelled in athletics. I lettered in four sports in high school: field hockey, basketball, lacrosse, and ice hockey. I also went to art camp one year when I was little, drama camp one summer; I took a photography class; I sang in the choir; I played sax, French horn, and later I took guitar lessons, but I swore the guy was a perv so Gma didn't make me go back. (Gma was the authority on three kinds of people: queers, pedophiles, and nymphomaniacs. If you wanted someone on her bad side, all you had to do was say the word, and *snap*—blacklisted.) I had completed every damn brownie badge before they even gave us the book. I remember flipping through each page—I was seven or eight at the time: *did that; uh-huh, done that too; yup, did that one; this one also.*

I'm not saying this to brag, folks; in fact, just the opposite. Believe me, there is such a thing as being *too* well-rounded. I was a perfect sphere, bouncing from one activity to the next when I got bored, never developing the discipline to reach any point near full potential. (Except maybe ballet—with that one, it was clear there was no potential and therefore no need to pursue further, despite my mother's desperate wish to have me develop into the pirouetting little angel she'd always imagined. We settled on a clumsy attempt at tap instead.)

When I was getting my master's degree, I took a course in which we discussed the culture of education in the US, particularly how we (parents and society) push kids to do well in every subject, encouraging countless extracurricular activities on top of an ever-increasing difficult subject load. We compared this to other cultures where they simply hone in early on their students' strengths and nurture those talents, worrying less about where they falter and more about where they excel. As with any discussion, we reviewed both sides of the argument, which typically left me more confused about exactly where I stood, but when we left the classroom on that particular night, I was certain I'd found my diagnosis. And there's really nothing I enjoy more than a good self-diagnosis.

Seriously, a search on craigslist for me involved the scrutiny of countless categories: art/media/design, customer service, education, food/bev/hosp, human resources, marketing/pr/advertising, nonprofit sector, salon/spa/fitness, tv/film/video, writing/editing, and that's just naming the fields in which I'd already held positions. It's exhausting. But with the ultimate goal of writing in mind and staying within the confines of not exactly having a "real job," personal trainer would do just fine.

THIRTEEN

THE QUEST FOR HIS NAME

I was so excited about all I dreamed up for Freeterrain that I even called Brooke, and after the polite *hello, how are you?* was feverishly describing my online blueprints, rattling away my big plans. I'd spoken to her off and on, sometimes I wished more off than on, other times, the contrary. It's like how scientists say that humans are great at forgetting pain, which allows women to have multiple children, and people to do other reoccurring painful things, like, say, go to the gym. At this distance, it was easy for me to forget the agony I had felt those last few months before boarding that plane, like I was just standing here now, barefoot and pregnant with the hope there might still be a chance. We had to talk, about money anyway, as the bills never ceased their endless cycle, and then I'd ask about Porter and before I knew it we were catching up.

I was still interested in her life—the portion that didn't involve Julie, anyway. I had begrudgingly accepted the fact that Julie enjoyed the comforts of my home while I paid the bills, but as I continued to learn with all my Oprah and Friends downloads, worrying about money would only perpetuate more worrying about money. Developing humility was the current lesson, which meant an awful lot of tongue biting. In fact, I think I had a perfect impression of my nice teeth imbedded in my tongue for at least a year.

Brooke always kept me hooked, though. Perhaps when she felt I had taken the liberty of my retractable leash a bit too far, she'd push the button and tug at the chord until I obediently rewound right back into her lead. One night, she called in a panic when she heard someone meddling with our outside shed just inches from our front door. Porter growled, fur on end, not letting her pass by him in the hallway. I calmed her down as best I could and told her to call the police—the basics—but we talked for some time until she felt ready to go. She laughed when she said, "I don't know why I called you. What exactly were you going to do from all the way over there?"

But I was glad she had and told her so. To me it said a lot that she had called me instead of Julie. It told me that, for at least one night, she was sleeping alone. Maybe dropping those clues were all part of her calculated, grand scheme. Or maybe I was just that much of a sucker.

∞

My brother was useless. I mean he was kind enough to support the idea of Freeterrain. He liked it, thought it was a good concept, but then he pointed me in the direction of online resources and took the proverbial back seat. I had really hoped he'd be more into it, but I knew he had a lot going on: school, work, annoying Hilton, scolding Boy Boy. So I dove in headfirst, obsessively, like I do all my new hobbies.

I'd work all day and then I'd come home and work all night. I had no idea what I was getting myself into. I just knew I had to act on the energy I'd felt that night. I moved forward on philosophies like, "If you're not prepared to be wrong, you will never produce anything original," from Sir Ken Robinson's *The Element*, stifling my doubts and fears. I shopped for developers to help with my vision. I didn't even know I could work with developers over-seas—and for cheap! which I know is not the *American way*, but clearly I was struggling here.

The developers and I went back and forth about the project agreement, and then before I knew it, it all started to come alive. I used a paint program to emulate the pencil drawing I'd scratched out the night of my vision to send my developers a screen shot of how exactly I wanted it to look. They'd send me back drafts, and I would e-mail them the changes, and with the time difference it would all show up by morning.

I was an ordinary hermit during the whole building process. I'd even started losing my tan. So much for dishing out all those com-puter nerd jokes; each night, Lea, Ben, and I sat stretched out on the sectional couch with our laptops slow-roasting our thighs. By this time, I had shared my idea with a few people, and they all seemed to think it was just as good a concept as I did—every light seemed green. Things felt like they were finally falling into place, for real this time.

Freeterrain became my baby. I was more and more awestruck with each recordable milestone. It took my developers only a few months to get everything up and running. Then they continued to do behind the scenes technical stuff while I started the fun promo-tions side of things.

All that time I played hermit, Steph would call and try to harass me out from under my cozy shell. One night, she finally guilted me into joining her at the First Thursdays Poetry Slam she'd been go-ing on and on about. Honestly, each month I had tried to make a point to go but something always came up, and for one reason or another, I'd talk myself out of it. This time though, I stuck to my word. I met her in town after work, and once I got there, I was stoked that I had.

It was really nice to see her. She flashed me that bright, crook-ed smile and grabbed me for a good, strong man hug—the usual. She had great energy and a good heart, a reminder every time I saw her how much I missed all those things. The place itself was packed. I'd never seen such a diverse group waiting in line for a poetry competition. The artistic energy was palpable just walking into the room. There was a sign-up sheet, jam-packed with names, where twenty poets would be selected at random for the slam. And this happened every month? I couldn't believe it was my first time.

I loved the poetry. I liked the witty ones, the abstract ones that wove their way into stories, the strong deliveries. I was less of a fan of the dramatic ones, the wounded ones, the weak deliveries. Regardless, the support for every poet onstage was commendable. People cheered, hollered and screamed for the effort, even if the poem or poet wavered. When a poet forgot her lines, the audience would snap their fingers or shake their keys, which I found far more compassionate than the shepherd's crook I'd seen used on TV. As I sat in the audience, enthralled along with everyone else, it dawned on me—*you know, I could do this.*

And with that, on the car ride home, I wrote my first poem. Well, the first one not brought on by the trite tides of a love struck high or grief-stricken low.

the quest for his name

Every Sunday, my entire childhood spent riding the pine of a painful pew awaiting the sweet dissolve of the bland, solidly stale, wafer that I let lie moist on my tongue for as long as it could hold on, cuz there was nothing better to do.

I Think I'll Make It

Falling into the trance of the traditional tide, reciting and mimicking words that mean so little to an ear that can't understand the intangible ...

"First he took the cup, gave thanks and praise, passed the cup to his disciples and said take this all of you and drink from it ... this is the cup of my blood, the blood of the new and everlasting covenant, it will be shed for you and for all so that sins may be forgiven ... do this in memory of me."

Is it blasphemy to ask him to poor a glass for me? What are the rules in this serenade, this parade of virtue, does it hurt you to believe in something you're not sure of—when you' re seven? Is there such thing as heaven? If so, are all of these white people invited?

Cuz they're all the same, they're so lame, following the leader like Marco—Polo,

"Blinded by the light," or just chlorine, flushed down the drain of tyrannical holy water. Cleanse us in the dunk tanks of biblical hypocrisy, cuz it's just not that hard to see that none of these people are paying any attention to the reflection being read to them.

I worked hard to hold onto a society that never tried to reach me, to a community as foreign as a Jew to me. I retreated and subsided and gave up on God and let it all go while others watched me grow.

And it wasn't until years later, I visited a new church. There was no stiff "Hosannah in the highest." This church was all ... "This little light of mine ... I'm gonna let it shine"... and before I knew it, it was like "Drop down sweet it go, let me see God tootsie roll."

I was all like, hold up ... wait a minute. This is church! This is motherfuckin' church? Cuz I felt God, I felt him rise up in me like never before. First it started in my toe, then my foot caught on; I got a little hip shake, a little shimmy shoulder, a hand clap, and a neck roll ... and by God this white girl had the rhythm of Jesus up in here.

It was the word; it was real; it was the real word. Open to freedom from the rules come a passion for peace, prisoned poverty. Why was this music robbed from me? This was praise. This was glory. This was the harmony that stood in front of me.

Now I got it. I understood; the what that could, the belief that should, the hope that would formulate the minds of the misunderstood. It was the music.

So last week I was in the club. And sho nuff, "It was like this n like that n like this n a"... I started to feel that same Jesus beat and I—couldn't help but move, feel the groove, the soul that thrives on the rhythms that drive, the heart is like a motion, picture of an ocean of ebbs and flows off highs and lows. Caught in the fervor of the moment I asked myself, the ever poignant question: What would Jesus do?

So, let me ask you, is this God too or am I still confused?

It just came out. It was half written before I even got home to a piece of paper. I didn't even flip my pencil once to use the eraser. I hadn't really been thinking about God or church or much of anything other than Freeterrain, for that matter. My guess is that I thought religion can be funny, and I wanted to make people laugh. I had joked for years about working on a stand-up comedy routine because I missed my time on the stage (two years of drama in high school had actually produced more than just false hopes). But this was better than stand-up, I thought. I had journals and journals of sappy poetry I could throw out if I could write animated, provocative poetry and get back onstage.

And Freeterrain allowed me to do just that. I could go anywhere all alone with great confidence, introducing myself as, "Kat, from Freeterrain.com." Now, choosing to have no friends was much more liberating. I went to open mike nights, poetry slams, art shows, surf competitions, all of it, passing out flyers for Freeterrain and talking to artists. It felt so good to be with *my people*, the creatives. I memorized my pieces and performed them, greeting the audience with a joke, and of course, a plug for Freeterrain. At night, I would go home and upload videos and pictures and URLs, and any other pieces I'd gathered to my site so it looked like it had several users. I emailed artists on craigslist to tell them how cool Freeterrain was so they'd check it out, and most of them did, with compliments.

For Freeterrain, I listed every category imaginable for artists. There was: Artist's Portfolio, Curtain Call, Writer's Block, Music Notes, etc. I really wanted to make it a one-stop shop for all creatives alike. I even had an Athlete's Playground category, because for months, I had watched so many *real* surfers carve the most beautiful lines in the water that the nuances of their artistry became apparent.

So, this was how it worked: if you were an artist you'd come to my site, click "create post," then select your category, and make an ad for yourself, not necessarily to sell anything, but just to get feedback on your work, put your stuff out there, or network with other artists. You could upload a picture, an audio file, video file, or if you already had a complete site yourself, you'd simply create a post with your URL, and boom, anyone interested could go to your page. See? Brilliant.

The problem was that Hawaii is a really small state, and I lived on only one of those eight small islands, hoping to reach an even smaller artist community. This was my first roadblock. Second, it was just me. That same *me* who knew very little about web marketing and development, and who was already devoting over forty hours a week to a job that actually paid the bills. And, yes—*I get it*—I knew all of this before I dove headstrong into the whole project, but I was just hoping it would be one of those "build it and they will come" sort of stories. I kept waiting for the artsy folk to come in droves, parading out from the parted cornfields.

Thankfully, I didn't hold my breath.

I did land a story in an online rag about entrepreneurs, though, "Early Signs of the Entrepreneur Within," since by now I was becoming an expert. I made it funny, thinking humor might dilute the fact that I was hardly an expert—I'm not a fan of dry business writing anyway. No fear, I think at last check that article had about sixty-seven views, so if I mistakenly misled anyone, rest assured it's a very minute percentage. And it was my ignorance to the fact that very few people would read my column, which got me puffed up enough that I began calling myself a writer—like a real writer.

Still, I had my own LLC, my own *company* credit card, my own new pair of big britches—and boy, did I march them around. Yet the real writing never came. Freeterrain was supposed to make side cash through sponsors so I could work less and write more, but since I hadn't made a dime and had turned down eager employees because I couldn't pay them, I worked more and more and wrote less and less. After a few months of loitering, even though it killed me to admit that perhaps I'd been living on too foolish a prayer, I was going to let it breathe for a little while. In the mean-time, I cleared the space and put Freeterrain on the dusty shelf next to all the other prolific ideas.

FOURTEEN

HEY THERE, MOON

For years I wasn't sure I believed in heaven, but I believed in heaven for her. Because she needed a place to sit, to hang out in her beach chair, with salt in her hair, enjoying the freedom the changing tide permits. She needed a spot to watch me get into trouble, and a star all her own to remind me she still existed. I've always reserved the brightest, or some nights the only star, for her. I never knew exactly which star it was, I never bothered to ask, but over the years people have given me a clue it might be Venus.

The first *sign* I ever got from my mom, I got looking up at her star. My first girlfriend, Whitney (flat tire Whitney), although we didn't call each other girlfriends at thirteen (better put, best friends with benefits), and I were lying in the grass of her parents' backyard one cloudless summer night. We were shoulder to shoulder staring up at the stars through the holes in the trees when I saw my bright star. I pointed, stretching my arm out in front of her nose. "That's my mom's star."

We lay there quietly, eyes fixed, more earnest than eighth grade called for. Then, from out of the still silence, "Take care of her for me," almost a faint whisper. I rolled my head toward Whit to tell her what she'd said, yet as I did, I saw that Whitney's gaze hadn't left my star. "I will," she said.

"You heard that?" I screamed, jumping up from the grass.

"Yes, I heard her." Whitney seemed less stunned but also got to her feet.

I ran around the yard like a maniac, smiling, crying, yelling. "I can't believe you heard that! That was crazy." I fell into Whitney's arms, and she held me, the two of us in tears.

Whitney, who to this day is still my godsend, was the first person to understand me, the first person to say, "Fuck, girl—you've been through some shit!" And it came at a time when I needed more validation than a soldier coming off the losing front line. I guess you could call us kindred spirits, Whit and me (even if that sounds so *Anne of Green Gables*). Perhaps soul sister is more fitting, considering there has never been a proper or innocent thing about us.

Our affair was intermittent until tenth grade, withstanding being caught by my aunt twice—once with my hands up Whit's shirt—both mortifying. We did not, however, survive the social pressures, the taboo, or the temptations with boys. And it took us years to even discuss our "relationship" and even longer to recount the night with my mom and her star.

I was in college when a girlfriend, who wasn't particularly kind all the time, mentioned that I sometimes pointed to different stars for my mom's. She had taken some astronomy class and was all of a sudden an expert. I told her I didn't care; it was the brightest one, and that was that. I was hurt, nonetheless, and I don't think she ever apologized. It *was* a matter of fact, I suppose, and apologies were scant from her for things of that nature.

All that said, I'm not exactly sure which star I looked at in Hawaii, nor do I understand how my location in the world changes my view of the stars, which still remains a mystery. (One that I'm sure Google could solve in minutes.) Yet there are several subjects in life in which I'm content to hover at ignorant, and this is one of them. I always think of Fievel though, in *An American Tail*, and Linda Ronstadt's "Somewhere Out There."

"It helps to think we're sleeping underneath the same big sky!"—the very song Gma wanted *us* (me and whomever willing) to sing at her funeral. She also wanted her body donated to science; both requests went politely ignored, with all due respect, of course.

In Hawaii, the brightest star had a cute little friend sitting just below, and to the left of its side. I couldn't help but put Gma on that star. Before they used to share but here they didn't have to! I got into the habit of taking long walks at night to escape the constant racket of cartoons in surround sound. On a rare clear night, I'd find myself saying, "Hey there, Moon," like Gma used to. Some nights the moon would be smiling back at me with that big Cheshire cat grin.

When the moon was all puffed up, dashing and dauntless, I'd wait for the man in the moon to saunter in for a smoky set or two. Not your typical dude, Hawaii has a different guy altogether. This guy's an uncle, with a chubbier face, eyes a little squinty. He had a ukulele (pronounced without the "y" in Hawaii), and I swear if you listened hard enough, you could hear him singing "Tiny Bubbles" (Gma's favorite). It scares me to think, as much as I talk about her, that I might grow up to be just like that stubborn old loon. Each night, grinning from ear to ear, I'd either walk or skateboard around the neighborhood and chit chat with my stars as I listened to my iPod tuned into Oprah and Friends.

One glorious star-filled night, I rode the motorcycle to the beach, parked right in front of the moonlit tide, laid back on the bike, and took the sweetest, silkiest, moon bath I'd ever sunken into. There were a few idle fisherman and a handful of guys at the tailgates of their trucks, who crushed cans or clanked bottles periodically, talking story, laughing, but it was all background, no attention spared. While I lay there, I couldn't help but feel so close, so big and so small all in the same.

Dr. Wayne Dyer, another amazing fellow I'd met through Oprah, the "father of motivation," as she calls him, had opened my eyes through his books to the concept that "energy never dies." Of all the greats: Rumi, Keats, Thoreau—or "pick your own hero," he'd say—their energy has never left. It's ours to tap into at any moment. I loved that. Staring up at the stars that night, I was grateful to all of those greats because what I needed most was some confidence, some courage, some conviction. And if they had any of that left lying around, I'd be honored to borrow some.

This coming from a girl who for years was accused of being overconfident. One night Steph called me out, in her eloquent manner. "You know, you're cute. I mean, you're not my type, but you kinda look like me, therefore you must be pretty hot," she said, laughing. "And you'd pick up a lot more chicks if you just showed a little more confidence."

I grunted at her in disagreement, considering my egotistical past, but she was probably right. I'd lost most, if not all, of that— mostly for the better. It had felt refreshing to shed that hard shell of ego, to finally step out of my footie pajamas, but I guess I didn't need the confidence to go with it. I was in the rebuilding and re-structuring stages, I assured her, exactly why I *wasn't* looking for chicks to begin with. She thought I was nuts.

One of the last nights she and I hung out together, we had all gone out—a whole crew of us—and nobody wanted the night to end. A group of chicks had piled into my car where the dance party and the groping continued all the way through the Jack in the Box drive-thru before we all headed back to Steph's apartment. I stopped in front of her door.

"Why aren't you parking, homie?" she said. Everyone else began to spill out of the back.

I Think I'll Make It

"I'm not coming in. I'm tired. I'm gonna go home."

"You're not serious, you fag. Come on."

"No, I'm cool. Have fun." I winked at her.

"Wait here a sec," she said in a huff, storming off to unlock her door and let everyone in.

She came back, poked her head in the car and talked sternly. "You mean to tell me that I have four hot chicks in my apartment who think you're cute and wanna get you naked, and you don't wanna come play?"

"It's all good; you know that's not my scene. You go. Have fun. Call me in the morning!"

"Homo!" She slammed the door.

I drove off, smiling.

∞

Between Oprah and Friends, and all the other reading I was doing on the side, I felt like I was back in school. Major: Me. Concentration: Me. Dissertation: Me. I battled constantly with my presumably selfish demeanor. I spent less time with my family. My offers to babysit dwindled. I spent almost no time with friends and was perfectly content waking up, asking, "What would I like to do today?"

This is the same person, mind you, who in college couldn't fathom my roommate, Kathleen, going to lunch by herself. I remember asking her, "Why wouldn't you just take it home and eat it in our apartment in front of the TV like a normal person?" It's not like Burger King had much ambiance to speak of.

And that's when she said the most baffling thing: "I like the time to myself."

I didn't get it. I hated to be alone. I hated listening to the nagging voice in my head that barged in when no one else was around. The same voice that spewed disappointment and failure into my cerebral cortex until I felt its shame run deep into my nerves. I had gotten used to it over the years, but through adolescence, I could keep it out only by nailing the door shut with loud TV, or telephone, or friends, or parties, or alcohol, or drugs. I rarely even smoked a cigarette alone: what? just sit there? by myself, feeling dumb for being so stupid as to smoke in the first place?

Only a few years before I had left for Hawaii, I found myself sitting alone in a coffee shop and I thought, "Look at me, I'm having coffee!" and I was instantly brought back to that conversation in college with Kathleen. It was the year Gma had died when I finally started to grow up a smidgen. I was still living with an ex-girlfriend, as friends, co-dependently, that no amount of incompatibility would shake—not even her straightness. Yet, that winter, in my very first act of independence since, oh I don't know, dressing myself in third grade, I got a job at Liberty Mountain as a snowboard instructor.

The schedule was odd; I worked weekends and some evenings. I spent a lot of alone time in my car and even more time alone on the slopes. Sure, I made some friends at work but mostly just guys to grab beers with at the end of a shift—yet, another job where I was one of very few women. I even toyed with the notion of dating a guy I had met up there. We had a few dates, we kissed a handful of times. No fireworks, but he *did* make me feel like a cute little snow bunny, so I kept him around for a while. But when Gma died, I couldn't be bothered by answering his embarrassing calls—basically, an abrupt, "Peace out, brother."

With Brooke, alone time was limited to her travel schedule, and not even because most times early on at least, we'd be strapped to the phone checking in. We spent so much time together that catty friends would tease and call us *Bathy* or *Krooke*, as if we were on our way to melding into the same person, if it hadn't happened already. We always took the jeering like champs, given that we didn't really care what people thought, or so we said. We had always floated around with this untouchable Brad and Angelina air anyway. Yet here I was feeling like a washed up Jennifer Anniston, except that she's way hotter and worth heaping piles of money.

I'll never forget when I came clean to some friends at work about how poorly things were looking for Brooke and me. "Not you guys," they said in some dramatic despair like we were the last of the surviving couples. "You guys always seemed like the most perfect couple."

That was where I'd usually drop my head in failure and say, "I know; me too—guess not, huh?" eking out a pitiful smile.

So as hard as it was with my family here, I knew I had to ride out the selfish wave for as long as I could because it had never felt so invigorating. I began to uncover truths that left the light on for me and lit welcome candles, illuminating the path I'd always, for some reason, chosen to stumble through hastily in the dark.

My girl, Oprah, through another series of podcasts, had me reading some six hundred pages of text on mindfulness in Dr. Jon Kabat-Zinn's *Coming to Our Senses*. I journaled daily in my gratitude journal after reading at least five hundred pages of Sarah Ban Breathnach's *Simple Abundance*. Jill Bolte Taylor taught me fascinating things about energy and consciousness in her book, *The Stroke of Insight*. Byron Katie's *Loving What Is* blew my mind with her methods that helped me dispose of guilt and anger. And, it was also through a *Soul Series* interview that I learned more about Vipassana meditation.

Given my struggle to come up with those four uninterrupted godforsaken breaths, the thought of a ten-day meditation course was completely out of the question. I had been plugging and prodding at my meditation practice, though, and was happy to hear that even Oprah struggled in this department. In an interview with O, Dr. Jon Kabat-Zinn, whom she refers to as "the source" of mindfulness meditation, made meditation sound like the twin I'd been separated from at birth; the void I failed to notice until I was made aware.

I went searching.

FIFTEEN

FALLEN SOLDIER

I was reading the same page of the *Tao Te Ching* tirelessly one evening at work when a friend and client, tall, skinny Brian, approached my desk and started right in on what I thought of it. "Of what?" I said, buying time.

"The book," he laughed, pointing at the obvious, missing my sarcasm. "What translation is that?"

I was embarrassed how little I knew on the subject—*translation?*—or, how little I'd grasped since picking it up. The creases from all the dog-ears tracking my progression were evidence I'd been plodding my way through, and he was the kind of person to pick up on that sort of thing.

The Hatch was super old school. Longtime executive members traipsed down the stairs into the musty basement for their methodical daily routine. The population was older, more than half Asian/local Hawaiian, the owner was haole, the employees, mostly haole, not that anyone noticed. Brian was one of maybe twenty members who were in their thirties or under. I was the only female trainer. I taught some eight-odd classes a week—from water aerobics to kickboxing, Butts-n-Balls to boot camp, and everything in between. Despite the few occasional complaints, that little dungeon basement was the best medicine any expert could have prescribed. I had more aunties and uncles down there than I knew what to do with. And they just thought I was the best thing since canned Spam. A true island ohana (family), really.

∞

It was in that basement gym where the scent of eucalyptus rose from the steam room greeted me as I came down the steps— blanketing any signs of mold or mildew—that I first found my own *true* breath. One of our yoga instructors, Shiva, had shown up to a nearly empty class, and while he waited for takers, he joined the conversation at my desk regarding the *Tao Te Ching* and meditation.

Sure, the three-minute preface and closure to yoga classes made the concept of meditation inviting, even trendy to yuppie twenty-and thirty-somethings all over, it seemed, but to sit all by yourself, without the stretch pants and matching Lululemon top, somewhere outside of the studio, was a whole different kettle of fish. So, when Shiva suggested we do a meditation class instead of his regular yoga class, in the comfort of our normal make-shift space, the four of us were all in to give it a try.

It wasn't the first time I'd spoken to Shiva about meditation. He had laughed at me on several occasions while I expressed my struggle to seize even three of those damn four conscious breaths that Tolle suggested to become aware of the present moment. I joked with him about my restless mind that entertained a constant barrage of images and a shuffling marquee of personal headlines.

Shiva was an experienced meditator who had traveled the world taking courses. He sat for three hours a day, morning, noon, and night. And, you could tell. He floated into the room, modestly dressed, accessorizing with only a plain necklace and a splendid smile. His charming Indian accent made each bit of phrasing sound boyishly inquisitive. His gleaming pearly whites confirmed my assumption that he was, in fact, fed by the universe—there was no sign of plaque or stains associated with our cultural interpretation of nourishment. His tender aura was clearly unaffected by the bustling world around him. His motto of "anyone can do it" didn't fool me—he rode a motorcycle; I would have bet he had a magic carpet hidden in one of those tiny compartments.

We followed his simple instructions, practicing stillness for a half hour or so, using physical, breath, and visual techniques. I squirmed during each attempt, adjusting in between methods, frustrated that my erect posture was so painful to maintain. His smile was playful, which I saw as almost demeaning. He promised the sitting part would get easier with time as he settled with ease even deeper into his own posture.

He prompted us with questions following each technique. "How was that one for you?" He'd open the floor then address each of us individually. We all got much of the same: his forgiving smile accompanied with a few suggestions to help ease our frustration in what felt like failed attempts. "It's okay, you'll be fine," he said, so simply dismissing our shortcomings.

My technique wavered, and I struggled to stay on task. Yet, I attained flashes of what felt like insight that branded me. Then suddenly it came. I softened, honing in on simple intentions to quiet the incessant traffic in my head—and it happened. My body began to tingle with a sense of presence I had never known. My eyes welled up with tears. A foreign stillness resonated in my limbs. I was looking from behind my eyes and could see peace like I had never imagined. I felt it—*all encompassing*—converging my concepts of divinity. It wasn't long; several seconds, maybe it was a minute, before flickering thoughts began to spark, barging back in, unannounced guests. Yet, the few moments of clarity I had for-tuitously grasped seemed to present themselves as elfin gifts in the divine package of unmasked awareness. It was then that I made a pact to begin a daily practice, any practice—mindful, I needed a lot of it.

∞

I clung to my pact with the fortitude of my own pinky promise, leading me to a committed daily practice of morning, noon, and night. First, stemming from simple gratifying instants of peace, which grew into minutes, then finally, when I was lucky, twenty whole minutes wrapped with ribbons at a time. Sometimes I felt like a natural—probably a guru in my past life. Yet, far *more* often than sometimes, I felt like a feebleminded child. For the record, arguing with yourself in half lotus is still *plain* arguing with your-self.

I enjoyed my simple routine: wake up with the sunshine, sit on the beach and meditate, read, surf, go to work, back to the beach, meditate—all while Oprah's self-help soundtrack played in my ear buds or car stereo. At work, I'd escape from the depths of the basement to the garden floor of the building. I'd sit on a rock over-looking the harbor and just breathe. My eyelids would flutter at first under the temptation to take in my surroundings, but *stillness* brought a calm in with the sweet coconut breeze, and more often than not, I'd have to run back to work because I'd gotten lost in thought, or on a good day, its absence.

One night I retreated to my room in hopes to do my meditation in bed. I would have normally been on the beach, but it was rain-ing; actually, there was a thunderstorm. As I sat there cross-legged, focused, earnest as a child learning to pray, I began to think about the sounds of the thunderstorm and how much I missed them. I hadn't recalled any thunderstorms at all since I'd been on island. Listening to the rain, seeing the flashes from behind my lids and then hearing the claps of the distant thunder I couldn't help but be brought back to my beach house as a kid.

We loved the storms. We'd get our sweats on and be all cozy while we watched the black take over the sky. Gma would have all us cousins rocking on the porch swing, watching the storm come in over the bay. She'd get out the candles and the matches, unplug the TV. We'd have board games going and forts built by the time the thunder rolled in.

The smell of the rain brought the tears. Thinking about the beach house didn't help. We'd sold it the year after Gma died, not first without a fight from us grandkids. I had always been proud to tell people that Gma, being an architect, had designed the blue-prints. It was finished the year I was born, which in my eyes left it somehow more connected to me. In fact, I can't tell you how many times I heard the story about my mom being so excited that she rode down to Bethany with Gma just to see it, pregnant—*as all hell*, in Gma's words—with me. My mom loved the beach. We all did.

I sat cross-legged with my palms up, hands open wide on my knees—open to the world, open to love, open to peace. I could hear my heartbeat in the silence between the thunderclaps. I felt a warmth in my palms, a now familiar warmth that sent my *alone* all away. It was stronger than usual though, the energy in my hands. It felt like someone was holding them, maybe even more than one person; I couldn't decipher.

The storm seemed to pick up, and with it so did my tears. I began to rock, forward and back, slowly, steadily, still crying but attentive. *Why am I rocking?* It was soothing, though, so I didn't stop. The movement came so naturally; the gentle force felt so real.

Then—it was obvious. *I knew.* There is only one person who would rock me, only one person who last saw me in pigtails with my coloring books, crayon in hand. *She* was rocking me. She knew just how like only a mother would never forget. She rocked me like the baby I still am to her in so many ways. She reassured me, rocking me, holding me so tightly. Her presence alone said, "Here I am, baby. It's all gonna be all right."

I sobbed quietly; I didn't want to wake anyone. "I love you; I love you so much; God, I love you," I whispered, taking in salty tears with each word. I felt the hum of a soft lullaby all over. The warmth went from my hands to my body, blanketing my skin—a quilt of unconditional love and compassion. I sang our favorite song softly, between sobs: "You are my sunshine, my only sunshine, you make me happy, when skies are gray, you'll never know dear, how much I love you, so please don't take my sunshine away."

We held each other for more than a few minutes, yet when I began to worry I'd lose her, she slipped away little by little. She left as gracefully as she came in and took the storm with her along with my tears. When I opened my eyes, there was only stillness. I sat stunned for a few moments, my eyes still blurry from the tears. Without even a hint of fear, anxiety, or loneliness to chase me in my dreams, I curled up in bed and slept like a baby.

∞

All along I'd thought to look outside myself for my mom, for God, for peace. I saw it as almost a travesty after so many years to learn that all I had to do was look steadily within. Many of my daily lessons carried that very theme, "So close, yet so far away." St. Francis said, "What you're looking for is who is looking." Simplicity right under my nose, yet all these years I chose to reach for the impossible.

I became devout. I never missed a sitting. My twenty-minute stretches of meditation turned into forty-five, sometimes without any awareness of clock time whatsoever. I had attained a level of trust that I'd lost at childhood. For many years, I argued that God had turned his back on me, but now I understood that standing back to back with God all this time wasn't such a bad gig after all. Besides, for someone who didn't much believe in God, I sure had an awful lot to say to somebody.

I listened to a program by Wayne Dyer and Deepak Chopra (Dr. Chopra is a medical doctor, a self-proclaimed quack who specializes in mind-body medicine). In the program, they double-teamed any doubts I was capable of pulling from my arsenal. Dyer offered this quote from *A Course in Miracles*: "That if you knew who walks beside you at all times in this path you've chosen then you would never experience doubt or fear." This was awesome. Not only did I have two hard-core angels, I had a whole squad! Playing the self-pity card wasn't happening in this round.

I remember sitting on the beach one starless night, where I always sat near the fence that separated Camp Smith's Marine Base and Ewa Beach Park, after listening to what felt like a long private sermon: "Let go of your personal history." Deepak Chopra was right; I clung to my past like a badge of honor. I paraded it around, dare I say, proudly and fell apart with every justifiable excuse it gave me.

When I'd sit to meditate, I would listen to the waves; I'd tune into my breath, my heartbeat, my senses, my stillness. But with the stillness came the awareness of mind chatter—and gobs of it. Thoughts I had always assumed were in my control, I realized were no more my own patterns than that of my breath. *Monkey mind*, they call it. And mine was a loud, obnoxious, chubby little bastard who pegged things at me for the sport of it. In order to attain some peace and quiet, I would often say a mantra, not aloud, just in my head, in an attempt to overwrite the noise: "Peace, harmony, compassion, joy, gratitude, grace."

On this particular day, I did just that. I said my mantra over and over until I found a rhythm with the tide. I could taste the salt from the sea on my lips and could feel the humidity carried on the island breeze sticking to my skin. It was past ten o'clock, a late meditation, but I never missed. "Peace, harmony, compassion, joy, gratitude, grace," became without resistance, "Let me let go, let me let go, let me let go."

I don't know how many times I said it, but I sat there determined. I'd never had more conviction about anything. I wanted to shed this skin, to drop the facade, to lift the weight off my shoulders, finally, after all these years. Exhausted tears fell into my lap, each one a tumbling release of relentless torment.

As I sat there, *letting go*, I was brought in memory to the table of my friend's dad's lake house. I was in Ohio on Lake Erie, for a mild August weekend; the last of the summer before returning to college, visiting a friend, Jess's family, for a reunion. Jess had mentioned on the plane ride up from Baltimore that her aunt Cheryl was a "free spirit." She was excited for me to meet her. "But don't be surprised if she offers to read your cards." I must not have looked thrilled because Jess simply asked that I wait to meet her before I made up my mind.

Jess's dad was parked in front of the airport in his pickup when we arrived. Stiff small talk and stumbling silence, peppered by Jess's nervous laughter filled the roomy cab as we made the short trip from the airport to his summer home. I was thrilled the sober part of our stay was over and done when we pulled into the tread marks indicating the driveway. The long and lean trailer home sat near the edge of a cliff, overlooking the ginormous lake, nestled cozy in a proper wooded trailer park. One look at the neighborhood and I decided it was par for the course—certainly tarot cards and single-wides pair like wine and cheese in some circles.

Turns out, Aunt Cheryl was pleasant and actually seemed rather normal. I was still doubtful of her *powers* though, but I thought *what the hell*, you only vacation in a trailer park on Lake Erie for a loony family reunion once in your lifetime. Besides, reading me would be impossible with the straight poker face I promised to keep.

She sat me down at the round, wooden table tucked in the corner near one of the windows overlooking the chilly, china-blue lake. With a warm, eager smile, she motioned for me to cut the deck. Then she took it in her hands, straightened the pile, and before turning the first card, she paused to look at me, her eyes smiling, and said, "You have a funny grandma."

I gave her a half grin—sure, she had my attention, but I was no fool, *everyone has a funny grandma*. She began flipping cards, full of vibrant scenes and bright pictures. And just like that, I was mesmerized by the esoteric imagery. I had never seen a tarot deck.

"You're an artist," she said, glancing at the first card with such certainty I almost cried. I had been complimented on my creativity before and was told I was talented, but to actually be called an *artist*—I was sure it was a first. She continued, "You will create great works one day, but …" she paused, heightening my curiosity, "the best of your works will come out of a deep depression." Then—nervous her projection hadn't come out right—she started backpedaling, hesitating with her words. She went on a tangent about artists and depression, naming a few of the greats who created such works under agonizing emotional pain, even referencing Van Gogh for lopping off his own ear (which I only recently read isn't exactly true, but at the time, I got the gist).

She didn't have to tiptoe, I wanted to say. I had long since grown comfortable with the concept of depression. (Let's be real, I was in college; most days I flipped through until I *reached* the Depression Network. Lifetime Movies were a sort of twisted therapy, a solid perspective—always depicting that things could indeed be much, *much*, worse.) Plus I was still stuck on the fact that she had called me an *artist*; I didn't care how it came—or at what cost. I never really liked my ears all that much anyway. If that's what it would take, I'd gladly sacrifice.

I sat up a little straighter in my seat, still listening. She described each card in great detail, making references toward my life, my personality, my past and future like a childhood friend who somehow knew me better than me. I furrowed my brow to reassemble my waning poker face. When we got to the last card in the row, she seemed to be more careful with this one. She took it in both hands and slid it nearer to me, stopping dead center of my chest, just so. It was a dark card with the image of a child standing behind a gate with a heavy lock resting on its bars. She spoke softer now, like a mom, and made vague references to a difficult childhood and a fear that I may have always harbored. She leaned in, and with the point of a finger, gestured toward the picture for me to see more clearly. "The gate is unlocked," she said. "All you have to do is open it."

∞

On the beach that night, *letting go*, I saw the card. I saw the faint figure of the defenseless child behind the gate. And I heard Aunt Cheryl's voice. "All you have to do is open it." It hadn't occurred to me till then, but that gate had somehow comforted me for almost twenty-five years. Now, not only did I have the strength, I had the determination to swing it open and step from behind its tall, thin, shadows.

Grief, Guilt, Shame, Fear, Pride, Anger, and Jealousy, like seven grouchy little dwarves, picked up and stormed off. "Come on guys, guess the party's over." Yup, that was them; the motley crew I'd been kickin' it with every time I threw one of my infamous pity parties. And I was sure there were others. I knew for a fact that Greed, Regret, Failure, and Envy had never missed a blowout—but they were gone too.

Peace never felt so vast, so wide open. I never knew quiet to be that comforting. I was brought back to my body. My head bowed; my breath steady. The night was still, except for the undulating sea. And then, out of nowhere, I couldn't believe it at first, I had never heard it sitting there before, and never again thereafter. I wouldn't have believed it myself if I hadn't heard it with my own two big, ugly ears. A horn from the base next door played *Taps*, in its entirety, without a stumble or missed note, as if only for me, right on cue.

I dropped my head to my knees and wrapped my arms around my legs. I listened to each crisp, clean note that cut through the cool, dense air. Liberated tears fell into a puddle of awe on my lap. Synchronicity had hung in till the grand finale just to let me know she was still around. And like a soldier who'd just been given a handsome medal, I followed orders. I laid it to rest—all of it.

SIXTEEN

TELL YOUR STORY

For someone who was considered laid back almost to a fault all the way up through college, I army-crawled, rather inadvertently, toward militant in my older age; closer to (I hate to even say it) Type A than I ever thought I'd comfortably tread. I had a certain way I liked to do things. I was clean (perhaps border-line OCD), precise, and for even more militant, I taught boot camp at the gym. I had a workout regimen, I had a meditation regimen, and I was starting to develop a regimen for my regimens.

Living with kids (my own personal little Zen masters), I learned to let go often. My things were never where I expected them. Germy little fingers touched me constantly. I was always a close-range target for wet coughs and surprise sneezes. And I almost died the time Boy Boy barfed on me. I learned patience, yes. It came in sudden spurts and then long lapses but grew nonetheless. Gavin could wear my heels because, let's be honest, I rarely did, and he looked cuter in them anyway. Hilton could have my favorite hat because it *was* just a hat that, sadly, she was also cuter in. Yet, of my time, I could not let go.

I had been the *yes girl* my entire life. It was as if I had never been taught the liberation in the word *no*. Sure, I may have uttered it once or twice before, with the authority of, oh, I don't know, a lamb.

"Come on, you don't really mean *no*, right?"

"I mean, *I did*, but I guess … no, I can't. I mean, I shouldn't. Well—I suppose I could stay for a little bit longer."

And then there I'd be, inevitably, drinking another beer, heading to another party, or going on a four-hour, 2:00 a.m. road trip.

I had a network of friends from high school and college right in and around Baltimore, so I had to make sure to "Keep up with the Joneses" as Gma would say. Plus I had the incessant need to uphold my duty as Captain People Pleaser. I would run around, burning candles and sticks and anything else I could set fire to from both ends, in an effort to save every last soul from the slightest disappointment my absence might evoke. I was a hamster on a wheel, a rat in a race, or just a feeble rodent who never grew a pair. Either way I sliced it, I was exhausted.

So, I took up being the *no girl*.

I drank less because I couldn't practice my evening meditation drunk. I tried once, but the stammering, awkward silence of my mind tricked me into believing I'd attained enlightenment. I rarely watched TV with the fam because I felt like I could be doing something more valuable instead, like say, reading. I had trouble relaxing, considering there was always a project I could be working on. I'd never been so hungry to learn. I worked out like a fiend mostly because it was a great way to pass the time at The Hatch, also because my body was something else I managed with some locus of control. Indeed, with much of my circumstances still lingering so far out of my hands, the few things I did have control over I coveted.

I'd been on Oahu much longer than anticipated, and I wasn't exactly sure when I'd leave, or where I'd go next, for that matter. I still spoke to Brooke on occasion, but I thought of her and us less and less all the time. That night on the beach, *letting go*, the tail of our two spirits that was *us* must have been caught and buried with the rest of the junk, deep and double padlocked because I felt great, never better, really. I still sent money home for mortgage, yet each signature of the virtual check carried much less resentment. In fact, worrying about money altogether had somehow become less of a chore overnight. Truly, I worried about very little in those days.

My noticing as much all started with the best surf session of my life that Steph and I had a couple of months prior to our last infamous night out. We had planned to spend the night at the home of one of her old clients, Ro, on North Shore. Ro was a petite and fit veteran pro surfer, with a surprising smoker's *sultry* to her voice. She had a beautiful house set on stilts, tucked back down a long drive off the main strip. I smoked a joint with a guy that night who'd been couch surfing at Ro's all week while the surf was up. He was lanky and tan, as I recall him, had a full thick head of unkempt curls and a pair of amber tiger-eyes, whose lids dipped lower and lower with each long drag of the passing joint. While the girls made dinner, he and I got into this rather shallow philosophical conversation about 2012.

Living on Hawaii, I had gotten used to people asking, "What's your sign?" I'd ignorantly offer, "Pisces," having little clue what it all meant, then I'd wait for the instantaneous recoil or sudden, awkward embrace, depending on their relationships to those of us born under the twelfth fish sign. And it's not only astrology they're into. Everyone in Hawaii seems to be more in-tuned with *signs*. I swear it comes up in casual conversation, with strangers even. There is definitely a general feeling of heightened *awareness*— must be from all the good energy spilling out of the equatorial seam. It's the natural mystic, man; they're all high on *aloha*.

Me and *dude* were absolutely high on some good, Maui Wowie *aloha* when he started in on 2012. Since I hadn't watched much

TV that was rated more than PG-13 in over a year, I scarcely knew what he was talking about. Steph had mentioned a little something about it before; she'd seen some movie and had been sold on every last word, but I wasn't buying it. Until of course, *dude* had me totally convinced "not to worry" because I was cool, and I was "going to the party, brah," because for believers that's all it was—"a big fucking party." He explained the Mayans and the calendar and all that jazz, but as high as I was, I was more into the party—that and whatever the girls stirred up in the kitchen.

We had a beautiful candlelit dinner on the second story wraparound porch, and with each bite, I floated like a leaf back down to just above reality. Norah Jones's mellow cradled my innocence as I stole sips of a sweaty glass of sauvignon blanc. I remember thinking that if my Hawaii could be like this all the time I would never leave. I was also grateful at dinner that we had switched the conversation from the Mayans onto something a little less apocalyptic.

When all the plates were cleared, I scrubbed the dishes to the sound of dude playing the guitar, singing in a low John Mayer raspy tenor. Charming measures strung together hung in the cool, comfortable silence, interrupted only every so often by a lonesome, staggering chord. The lullabies lured me to bed, and without so much as a "good night," I ducked out downstairs to the guest room.

We woke up early the next morning, too lazy for dawn patrol (early early surf), but early enough still for glassy morning waves. It was a typical gorgeous Hawaii morning with steam rising up from the grass, the eager sun baking off the early morning dew. Ro was kind enough to take us to one of her secluded spots since the over-amped surf report had already brought *choke braddahs* (plenty dudes) in, crowding the swell. She parked somewhere between Sunset and Turtle Bay where we walked along a trail to get to the beach. I was stunned when the skinny bamboo and tall trees opened up to a magnificent empty break.

It was just one glorious *left* after another, and since I'm goofy footed (right foot forward), I was in pig heaven. Steph and I paddled out. It was easily a twenty-minute paddle, maybe more. I had barely listened for instructions from Ro before my willing toes were already in the water. Steph made sure to remind me that I'd acted too hastily. She was probably right, but *whatevs*. On that morning, nothing could stop me from taking in the North Shore in all its splendor.

The ocean sparkled in the sun, spreading lavishly before us, rippling silks of green tourmaline gemstones. The palm trees bent to and fro gracefully in the breeze. And the sun warmed our backs in the water's early-morning chill. By the time we paddled out, Ro and her two labs were gone and it was just Steph and I, and lefts, lefts, lefts, for Sunday morning brunch.

They were the kind of waves with such perfect shape that paddling was made easy, and before we knew it, we were up and riding. They crumbled behind us gently, with more of a pat on the butt, "Go get 'em tiger," than the ferocity of a thick barrel break that can get to feeling more like a big bully chasing you down—"You wanna see surf! Huh?" Still, they had force and speed, and with each wave, there was plenty of face to carve out our own intimate dance. Then there was a nice cushy shoulder to sail off on and drop back down to our board to paddle back out for the next set.

I thought Steph might have been a little grouchy because she didn't like all the lefts. She was regular foot and would have really loved a right or two. Or she could have still been harping on the fact that I was a *pussy* (her word) for not partaking in the master cleanse (that lemon juice, maple syrup, cayenne pepper thing that had her shi-shying out of her rear for ten days). "Fag," she called me for not wanting to attain enlightenment through mild starvation and sheer loss of water weight—she swore she had more clarity than ever.

It could have also been that she was getting spooked that it was just the two of us (no lifeguard, no nobody), and the sets were starting to break a lot bigger and farther out, becoming more inconsistent. Who knows?—she was always such a mystery to read. But after about an hour of the best surf I'd ridden since coming to Oahu, she said she thought she saw *something*. As in *shark something!* And you just don't just say something like that. I didn't budge, though. I paddled back out to get in line for the next set.

"Did you hear what I said?" she yelled over the roaring break.

"Yeah—I'm not ignoring you. I just don't care," I said, still paddling.

"That's fucked up, dude. What'ya mean you just don't care? I said I think I saw something!"

"It was probably a turtle." I was sitting up on my board now, one eye on the break, one back on her.

"It wasn't a fucking turtle, dude. I've seen fucking turtles!"

"Well, if I'm gonna die, brah, I see this as the perfect day to do so. Look around you, Steph. This is fucking amazing. You can go in, dude, but I'm staying."

She huffed off, taking the next wave in, and then paddled to shore just as two other surfers emerged from the head of the trail. *Pfff ... shark.* I rode several more perfect waves, without a fear in the world, all by myself. And it was on the face of those waves I realized I had little trepidation of dying anymore. In fact, my biggest gripe with the whole 2012 debate was not that we were all going to die. It was that I hadn't yet accomplished what I believed I'd been put here for. I didn't want our whole species to disintegrate to dust before I'd gotten a chance to do whatever *that* was—that magical piece I had yet to figure out—but *God* I wanted it; more than anything, I wanted it.

Steph was right to be huffy; shark attacks were real and not all that uncommon. A friend of hers, another pro surfer, Bethany Hamilton, had lost her arm to a shark a few years back. It was a risk we all took every time we strapped on our boards, paddled out, and sat with feet dangling in the water. A friend of mine once said, "You *do* realize that they have seen you?"—*they*, of course, being the sharks.

I thought: *Well no, actually, I never thought about it like that.* But because he was probably right, I said: "Sure, I knew that; duh, everybody knows that."

As a kid, I'd imagined it would be a great way to go, either that, or struck by lightning. I thought at least I'd make the local front page. I'd like to imagine that sort of talk was due to the fact that I've always had a desire to make an impact somehow, or perhaps more likely, that I just didn't get enough attention as a child.

∞

With all my budding alone time, I got good and comfy with my flooding emotions, including overwhelming instances that regardless of my whereabouts brought on the tears—and cry I did— regularly. A man helping an old lady across the street, a rainbow in my rearview mirror, a song on the radio, a quote from a book. And not one tear was shed out of sadness. My gratitude journal teemed with joyful moments. "And the day came when the risk it took to remain tight in the bud was more painful than the risk it took to blossom," from Anais Nin. See? How can you not cry?

I found all my spiritual beliefs tucked so masterfully into the ninety-one minutes of *Kung Fu Panda* I thought it must be a *sign* as I watched intently in the theater. The line, "Yesterday is history, tomorrow is a mystery, but today is a gift. That is why it is called the present," made me cry even though I'd heard a rendition of it before, but never from a wise, wrinkly old turtle. And *Wall-E*, I can't even stand the parallels, a cute little robot finding out what he was meant to do in life—the love story!—I lost it.

I even found myself *crunning*—crying while running—for the first time one afternoon while I was out on a six-mile jog. I ran toward the beach, and just as I got to the path along the ocean, it began to rain. My iPod blared Kelly Clarkson, "I'll spread my wings and I'll learn how to fly, I'll do what it takes till I touch the sky." I was singing and smiling and crunning; quite the spectacle, I imagine. Tears fell to the beat, soaking my lashes, making it impossible to see in the rain, yet with focused attention, I didn't lose a single stride.

It was as if I'd been lent a pair of rose-colored glasses and everything before me was suddenly and lustrously illuminated by love. For even more profound, I recognized that love as myself. I'd end every meditation with, "Thank you—I love you." Meant for God, I suppose, originally, but the more and more I said it, I realized I was thankful for and loving more the divinity in me. I never imagined this relationship with myself would get so intense: *the next thing I knew, we were living together ...*

I'd cry because every day I felt more alive. I felt more on purpose, even though I had little clue yet what that purpose was. All I knew was that, like Thoreau, I wanted to "Go confidently in the direction of my dreams and live the life I imagined." Yes, I was an artist. I felt most alive doing anything creative, including all my work on Freeterrain, on stage entertaining, or writing; I knew I had a book in me somewhere. But where to start—again? What to do now? In what order?

I didn't want to be a personal trainer when I grew up, that much I knew. *The Secret* told me I could manifest whatever I wanted, but

I couldn't visualize or even wrap my brain around something I didn't yet have the compass for, or God forbid, a map.

I sat in my spot on the beach one morning, first with my mantra and then, all of a sudden, another: "You are the shepherd of thine peace, lead me to the way and I shall follow." (*Um* ... Yeah, don't ask me—I have no clue where that came from.) I shortened it a bit, taking the edge off archaic to sound a little more like me. "Lead me to the way."

After a good while of asking, I finally just started begging. "Please just tell me what to do. I'll do anything. Just tell me."

I read a book, years ago, that started me on this rather capricious journey of finding my passion: Po Bronson's *What Should I Do With My Life?* It's a great book, and I highly recommend it, even if you're only half the mess I've described myself as here. In the book, Bronson shares several stories of people he had interviewed at numerous points along their path in the pursuit of passion, some later in life after delving into solid careers even.

I'll never forget the story about the young guy living in Manhattan who received a letter in his apartment mailbox, revealing to him his destiny. I will let you read the book to find out what happened, but I will say, I walked away from those pages wishing someone, or something for that matter, would do *just that* for me— send *me* a letter—please! Spell it out, in all bold, so there is no discrepancy, and make it look fancy, *will ya?* so I don't recycle it with the junk mail. I didn't want to be the jack-of-all-the-stupid-trades anymore. I wanted to be standing at the proverbial doorway ready to master at least one.

I begged on the beach that morning, "Please tell me what to do. Please ..." And then, after all that begging, there was a voice. It sounded a lot like Wayne Dyer, truth be told (an obvious side effect of being plugged in all the time). The voice said, "Tell your story." I thought about it for a second before it began to resonate. *Oh yeah, I have a story.*

I immediately thought back to the last time I was asked to "tell my story." My faculty chair at St. Anne's, Barbara, had approached me about presenting at the senior retreat. I remembered having said *yes* even before I'd gotten the chance to ask what I'd be presenting. She said, "I was wondering if you'd be willing to share your story?" Funny, because I had never told Barbara *my story*. Perhaps a parent had offered it at one time or another. There were a few parents who had recognized my name in the *new teacher* newsletter, Barbara later confided. One mom revealed that my grandfather (my mom's dad) had been her family doctor for years, and as our case was going on in the local media, she had saved some of the newspaper clippings. She asked if I wanted them—of course I did.

I had left the DC area for Baltimore in elementary school, taking with me our family's haunted history, leaving behind the palpable memories embedded in our community. I didn't realize when I started that working at St. Anne's, just outside DC, would unearth a smattering of those who hadn't yet forgotten.

Not only was I happy to share my story, I was honored. And when I did, I was exhilarated by the overwhelming response of the students, many of whom later, shared with me their own stories.

∞

That's why I'd gotten into teaching in the first place. I actually thought I might be able to help the kids, save them from the many mistakes I'd made—inspire them somehow. I was a good student and athlete but wavered in every other aspect of adolescence. I thought my ripe wisdom at twenty-three could harbor them from their own ignorance. The only problem was that the classroom didn't allow for much personal discussion. I rarely felt comfortable saying, "I know; I understand; I've been there." If students came to me with a problem of significant magnitude (*significant* being nearly everything), I'd inevitably be required to shuffle them along through the system to a guidance counselor, or report *the incident* to the principal. Even in a private school where there was less red tape, I still found myself in sticky situations that made me want to get out of education altogether or at least the confines of the classroom.

So when the Wayne Dyer voice said *tell your story* I assumed that's what he meant—a motivational speaker of sorts. Go to schools, crack a few jokes, slam down some poetry, get their attention, and then lay it on thick, the *Scared Straight* facts. I had dealt with divorce, depression, domestic violence, sexual identity, alcohol, drugs. I had a friend in high school who committed suicide, another two who were murdered in gang-related violence. I had the bases covered.

∞

The notion of having a *real purpose* made me well up with honest yearning, and hopeful tears spread to my cheeks, then to my lips. "Thank you," I whispered. It instantly gave meaning, not only to my life and its series of stumbling hardships, but to *hers*—an inkling of justification for being robbed of her children, her loved ones, and so many unfettered years. The tears came more surely and from greater depths, imagining giving her a voice and making her proud. "Thank you." I shook my head in disbelief. "Thank you."

I worked on a script for three or four weeks at least, feverishly. I'd meditate, and with every worthwhile disruption, I'd stop and scribble it all down, then go back to meditating. I wouldn't go anywhere without a notepad for fear I might come up with something good and lose it forever. I had scratch sheets of paper, receipts, corners of recycled brown bags stuffed in my pockets with key words or quotes or phrases.

I was excited to be moving in the right direction—at least it felt like the right direction. I thought if I could only share with my audience an ounce of what I'd learned in Hawaii—"You are not your thoughts"—how powerful that would be. I'd been imprisoned by mine for so many years.

And, I found, it wasn't just me: "Why then 'tis none to you for there is nothing either good or bad, but thinking makes it so: to me it is a prison," from Shakespeare's *Hamlet*. Einstein also agreed: "[A human being] experiences himself, his thoughts and feelings, as something separate from the rest—a kind of optical delusion of consciousness. This delusion is a kind of prison for us, restricting us to our personal desires and affection for a few persons nearest to us. Our task must be to free ourselves from this prison by widening the circle of understanding and compassion to embrace all living creatures and the whole of nature in its beauty."

If I could only convince them of this valuable lesson from William James, "If you change your mind, you can change your life," what an impact that might make. I was walking, talking, breathing evidence of such an incredible shift—one of many brave souls, I was discovering, who refused to accept the initial cards we were dealt as a shattered destiny. I could save them from that torment—their very own motivational superhero!

I could see it already. I would come out onstage dancing like Ellen, because I can dance, and that's pretty much universal—everybody loves a white girl who can dance. I'd introduce myself, spit out some poetry, and then head straight in for the kicker: "Be Somebody!" I could somehow fold Freeterrain in; in fact, I would give them Freeterrain. I would let them take over, by some means, and have them figure it out like through computer classes and business classes. Sure, it was a rough sketch, but the wheels were turning—and it would happen—I could feel it.

The only issue was that I hated everything I wrote. It all sounded so contrived, so not funny, not cool. It brought me back to my last two years of teaching, when it was obvious I was no longer the young, hip teacher anymore. I watched the students dote over the young, hip, inexperienced, cutie-pie teachers. (The ones who still woke up an hour before work and actually did their hair, applied proper makeup, and most likely fixed a balanced breakfast and packed a wholesome lunch while watching the *Today Show*. The same ones who were still young enough that their moms took *them* back-to-school shopping.)

My jokes were stale, if the students got them at all. They'd look at me with those obnoxious blank stares and give me that tired, forced laugh like it was too difficult to exert more. I didn't want to get up onstage and try to impress a young audience with my old school badass that was probably just more *bad* than ass. I pictured Michelle Pfeiffer in *Dangerous Minds*. Now, she was badass! Under her duress, I would have curled up in a ball and cried in a corner. I wanted to be more authentic to my thirty-year-old self, not a washed-up twenty-three-year-old wannabe.

All I had ever known of my image was based around ego. I couldn't imagine creating an on-stage persona without it. It hadn't dawned on me how I would look to others, how I might appear. An average day in Hawaii called for board shorts, tank top and slippers, usually with sand still in my hair. Days of blow drying and flat ironing were long gone. I don't think I even owned a comb in those days. I wore a little mascara, but besides my visits to my smoking-hot hairdresser, I did very little in the way of maintenance. If it weren't for year-round bikini season. I might not have even shaved.

∞

My hairdresser, Tanya, was part Native American, olive skinned, bright blue-eyed, and brunette, with the whitest teeth next to my yoga instructor, Shiva, I'd ever seen. She would walk me to her chair and sit me down in front of her, take my hair in her hands and ask, "What are we doing today?"

My response was always the same. "You can do whatever you want with me," and I meant it just as it sounds.

She'd escort me to the shampoo station and give me the most ridiculous head message. (I suppose *any* massage at that point would have felt ridiculous.) She'd give me all her boyfriend drama, and I'd give her my ex-girlfriend drama, then we'd talk about family, and I'd catch her up on all my creative pursuits with Freeterrain. The first few times I left her chair I was short haired, spiky and blonde, the last few times I was back to my natural color, brunette, mid-length with her signature blonde chunk, and each time I left smitten and could have cared less what she'd done.

Needless to say, working on an onstage presence wasn't exactly coming together for me. I had yet to develop my own presence. I had never felt more comfortable in my skin, but this was me outside my scene. This was me in never-never land.

SEVENTEEN

HOMECOMING

It was October 2008, a month before our big presidential election and a full year since I'd left Baltimore when I decided I was due for a trip home. I had earned, after almost a year at The Hatch, a week's worth of vacation, and with my sincere promise that, yes, I'd be back, I was granted early leave. The island buzzed with "Obama Ohana" anticipation. The island-born future president had been home this summer, caught by the local media bodysurfing at Sandy's and doing other local kine stuff—throwing shakas.

At work, the gym seemed split, half local Hawaiian rooting for Cousin Obama and half haole Republicans rooting for McCain. I didn't share my left wing politics over Fox News' constant blare, nor did I offer my left wing sexuality (not that I had much of a sexuality to offer in those days). So I hid the tears when I would eventually watch while leaning on a treadmill as Obama gave his victory speech. Not only was I thrilled to have an articulate president back in office, I was excited for change. I was excited for new beginnings, my own and that of our fine nation. I was a believer. "Yes, We Can!"

The bite in the air on the ground in Baltimore was a startling wake up. My bones shivered as I stepped out of the airport to meet my dear friend, Cindy, who was kind enough to retrieve me in the middle of her workday. Originally, Brooke was going to do the honors but couldn't fit it in around her work schedule. Just as well, I was glad to see Cindy. She and I had kept in touch fairly often while I was gone, mostly her calling to check in. And when she did, I never missed the opportunity to tell her what I was reading, suggesting what she should pick up, often with the promise, "This one will change your life, I swear." She was always a great ear, a good support, and proudly still one of my biggest fans. She and I gave dating a go after nearly five years of friendship, but a rocky year and a half later we decided cheering from the sidelines suited us far better than trying to beat each other at our own game.

∞

I had twenty-four hours to sleuth around Baltimore before the big surprise. Dana and Jay had planned a joint thirtieth birthday celebration for their wives, Whitney and Katie, respectively. Dana and Jay had me on speakerphone back in early September, double-teaming me, making sure I didn't punk out by not doing all that I could to make it home for the soiree. Their plan was for me to arrive after the honored guests as the *ultimate* surprise. I had no money and therefore no business making even a three-stop Pacific hurdle, but it had been way too long, and I would have hated to miss such a big occasion. Besides, even with a shrinking ego, I could never turn down an opportunity to be the *ultimate* surprise. So I got out the shiny new business credit card that when held between forefinger and thumb reflected my big grin back at me as I expensed the trip away—for marketing purposes, of course.

I Think I'll Make It

Cindy and I caught up on work drama, life drama, and lesbian drama, finishing in the half hour it took from the airport to my aunt and uncle's house what could have probably gone on for at least a few beers and a couple of more hours. My truck had been parked in my aunt and uncle's driveway for several months now. They'd gone to retrieve it when they realized I wouldn't be home any time soon. My uncle drove it to the post office or Home Depot every once in a while and got the oil changed; it was their way of taking care of me while I was so far away.

My uncle Paul was home at his desk in the back room where he greeted me warmly as soon as I walked in. He and my aunt Mary have been such a great encouragement for me over the years. I lived with them through middle school and early high school—God bless them—before Gma decided to take me back and set me straight. ("See this fist?" she'd say. "The hell you will ... over my dead body.") Ever since Gma died, though, when I report home, I call Mary and Paul.

Paul had encouraged me to go to Hawaii in the first place. He insisted that I travel and explore as much as I could before I settled down. I suppose he resented that he hadn't done more himself. Funny that there was a time when I would have done exactly the opposite of what was suggested, but it was nice from this perspective, being on the same page, looking eye to eye.

Growing up I always considered my friends my family. They seemed more constant, more reliable, less judgmental, but now looking back, I've seen friends come and go. I've had a solid crew since eighth grade, yet others have changed with jobs, with moves, with maturity. I'll admit that over the years my family has turned out to be quite the damn good time, much more so than I was willing to credit them at fifteen. I think we've all grown to accept one another's glaring idiosyncrasies, or it's that we've discovered with the right amount of wine they're hardly noticeable anyway.

∞

With little thought, I drove to my old neighborhood, turned onto my old road, parked in my old spot, went in to greet my old dog, and sure enough, he peed on me. Well not exactly *on* me, but he got so excited he shi-shied on the floor right in front of me and it totally splashed. And he just wagged and wagged, tap-dancing like old times. He hadn't forgotten me at all. My cat, Lucky Badass, was there too, masking her excitement as always. The smell of the house was the same, the 409 and the paper towels (to sop up the dog pee) were still in the same place, the furniture was rearranged, but everything else was just as I'd left it.

Gma's china cabinet was in the dining room, seemingly untouched. I opened the wood-framed glass door, stuck my nose in, and was immediately brought back to our old front room at Manor Club where we used to play church. (I was always the priest, of course, blessing the Eucharist, preparing the chalice with grape juice, telling people where to stand. I had to be the priest—I was the only one who knew the whole Mass by heart. I'd break the bread and pass it to my disciples, whichever cousin or friend was a willing disciple that day.) The familiar musky smell had me standing in the room, taking it all in—the Oriental rug, the stiff antique couch with the giant paws for feet, the long bay window with its sheers wide open, casting light on the dusty, mostly forgotten grand piano—(except for the occasional *flat* "Heart and Soul").

I looked over the little trinkets I had collected in my travels, mine next to Gma's. I saved the card I'd left standing on the top shelf for last. It was the sweetest card I'd ever received from Gma, not counting all the cutout Peanuts Valentine cards she sent me in college that I wish I'd saved. This card said something I'm not sure

I'd ever heard her say, the one thing that maybe I needed her to say A LOT more: "I believe in you." She had triple underlined each word. And reading it this time, like most times but holding more weight here, now, I fell to pieces all over again.

I held Lucky "Furball" Badass as I walked around the apartment, reacquainting myself with my old life, spitting out tufts of fur that floated off her back, plotting a course to my unsuspecting lips. Both bedrooms had been rearranged, but all the art we had chosen together was still right where I'd clumsily nailed it in. The monogrammed "hers and hers" towels we had picked out were still on the racks, turned inside-out. It was all still mine, oddly enough. I went through some of Brooke's drawers, looking for things I may have forgotten I owned. We were notorious for stealing each other's stuff. I slid open the mirrored master closet to see my side, nearly untouched; my whole teaching wardrobe hanging there, bored and lifeless, most of which I would never wear again.

With Porter at my side, I climbed up into the closet to pull down the boxes of pictures, albums, and all sorts of junk Gma had cataloged and saved for me over the years. I had this overwhelming urge to see all of it—to touch everything. I wanted the intimacy and affection that came with those memories I was afraid I had forgotten. I spread it all out on the floor in *my room* (the office with the futon) and went through each piece, smiling, crying—laughing, crying—crying, crying.

When I finished flipping through every last album and re-zipping each Ziplocked piece of cloth memorabilia, Porter and I put the boxes back up in the closet, and then he and I went for a long walk. We talked the whole way like old times, except I was much more patient with the array of distractions: a passing beetle, a fun stick, a panicked squirrel. Afterward, I sat on the patio and watched him roll around in the grass, content as cotton candy.

Even Lucky came out to tell me how much she loved the fall. "Me, too," I said. "Me, too."

I missed it like an old friend—all of the seasons, really—the way they keep rhythm. The changing leaves. The birth of spring. Hawaii had begun to feel like Groundhog Day. "Good morning, Hawaii, today it will be beautiful, and tomorrow beautiful as well; in fact, all through the week we should expect nothing but beautiful." The grass is always greener, I suppose. I posted this reflection on my blog a few days before I left the island:

I miss the fall ...

Current mood: envious

I miss hooded sweatshirts, fat pants, huge glasses of red wine, football at a normal hour, shitty-ass cold rainy days, Lifetime movies, a good excuse just to eat and couch all weekend, a few long dark months to not think about a bikini, ridiculously decorated spooky houses, high-calorie hoppy fall beer, squash that didn't come off a boat, redundantly sweeping my four leaves, meat on a stick, a guiltless reason to drink whiskey, overalls, red handkerchiefs, rubber boots, lawn ornaments, John Deer, southern twang, and Rosh Hashanah.

I noticed those "four leaves" on our sidewalk when I drove up, but as it turns out, that wasn't my job anymore. There might have been six even, and I stepped right over them. *Ha!* I also noticed that the garden looked a little shabby, and there weren't any nice mums in the pots that I would have planted. *Sucks to be you!*

So much for my mantra. "Peace, harmony, compassion ... "— yeah, yeah—that's the one.

Brooke came home after work to get Porter and some clothes; they were going to stay the night with Julie. She gave some excuse, but I didn't care. Or if I did, even just a little, I tried really hard not to show it. But when she left, and I was ready to be bothered, I stood in the cavernous hallway, frustrated because I couldn't even call my friends and bitch—most hadn't a clue I was even home. So, without Brooke and Porter, me and little Lucky Badass had the whole, cold, empty place to ourselves. I ran a bath in our giant tub (originally, a big selling point for the house). Pleased by the thick layer of dust I rinsed out first, I sprinkled some smelly blue salts, lit some candles, and with one of my many books on mindfulness, sunk in. Lucky purred at my head, prancing along the edge of the tub, trailing wet fur behind her. "I know it. I missed you too," I said. "But stop moving, will ya? You're shedding all over me."

∞

It had been way too long since I'd seen my ladies, so of course I had to step up my game, i.e. no board shorts and slippers. And as it turns out, shopping isn't all that bad when you're slipping into smaller sizes than you're used to. Since I got paid to work out and because I was drinking a lot less beer (perhaps more the latter, honestly), I was down to about sixteen percent body fat; still *chubby* according to Steph, but she was a freak genetic specimen—no comparison, really. I had a little four-pack working (which I'm grateful was documented in a couple of photographs because I haven't seen it since). I felt good. So, I showed up to the party in cut-up jeans, a vest that didn't cover much more than necessary, some slutty heels and a pair of big incognito J-Lo frames to make my *ultimate* entrance.

My girls were thrilled. They made such a fuss when I arrived that I totally lost touch of any burden I may have carted in with me (that also could have been the champagne). It felt so good to be home where I didn't have to explain myself or talk at all if I didn't want to. I could act a fool all night and not one of them would even think to bat an eye. In case I haven't clarified, these girls aren't just my sisters, these girls are My Shit.

By the end of the night, I was carrying my heels. My feet, evidently pissed, were swollen and red at the edges from all the dancing (I have no clue how Beyonce does it). Many of us spent the night at Whit and Dana's. And after another cocktail, an extended dance party, and a frozen pizza, we all slept wherever we landed.

The stale few of us left over the next morning vegged on the couch all day. I'd fallen into a coma with a ceaseless marathon of the Kardashians until I guilted myself into a late afternoon run. I ran a couple of miles down to my favorite spot, Tide Point Pier, and tried to find a little peace in my head after all the commotion, a.k.a. vodka, from the night before. Meditating on the beach on a beautiful island charged with an abundance of natural, spiritual energy was not quite the same as sitting, albeit hungover, on a Baltimore pier among power plants and police sirens.

The sweet caramel of the Domino Sugar factory tickled under my nose in the cool harbor breeze. My mantra, "Thank you, thank you, thank you." Thank you for my amazing friends, and such a great party. Thank you for this beautiful fall day, for the harbor, for this pier. Thank you for my house that I don't live in anymore but is nice just the same and according to the deed, I still own. Thank you for my truck. God I love that truck. Oh, and thank you for not punishing me too much this morning for the disgusting amount of alcohol I consumed last night. Thank you.

I'm pretty sure that was the only time I meditated all week. As I imagined, all the distractions got the best of me—so much for the notion of coming down from the mountaintops, going into the marketplace and remaining grounded, centered, and wise. My *Buddha*, instead, fared better on a remote island. It was a weeklong binge of food, alcohol, and friends that in many ways I needed, soaking up every excuse to indulge. But when I got on the plane to go back to Hawaii, I was ready to return to my regimens, my quiet, my solitude—me.

EIGHTEEN

CHRISTIAN ROCK

I believe this was about the time when I discovered Christian rock. It was an accident at first. I'd been innocently flipping through the channels on the car stereo when I came to a song that I thought I knew. I even starting singing it, or mumbling it rather, before I realized that I didn't know the words at all. *Holy shit!—they're singing about Jesus.* At first I felt betrayed; pulling the wool over my eyes like that, they should be ashamed.

Like the time I was in seventh grade when I went to a church event with my friend Chelsea. It turned out to be a "motivational talk" in a big auditorium. Several speakers took turns sharing their stories, some compelling, others rather so-so if you ask me, about their paths to Jesus. I remember sitting there thinking about how these stories would go in jail because that's where my dad had found *his* Jesus. No sooner had he been incarcerated when Bible quotes and religious memorabilia started showing up in his letters. I remember feeling skeptical, even as a kid, and rightfully so, considering he'd never been much of a Jesus freak—Catholics don't typically dote all over Jesus like that anyway. When he was released, I took note that he must have forgotten his faith back at the big house. All those years later, I never heard him mention boo about Jesus.

The last speaker of the day was a young girl, slightly younger than I was at the time, in a wheelchair. An accident? Palsy? I can't remember. She had a small, yet confident voice, clear as day, with impressive conviction. She was precious, really. I'd buy her Girl Scout cookies if that's what she was selling. Shortly after her standing ovation, I noticed I was being shuffled backstage with a group of others (sinners probably, like me). They sat me down in front of a sponsor, and before I knew it, I had given my heart to Jesus. Turns out that clever little girl had sold me a slice of the Kingdom, and I bought every last bit of it—bait and switch.

I even got a big brown, ugly Bible as a souvenir that didn't go un-scrutinized by my aunt when she saw me put it on my bedside table. "What'd you do, join a cult?" I had been defending the church since I started attending youth group with Chelsea. I really wanted a part in the Christmas musical, and I thought if I had to give my heart to Jesus in order to land the lead, well, so what.

In the end, I didn't get the part, nor did I remain a member of the youth group long after Jesus's birthday. The Bible got stuffed into the drawer of the night table, never to have its thin, crispy pages thumbed through again. I had completely forgotten about the whole episode until this tomfoolery of the inspiration station, 95.5 FM *The Fish*, tricked me into listening to its so-called faith-filled lyrics exploiting my homeboy, Jesus.

But I hadn't turned it off. With all this reflection I was about three songs in, and I hadn't switched the channel. I'm afraid to admit it, but I was actually enjoying the melodic, catchy motivation. It was very *Godspell* or *Jesus Christ Superstar*, very show-tuney, and I do love my show tunes. I spent two whole college years blaring and belting out the *Rent* soundtrack in the shower.

It's a wonder my roommates didn't take the set of tapes and back them over with their car.

I've always been a fan of gospel. I was practically a *sister* in *Sister Act*. And the hymns we sang in concert choir were always my favorite. In fact, in college I was rather determined to audition for the gospel choir. It was an all black choir, but I had several dreams of my white ass, swaying and clapping in my velvety robe, right along with them. My friends convinced me not to join, justly so, being that rehearsals clashed with *college night* (dollar beers and 25-cent wings). Yet every time I sat through Mass at St. Anne's, listening to the *soul* rise up from the gospel choir, I wished I hadn't listened.

It was also around this time that I accepted the fact that I might become a Christian rock headbanging Buddhist monk—the alternative to taking a stab at the daunting thirties-plus dating scene. In those months that I began thinking about dating again, it had dawned on me that I had never actually dated—ever—in the sense that I never went out seeking a relationship. *Relationships* had always just shown up, usually right on time for me to leap right from one lap into another. I had never been on a blind date. Now that I think about it, I hadn't been on a legit first date since high school.

So, embarking on a whole new set of dating adventures at the ripe age of almost thirty-one seemed preposterous to me. The last few ladies' parties I went to I had started to realize that I was in the upper echelon of the age groups present, maybe even eking toward the *creepy watchful ones* we used to talk about at Coconuts. I had begun flirting again, finally, and perhaps was a little more forward than I'd been in a long time, but I can't say that I wanted it to go much further than a good conversation. I felt like confidence had shown up by the armfuls; perhaps because I cared less about the outcomes, I was less pressed about the game.

There was one problem though. Not one woman on island, even in the slightest, resembled Brooke. Not that I needed an exact match but someone at least in the same genre. Taller, for one, which was nearly impossible here; the island really started to give me a tall complex, like I had from about fourth through seventh grade when I was taller than all the boys at school. I was convinced I would have to carry one of *them* over the threshold on our wedding day because not one of those scrawny boys would have done me any justice.

I didn't want to be the spoon-er, I so enjoyed the years of being the spoon-ee. I also wanted older, hoping that with older came wiser, beyond the drama—although more and more evidence seemed to prove that wasn't necessarily the case. Lastly, I needed rich, or comfortable rather; actually, comfortably rich would be nice. I had big dreams that paid very little to start, and we wouldn't want the worry of money to interfere with all this creative genius. I needed a sugar momma to bring home the bacon, and I was okay with that. I'd even cook it if need be. Shoot, I'd scrub the toilets if I had to.

∞

My little Zen masters made me smile when I came back from my trip. "Auntie!" they screamed, tackling me before I could put my bags down. I was giving Ben the silent treatment because he had forgotten to pick me up from the airport, again. I brooded in the cab ride home, thinking perhaps all our family time was starting to wear on us.

Brooke had bugged me when I was home about my plans. But the truth was I didn't have any plans yet; I hadn't gotten that far. She and her dad had been trying to work something out with the house, and it was starting to look as if our only option was to sell. In one of our more heated debates, I reminded her, "IF WE WERE STRAIGHT, BROOKE, AND MARRIED, YOU KNOW GOD-DAMN WELL THAT HOUSE WOULD BE MINE. NO QUES-TION!" And then I went for the gizzard: "THE HOUSE AND THE DOG!" Yet from less of a finger-pointing perspective, I agreed we could do this amicably. But just not yet.

I had started a new chapter here, and I had no idea how to end it. I was still at The Hatch where I had great clients and good friends. I was still surfing any chance I got, running through flaw-lessly bloomed lush-lined trails, hiking to see grand, majestic falls, and climbing really frickin' big rocks just to have my breath taken away for as many more times as I could muster.

I had given it about a week before I fully forgave Ben. I might have let the grudge hold a little longer, yet he broke my heart one night in an unexpected display that made me melt for him all over again. I should add that it was under truly unfortunate circum-stances that I dropped my weakening defense. He had lost a friend, a twenty-nine-year-old acquaintance, to drug-related violence. Ben's relationship with his friend was loose and nondescript, but I'd gathered they'd shared a few joints in a smoky living room among friends on more than a couple of occasions. I could tell he was upset at the first hint of hibernation to his office with a handful of beers.

Pearl Jam played incessantly from his computer speakers, along with several other somber melodies. I think the cryptic email messages to my ENTIRE family began just before 9:00 p.m.— titled "Irish Wake: no body, just beer." YouTube video after YouTube video of Shannon Hoon, Bradley Nowell, Brian Jones, J. Hendrix, J. Joplin, J. Morrison, Kurt Cobain, littered the screen in a succession of emails. (My brother is notorious for sending strange mass messages that yield no reply.) I was in my room reading while I watched him go down and back up the stairs, with more fistfuls of beers, shirtless, before he'd fade smaller into his room, stepping on his baggy, unbuttoned jeans, revealing, shamelessly, the top shadow of his crack.

Had I known that emails were spreading like wildfire to the far reaches of distant cousins, I may have justly interfered, yet by the sheer tone of the music, and witnessing his periodical, singularly pitiful funeral procession, I kept my distance. Lea was out of town (to everyone's misfortune except, evidently, her own). The kids were passed out, contorted figurines, in front of the dim, flickering light of the TV when Ben came to my door blubbering like I'd never seen him before.

"He had two kids, you know?" (awkward silence) "You never know, that could have been me ..." (more awkward silence.) "He was a really good guy—a good father ..." He then began to laugh at his own spectacle, choking, laughing. "I know this is ridiculous, but seriously, he was really cool ... Don't look at me like that ... For real, I'm just tippin' my forty to my homie ... you with me?" He held out his beer toward me in a rhetorical offer.

When I gathered he had gotten it all out of his system, I told him I was sorry as I stared bewildered at the clumsy shadow he cast, swallowing the glow of the doorway. Tears and snot and sweaty beer glistened on the portion of his face visible in the hallway light. The button on his jeans, clearly bought when he was two sizes bigger, was undone; his boxers splayed out. I had no clue what to do with him. "I'm sorry, Ben."

He just stood there, going on and on about this guy whom I'd never heard him speak but two words about. Yet, I knew this had less to do with his friend than with Ben. This was Ben mourning someone who, at the slightest turn, could have actually been him.

I think the last email was sent about 2:00 a.m., when I had long since fallen asleep to the wake's droning soundtrack—taking a turn to Seu Jorge covering David Bowie in his husky Portuguese—although the Irish mourning went on till 4:00 a.m., he later confessed. Five unanswered emails in total that my family must have simply written off as "Ben being Ben."

Needless to say, when he asked me to go surfing with him a couple of days later, all had long since been forgiven. And, remarkably, he and I had one of the most amazing surf sessions on North Shore—celebrating life. I didn't miss the opportunity, however, to get in a few jabs about just how pitiful he was that night. I even told Lea on him shortly after she walked through the door from her trip. "I cannot fathom how you find it in yourself to leave me *and* your helpless little children alone with this man. You will not believe what he did this time …" He too was laughing about the whole thing. Yeah, real funny now, a few days later. I, on the other hand, was still scarred—Pearl Jam, for me, has never been the same.

A small north swell led us to Ehukai Beach Park just down from Pipeline. The waves weren't crazy big, which was good for us. The wind had started to taunt us though, so we lay low on our boards while we waited for the sets, water being warmer than the cool air above. Everyone else was smart, in a wetsuit top, at least. I even recall smelling a fireplace somewhere off in the distance. We were thinking about calling it a morning after a few more waves when it started to sprinkle, which sealed it. Pau (done).

Before we could take our last wave, though, a double rainbow shot up and painted itself across the sky. I had seen plenty of rainbows in Hawaii. In fact, there's a joke about spotting tourists by their fingers constantly pointing to the Crayola-lined sky, but I'd never seen a double rainbow. Ben admitted, in his thirteen years, to only ever having seen one. And then, as if it wanted to prove just how badass of a rainbow we were dealing with here, it spilled out like paint in the water and wrapped itself around us. Ben and I, and maybe six other surfers, were mesmerized by the royal ring we floated in. It was stunning.

And it was moments like this when I knew Synchronicity was still giving me shout-outs every chance she got, the Universe, whipping out high-fives. And the more in tune I was to finding them, the more they insisted on showing up.

∞

My obsession with nature went beyond the surf, sun, and sand. Trees with trunks as wide as my first car was long called me to their roots where I'd stand mystified, wondering about the stories they held within. I'd hike trails deep in the rainforest or lush valleys and stop every so often just to lay my hand on one of those magnificent trunks in an attempt to pay respect. It didn't feel hokey or contrived, I was well aware this was "tree-hugger" to the max, but I didn't care. The more I read about the interconnectivity of nature—the universe—the more I became aware of its unyielding splendor. As if someone had switched on the High Def, I experienced it all for the first time.

Hungry to hike and explore as much as I could before I left the island, I set out to find a good running trail one afternoon. There was a popular one that somehow I could never find, all the way up the hill in Aiea. After asking for directions, I cruised up Aiea Heights Road to the end jamming the whole way to my inspiration station, my new go-to when I needed a break from audio books. Ben had told me the trail was a loop, and he'd run it before, so I knew it couldn't be all *that* long. I went for it.

What I hadn't taken into consideration though, was how late in the day it had gotten to be. At first I started along the path and then stopped every so often to take it all in. Cliffs overlooked a deep mesmerizing canyon of puffy lush green, so inviting it appeared as though you could dive on in. There were rubber trees (one of my favorites) everywhere, and with the tall pines and enchanting eucalyptus, it was a soothing aromatherapy and meditation, a charming combo meal of wellness. I would stop for thirty seconds, flash a mental photograph then continue on as the sun sank heavily behind the trees.

For a time, the trail was rocky and wide, then narrow with jutting roots. I ran and jumped over fallen old logs or big puddles of mud. Suddenly, it dawned on me that no one else was on the trail—just my quickened breaths and mind racing along with me. I darted around corners and dashed through flat sections, picking up pace with each passing moment of light. My mind started in on all its nasty tricks: how I would fall and twist something (flashing gruesome images across my mind's screen), and with no cell phone, of course, I would be left in the woods until morning. No one knew where I was, or would even think to look for me until tomorrow. *That's it*, I was a goner.

Waking me out of my own maddening thoughts, a loud stir came from the forest lining the trail. Feet—several of them—scrambling, faster than mine, pounded alongside me. I didn't stop running. I figured whatever it was would sense my fear if I stopped. Thankfully, the wild boars (I later confirmed) stayed out of site and were probably just as scared of me as I of them. But perhaps *not* if I were on the ground, injured, bleeding to death like I could easily be if I didn't *get the hell out of here!*

I tried to tap into my Suzie Sunshine, but to no avail. She continued in my ear anyway, "This is beautiful. Seriously, look around. You have the whole place all to yourself. Just enjoy it. Breathe. Do you smell how amazing that is?" If I could have smacked her, I would have. But she was right; I gave it a go. *Breathe, damn it; breathe.*

Just as I started to relax and maybe even muster a smile, I turned a corner too quickly, lost my footing on a blanket of pine needles and slid off the edge of a deep ravine. I wasn't cliff-hanging by any means, but I *was* digging into the crumbling earth with only my fingertips, white knuckled, while my feet struggled to gain solid footing below. I tried not to think about the trees and rocks and debris beneath me that would do me no favors padding an awkward landing. Instead, I focused on my fingertips, my nails digging in. "Trust, trust, trust," I whispered in every effort to will my way back onto solid ground.

It was much like the incident when I stopped to shi-shi that one infamous day when I was trying to teach Brooke how to snow-board. I had rolled myself over the edge of the slope near a tree where I could easily pop a squat. It was initially a shi-shi success, but when I got all geared up and started back over the edge, I fell, screaming for Brooke, grabbing hold of a branch of what looked like a small sapling, hoping I hadn't landed in the freshly stained, steaming yellow patch. When I tried to hoist myself up though, I tugged at the branch I had gripped for dear life, and the dumb loose stick came out of the snow just like that in my hands—complete false advertising—and Brooke just lost her shit over it, doubled over laughing hysterically. In truth, it may have been my saving grace from the audible temper tantrum she had thrown on that crowded green circle (beginner slope) she had cursed her way down, walking, board in hand. I, too, laughed, but not on purpose because I really should have been in tears to better express the magnitude of the situation. She hadn't seen how steep of an incline I was hanging from, and she just laughed and laughed until I dug my way out of my own mess. I have to admit it was kind of funny, especially when all the kids came by to peek their bobble-helmet-heads over the edge to see what all the commotion was about.

But this wasn't exactly like *that* time because here I was by myself with no cell phone. No ski patrol to rescue me if I took an gruesome plunge. I'd been dangling for a few minutes, contemplating, not wanting to make a false move. Eventually, I closed my eyes, "Trust, trust ... "—and somehow that did it. I found the footing. I heaved myself over the edge and crawled to solid ground, shaking, kissing the dirt under my nose. "Thank you," I whispered as I got up and started booking, grinning from ear to ear. "Thank you."

NINETEEN

HOLIER THAN THOU

Since seasons didn't move me along in Hawaii, the monthly news articles I dressed up at the gym kept me convinced that time actually passed. I wrote health- and nutrition-based articles, updated clientele on fitness challenges and events, and selected a Mr. and Mrs. Fitness to be recognized in the monthly newsletter. It wasn't a glamorous writing job, but I guarantee health and fitness hadn't yet seen that much color—well, at least not down here. I changed my bulletin board each month with as much fervor as I felt for such tasks as a teacher, about as excited as I'd be to pierce my own eyelids with a pitchfork.

I was never one of those teachers who couldn't wait to decorate her room with all that cutesy, color-coded laminated crap. Even after a summer's worth of rest and relaxation, I clashed steadily with all the chirpy empty promises and juvenile wishful thinking, counting the days on my fingers till Rosh Hashanah, walking out of the *Welcome Back* faculty meeting. I was clearly better suited for high school, where I could get away with *not* doing all that stuff. Plus, one of my favorite students, Zach, was an artist who had a series of "Dirty Kindergartners," which I loved because they resembled the old Garbage Pail Kids cards that somehow Gma had not deemed sacrilegious and we were allowed to collect. It might have been like the Badass Board Company T-shirts she bought for us because we had convinced her that the B.A. stood for "Bad Attitude." Or perhaps after already raising six of her own children, she cared less about the small stuff. Either way, we were stoked because deep in our decks were the likes of Jay Decay (pictured crawling out of his grave), Acne Amy (painfully pizza faced), Mugged Marcus (beat up and bruised), and Fryin' Brian (being zapped in an electric chair), all grotesque versions of the adorable Cabbage Patch Kids with their Xavier Roberts stamp on the tush. Anyway, Zach's "Dirty Kindergartners" were all over my walls, as well as Jared's dragons, and David's God-knows-whats. Who needs bulletin boards, banner tape, and stenciled letters? Where's your originality, people?

I remember sitting in my elementary ed grad school classes with all the other teachers, watching them highlight their notes with precise lines, switching colors for each topic. I sat in the back, usually with my feet kicked up on a nearby chair, no highlighters, no pencil case. I could never understand what they were taking notes on; the professor had just begun, "Today we will go over ..." I'd already be indignant, *What the frick are you writing down?*

Another quiet woman sat on the other side of the room in the back row, too. About my height, dark hair, confident, as *thrilled* as I was for group projects, just as confused about the company we were forced to keep, and I couldn't help but notice, took as few notes as me. One day after class, instead of bolting like she usually did, beating me out the door, she met me in the hallway to ask what I knew about bartending. All the other teachers were still in the classroom discussing, oh I don't know, their Trapper Keepers loaded with interactive lesson plans or the latest online discount for teacher supplies, while I walked with Lisa down the hall. "I've never bartended before, but I've waited tables some, and—I drink a lot."

"Perfect," she said. "Can you start Saturday?"

And that's the story of how I became a *Coyote* at Coconuts.

∞

I've always had a tendency to do things a little differently. It never much appealed to me to stay within the lines. I picked up and ran from any job where I felt even the faintest loss of space or suffocation of micromanagement. I've always needed to know why. Doing things just for the sake of doing them still makes me batty. So does following rules that don't really make sense, which I've paid the price for on occasion. I have a bad habit of questioning everything; and maybe it's just a further extension of my ego that I most often believe I have a better way. It should be noted that I've run into many difficulties upholding such a level of stubborn pigheadedness. Yet at least as I see it, I haven't fallen between the cracks of the mundane and mediocre that I continually step over and feel sorry for—with as much compassion as a *beginner* might offer, I should add.

I'll just put it out there, hang it on the line, if you will, for some fresh air and all the neighbors to see. The general acceptance of boredom, poor health, preventable chronic illness, even fatigue, and overall unhappiness has become more and more difficult for me to swallow in recent years, and in Hawaii my patience for such unconsciousness wore Thin Mint slim. I'm not trying to get all high and mighty here; it's just that you notice these things when you invite a little Grace into your life. I'm just sayin'—there are a lot of people in dire need of some goddamn Grace.

I simply could never understand why I, and only handfuls of others I met along the way, sought in some way or another, a more fulfilled, more balanced, healthier existence than many people I've encountered in both Hawaii and on the mainland. Believe me, I've had my years of dissatisfaction and self-destruction following me around, tapping their pesky little fingers on my shoulder. "Hey stranger, remember me?" I have self-diagnosed my mind and body at least one hundred and seven times over, but I have always maintained a level of introspection to do so, and I can't understand those who either aren't equipped with or ignore their own self-monitoring system because only a couple of words come to mind—bored and lazy.

While on this soap box, I'd like to introduce my friend, Darren.

Darren was one of few friends to visit me on island, and one of even fewer to visit twice. He is a good guy, whom I met at the dog park that first year raising Porter. Darren had an adorable boxer, Casey, and we'd meet on top of Federal Hill for play dates almost every evening. The dogs would run and play, tiring themselves out (which is why we hardly missed a date), while all of us doggie parents stood around and talked in between the glamorous jobs of picking up poop and tossing slobbery sticks.

Darren looked *hard* when I first met him, with his shaved head, wearing an old school Triple F.A.T. Goose jacket, but to see him with Casey, you could tell he was a sweetheart underneath all that down. I had joked with Brooke that one day he'd be our baby daddy, considering I had fallen in love with his puppy-dog eyes and Crest White Strip grin. I ignored his past, his rather severe version of self-medication: drugs, alcohol, Johnny Law, and yucky menthol cigarettes, because really, who doesn't visit all those things.

He's the kind of guy who gets along with everyone; prop him up on a bar stool and he'll make friends in no time. He goes with the flow, and despite his steamy forty-five minute shower routine, is relatively low maintenance. For all those reasons, I invited him to stay at our house on his second trip out to the island. Unfortunately, the beach front North Shore cottage where he'd stayed the year prior had fallen through, so our humble suburban abode on the hotter, drier side of the island would have to suffice.

He would have been happy with a tent, or better yet, the garage, so the whole house with kitchen and toilet might as well have been the Four Seasons, especially with our self-appointed greeters. "Uncle!" Hilton was thrilled to have a handsome man in the house, but curious—you could tell from the looks—how he ended up coming home with me. Boy Boy climbed all over him like a jungle gym, no period of shyness or quiet like I see other kids go through with strangers, standing behind their moms. My two just jumped right in on the, "Who are you? Why are you here? Where did you come from?" line of questioning. Nothing got by those kids.

∞

Like the first time he visited, Darren talked all kinds of shit about how he'd mastered the water and just watch out because he was gonna *do the damn thing*. And just like the last time, I watched him punk out and get washed ashore more than he didn't. He huffed and puffed his way through panic while I yelled over the crashing waves, "I thought you said you quit smoking?"

I have much of the same relationship with Darren as I do with Ben. We talk mad shit to each other, we duke it out a bit, and then we drink a lot and laugh and make up: wash and repeat. But nothing was funnier to me than watching two-sleeved, hard core lookin' Darren wash ashore with sand in every crevice, walking that surf rash, chafed, wide stride with his pecker between his legs—especially after all the shit he'd been serving.

In all fairness, I will admit that I had one of my best wipeouts while Darren was in town. We were at Maks, body boarding, and I don't know what happened exactly. I imagine that my back was to the beach when I saw the wave coming and quickly turned and caught it. Which would be the only excuse for my poor lineup and sightline, because I knew those rocks on the right were there; they've never moved. But somehow I found my way smack dab in the midst of them. I felt first the instant burning and tearing of skin, then the thud of the rocks under my board. When the water receded, I swear I looked like the Little Mermaid sitting perched in all her glory, stuck for a few seconds. As I yanked my tangled leash from the rocks, I nearly had to stand in my fins (which are not an attractive accessory) and jump to scramble off back into the water before anyone, especially Darren, caught sight of me.

Thank goodness Darren was busy playing "uncle," as I called it, and had missed the whole thing. (Some of the older, bigger uncles are notorious for paddling out and rarely exuding effort to catch waves. They are just as content lying on their board, stomachs falling to either side, hanging out in the surf, talking story. That was Darren—well, a smaller haole version, at least.) He was too distracted waiting for that one perfect wave to form in front of him—and him only—that he hadn't seen me. Later though, as we toweled off by the car and I assessed the damage of my gaping wounds, I happily poked fun at myself with a padded play-by-play, exaggerating all the good parts, naturally.

And each time I told it thereafter, the story got better. In one version, I described the snapping of my head back while I sat perched on top of the rocks, the spray from my hair raining down my back just like a moment in Disney's version, full of "Up where they walk, up where they run, up where they play all day in the sun!" Unfortunately though, we hardly resemble each other, Ariel and I. Sadly, I'm afraid, I couldn't even fill her seashells.

∞

After a few days of getting his ass handed to him, Darren finally started blaming it on the smoking and admitted to being out of shape.

"Why don't you just quit then?" I said like a nagging sister on our drive back from dinner one night.

"I just wish my girl would quit."

"Oh, for shit sakes, Darren, why don't you just man up and stop making excuses for yourself?"

"I'm not making excuses," he said, a defensive younger brother.

"Well, do you actually want to quit? Because all I've heard all week are excuses."

"Yes." He paused. "Except not if it's gonna make me wanna kill people!"

"What?" I said, laughing. "Are you for real? Seriously—kill people? You're full of shit. Do you want to quit or not?"

"I am serious! I don't want to quit if—after two months I'm gonna feel crazy and wanna kill people!"

"Well," I said, peppering in a chuckle. "It takes more than a couple of months. It took me about six months or a year when I quit before I felt fully over—"

"Well, I'm not you!" he interrupted. "And I'm not perfect, and I don't eat rabbit food!" He was totally serious.

I laughed desperately. "Right—I wear a cape. I'm perfect." *Are we really having this conversation?* "So I still haven't gotten from you whether you actually want to quit or not."

"No damn it! No! I don't frickin' wanna quit!" He may have banged the dashboard with this emphatic display. I can't remember because the whole tantrum was a spectacle either way.

"Okay then." I couldn't help but grin. "Then why are we still talking?" He seethed, but I couldn't miss the opportunity to seal it. "You're wasting my time."

Here I was getting an ego while dropping an ego. It had become obvious that I was obtaining an allergic response to apathy. I didn't understand how people didn't feel more called to action, especially with the halo of truths I could help shine on their lives. I wanted to fix people, my clients, my family, my friends, yet I found out more and more that people didn't really want to be fixed. They were just as content ho-humming along as they'd always been. I started to think the monastery wasn't such a bad idea after all, or that 2012 party where *my people* were headed, *brah.*

∞

Before I knew it, Halloween had passed with a tiny little masked Batman and a blinged-out convict (it boggled my mind how she could turn a convict costume into something chic and seven-year-old sexy). I spent Thanksgiving house-sitting for Sheila and Michelle back in my vacation home with Suki, the parrot, and the dogs. Thanksgiving Day I celebrated with friends and family, Filipino-Hawaiian style, "up country" (North Shore), surfing all day and then eating choke Styrofoam plates of food while watching the kids (of age and under) fight over their turn at XBox's Rockband.

It was when the rockers and groupies eventually began to trickle with waning interest that I jumped in. I preferred my place as the lip-biting drummer, except for my one Oasis solo, "Don't Look Back in Anger," which I was always happy to belt out.

Christmas came and went rather inconspicuously—we lost hours as a family to our own new Rockband set. Lea wouldn't let go of the microphone except to fill her wine glass—Radiohead's "Creep" kept calling her back—and Ben and I took turns on the drums, me rereading the same page of my latest book in an effort to retain something in between.

Hilton was decent at guitar, but like her mom, would rather sing—a breathy, mumbled, goth-style rendition no matter what the genre—I thought I'd die if I heard Garbage's "I think I'm Paranoid" one more time. Boy Boy circled us, scooting on his truck, sometimes opening up the floor with his surprisingly natural breakdance moves.

Not much else happened that Christmas except, I should say, I took notice of more couples arm in arm being all kissy-face during the holidays as I grinched my way around the island, losing all sense of compassion at the sight of each obnoxious couple. It's amazing how many people you notice holding hands when you're single. And I found myself being both happy and horrified, watching couples who I swore were tipping near a century, all cute and cuddly. *Even they're having more sex than me.*

Other than an insane half marathon trail run I got suckered into, which I had to cuss my way across the finish line, and being commissioned to write web copy for a random lawyer, the best thing that happened all winter was the opening of the new Whole Foods on island. The lawyer was random, only in the sense that I had been back on craigslist looking for jobs in California. I wasn't really interested in going home empty-handed. I had already started losing steam for Freeterrain, and the thought of relaunching it on the mainland seemed more daunting than just accepting its limbo status for the time being.

I hadn't lost my resolve for speaking to schools; I simply feared I didn't have a platform to speak from just yet. I wanted it to happen organically, not force it. Somehow, having an inkling of insight as to what I should do made it even harder to go after. The stakes seemed higher all of a sudden. Failing at something that wasn't my destiny was easy, but failing at this—no, I wouldn't dare. So, I backed up a few steps and just admired it from a distance, gaining perspective while I continued to do the little things that needed to come first anyway, I reasoned.

Like before, I searched and searched for gigs, first in my field(s), but California is full of personal trainers and bartenders. I started back in on the jobs that came with housing and found what seemed like the most perfect listing. It was a live-in health coach/mentor job for a struggling teen who had just gone through her parents' ugly divorce. After a few résumé emails and a phone interview, the job was practically mine. In the several emails that moved quickly back and forth, pictures of my new room, get to know yous with the daughter, the fact that I'm a writer surfaced. "Oh, my ex-husband is looking for a writer," the mom, Tracie, said. "Is it okay if I give him your info?"

"Of course, please. I would love to help," I said, perhaps more enthusiastically than necessary given I already had the job.

So, two more emails later, I got commissioned to write web copy for the defense attorney dad. Kind of a sleazy "first" for a paid gig, but a gig just the same. Plus anything I could do for this family who was willing to offer me my very own grown-up room and an adjoining bathroom with no little boys barging in, I was all for it. (Not that I hadn't been grateful for my room and especially for that curious little boy.)

As it turns out though, the teen had (surprise) a lot of issues with her dad, and when she found out he and I were getting chummy through our loose work relationship, I got canned. Fired!— before I was technically ever hired. I'd *never* been fired from a job. Well—except that one time, the stupid Olive Garden. I nearly did everything but beg to be fired from that ball-busting joint, which was different. I continued working with *dad* and finished the copy for his site, never to hear from Tracie or troubled teen again.

I guess that was my *sign*. I was befuddled, but with "everything happens for a reason" practically tattooed on my forehead, who could deny the oddities pointing me back home.

TWENTY

SIX WORDS OR LESS

New Year's Eve I sat happily with a Guinness in a beach chair in the driveway, watching the kids (the old outnumbering the young) pop fireworks in the cul-de-sac until the smoke sitting still in the dense air sent me inside, choking. We watched the ball drop on TV, six hours after my friends back home. Some of them had already called as we were sitting down for dinner, high on bubbly, yelling into the phone, "Happy New Year! What? We can't hear you. Love your guts! Huh? Miss you, too. Come home soon. Bye-ee!"

Despite my continual efforts, responding to endless job listings out West, I was excited by the prospect of going home and reconnecting with friends and family. Still, I was in no rush. It's not that I was stalling, but I'd built a life out here and couldn't just pull the plug and roll out. There's a way to do this sort of thing—somehow. Brooke was beginning to get irritated with not knowing what was going on. She kept trying to organize and delegate things every time we spoke, usually on Google Chat.

"Do you want a dresser in your room for when you come home?"

"Since I'm not sure whether I'm coming home, why don't we wait on the dresser?"

"Well, if we're gonna put the house on the market when you come home, I'd rather you not be living out of your suitcase."

"Again, I'm not sure when I'm coming home, or IF I'm coming home, so why don't you hold off on moving things until we know what's going on."

"Well, I know you're just fine waiting for the wind to blow you around in any old direction, but I prefer a little organization in my life."

"Hence, where we are right now."

"Exactly!"

"I don't know why you're getting all worked up. All I said was that it doesn't make sense to worry about anything until I know what I'm doing."

"You just think this is all a big joke, don't you?"

"No. I just think your worrying about essentially nothing is rather amusing."

∞

I tried to be compassionate, but it was difficult indeed *not* feeling like I floated along in this ephemeral realm, looking down on these poor people who just didn't get it. By then I had already read almost forty titles on spirituality and mindfulness. More books than I'd read in the classroom, on vacation, or at bedtime combined. In fact, my last true passion for books ended with the *Sweet Valley High* twins in the fifth grade. There were a few winners thereafter but nothing that lit the fire like my budding new library.

Having had some of the simplest questions answered—What? I'm not crazy?—was so profound. The only problem now, I swore, was that I was surrounded by crazy people. Okay, perhaps not all, but I think it's fair to say that *most* people couldn't be any more

UNaware if they tried. In traffic, at the grocery store, at Starbucks, even relaxing with a book, they're checking their cell phones, listening to their iPods or feverishly chewing their nails. I'll admit, they probably thought I was crazy as a loon, as much as I insisted on smiling at everyone and making lasting eye contact, carrying on personal conversations with cashiers, holding the door for someone far longer than necessary, and remaining patient as a peacock in the most ridiculous of circumstances.

(Months later, I would make a friend, Gretchen, cry-laughing when I told her that I hadn't had a bad day in over a year. Sure, I'd had my episodes, but to write a whole day off as *bad*, I wouldn't think of it. She wiped her tears and laughed at me like I was a naïve little school girl. Then we just went back to conversation as if nothing had happened, sidestepping any further disagreement from either end of the spectrum.)

And that was the real bit for me—that it all made sense. I felt good, better than good even, and I could tell that other people felt good around me. This wasn't the people-pleasing routine I had perfected before; this was authentic. This didn't deplete me; this was true compassion. Despite my quavering moments, I twirled my sparkly baton way out in front, leading the Positive Parade. Even with failed job attempts and California housing opportunities falling through, I was still high as a kite on sunshine silhouettes and mystical moonbeams. I knew there "are no accidents," and I would be taken care of accordingly when it was time, so I waited patiently—for the *signs*.

∞

I woke up to a curious email on MySpace one mid-January morning. I hadn't yet made the switch to Facebook—the thought of learning a whole new set of social networking skills seemed like far too great an undertaking. The email was from a chick named Elisa (Lee), who had been to Hawaii and had seen my picture on a friend's page. Before I emailed back, I shuffled through her pictures and read her profile to see if she was just another bored, lonely creep like all the others. Her pictures were kinda cute. (My friend Erin, later, pointed out that she had bad shoes, to which I totally concurred.) It was hard to tell, her profile looked normal, *wait—a teacher, shorter, younger*—yikes! *Shit, she's from New Jersey!* fail, fail, fail, fail!—but it *would* be rude not to reply, I supposed.

I sent her a note, rather noncommittal. She replied, sounding surprisingly normal and nice enough. Soon, messages flew back and forth for a few days; *am I really engaging in some sort of cyber connection?* She passed several discreet tests before I went in for the kicker: "In six words or less, why are you single?" I woke up the next morning to, "I do not settle for mediocrity." *1, 2, 3, 4, 5, 6*—PASS!

She, of course, replied with the same question, although I found it funny that *my* character was in question. Me? Really? I was just innocently going about my business until YOU showed up stalking ME, remember?—but I obliged with, "Learned to love myself truly first." For me it had been almost two years of being single, since I'd kissed someone, or even held hands, which I imagine constitutes *born again virgin* under several doctrines. Lee's last relationship ended a little over a year ago as well. She had done some dating in between but nothing serious.

Talking to Lee was indeed the breath of fresh air I needed, although I never imagined it would come in the form of a cyber girl. I always teased her about how many other women she had corralled online before I responded. The best part was that she read all the same books I was, and the concept of meditation didn't scare her off. Actually, the real best part was that she had a twin, Catherine, and on Catherine's page were pictures of the two of them together that made all the difference. (Not that I'm completely shallow, it's just that when there's five thousand miles of land and ocean between you, and bad shoes to ponder, there's not a whole lot to go on.) Turns out, Lee would just put up any old crappy picture, but Catherine, the prima donna of the two, knew better which ones to delete. The twins were stunning in pictures from a recent wedding and other events—sold!

I woke up early just to read my email, and then I'd run out on the beach to meditate and then I'd run back home to check my email again. (Remember, this was B.S.P.—Before Smart Phone.) I found out that she was a little baller, a point guard in college. So, I pumped up the saw-dust covered basketball in the garage and started shooting around in the morning after meditation to freshen up my game. I listened to music I hadn't dared to in ages, smiling wide, thinking about this cute and curious chick prospect I was getting to know from the questionable state considered the armpit of the US.

∞

Lee assured me that New Jersey had finer qualities than what is advertised by the incessant billboards and smoke stacks lining either side of the turnpike. She had to convince me of quite a bit early on. Like how it was cool to talk on the phone after we'd been emailing for a couple of weeks. *But what if her voice is strange?* Plus I was shy all of a sudden—weird, I'd never been shy.

The day of her Nana's funeral, I decided I could look past all my neurosis and finally call her. I had driven out to the east side of the island and was overlooking Makapu'u from the lookout on

Kalanianaole Highway when I dialed her number. Her voice was normal, thank God, cute even. I drove down to the beach and sat on the rocks to watch the body boarders and assess whether I was getting in, while we had what felt like an effortless conversation about her day, the movie she was on her way to see, and her quaint little town. We laughed naturally; there were no uncomfortable pauses, no awkward tangents. *Was this girl for real?*

Lee and I had been talking for about a month when my dad came back out to the island. Under normal circumstances, which I'm not sure I believed in anymore, I might have waited to explain my family situation to her, but since I'd be uprooted again, I figured over the phone was as good of a time as any. I told her the basics one afternoon as I rushed off to work. *Way to go, jerk,* I thought as I left her sniffling and speechless, while I hung up the phone. I later apologized, but she didn't want to talk about it, any of it for that matter. She hurt too much for me to think about it, she said. I understood; I guess it is a lot to dump on someone. Especially a cyber someone I had yet to even meet.

I went to stay with Sheila and Michelle again, who approved of Lee's pictures and listened patiently while I told them all about her, always adding the disclaimer, "She's probably psycho in real life, but so far so good, right?"

Lee was an English teacher whose vocabulary made me smile, although she used prepositions at the ends of sentences and sometimes conjugated her verbs incorrectly—which I teased was the fault of New Jersey. I appreciated her passion for literature and thirst for knowledge, though. She taught poetry at the time and left me with a cryptic message one evening, "Give me three things you crave." I had just come back from a poetry performance when I got her email. Energized and awake, I replied with this:

I Think I'll Make It

Just three things

Just three things to delineate, to try to operate and coordinate. No can, simply can-not, in this ever-developing sweet adventurous plot. I gotta start at the beginning cuz that is what I know, where it all derives, and where it all flows. From the heart and the soul, the mind and the time, the fervor and freak, the passion and the meek. From the midst of the moment, the conscious presence ever poignant ... what do I crave? You say, we should play—the games I so enjoy as we are delving into each other's pasts, presents, and futures. Our lives intertwined and digitized through computers and cell phones and hopes and dreams. Fears of current everythings and timeless nothings. Scattered and shattered memories played through music echoing in the airwaves of our battered hearts. Trusts tainted, plots fainted, developed and thickened only to be stricken by exactly ... what was meant to be. For us to be free, so I could tell you my three. What do I crave? You say, we should play.

I crave Sunday mornings, cuddling yearnings, hands clasped content, knowing your scent, feeling your breath on my chest as I cradle your internal sunrise. I crave a heartbeat close to mine, the feeling of skin that touches you right back, divine. I crave waking you up to kisses that seduce, and may even produce PANCAKES ... later, after I cater to your succulent Sunday morning intrigue, give me your three; what do you crave? I say, we should play. Tell me your needs, your wants, your desires, let me conspire, cuz I got all day to play and stray from the way the outside world might think we should be ... if they only knew we had three.

What about those pancakes, I've earned? Did I mention the toast that I burned? — let me help you outta' bed, baby ... dress my lady. Send you off with a smile, I'll be a lil' while ... I'm gonna

earn some more points making the bed, picking up all the clothes that were shed, last night when we didn't have to play, what do I crave, cuz you were brave and you just showed me, cuz you felt like you know me, and as you should because it's just, well, ... understood.

Cuz two hearts in pain, protecting themselves in vain, move in such a way, strategizing careful conversations, predictions of emotions, not wanting to fall into the notion, of what could be or could not, what we could see if we just gave love a shot—again after patching up our mendings of last endings that left us broken open, needing to be lifted up from the ashes, choking from the smoke suffocated in past passions. So if you ask for my three, one is ... let it be me, to change your mind, give you the time to trust, to lust and dust off the child that's not afraid to fly, to cry or to crash and burn.

Speaking of burn, can we still have pancakes? After my chores, following your lures, I'll help you cook, playing the distracter, inhibition no factor. Picking you up onto the counter, just for a few, cuz, God, you make me want you. Eye to eye, stealing your attention, I don't even have to mention, what I crave, cuz you can see through to my sincerity, and realize we don't have to play games, cuz I come with a money back guarantee, a warranty that promises three if that's the way it needs to be.

Homework. *Check.*

∞

When that didn't chase her away, I knew I was in. God knows what she said to Catherine after opening her inbox to that. Perhaps they discussed, instead, one of my more eloquent expressions of my situation: "Oh, and by the way, not only am I a vegetarian, meditating, poetry-slamming, fairy god-child, I will also be moving in with my ex-girlfriend, whom I may or may not still be in love with, whenever I decide to move home and start selling the house that we may end up losing anyway—cool?"

My dad sort of came and went without me thinking much of it. I had come to terms with so many essential pieces of my past that it seemed almost silly for me not to meet up with him and at least have coffee. But every time I thought about it, my interest fell neither here nor there, and then the next thing I knew he was gone and I was back in my trusty ol' room again. One of my clients at the gym, Rayanne, a tall local Hawaiian with a bigwig banker job, whom I teased because she slept with her Blackberry, was one of very few at the gym who had asked me about my family. She felt so strongly about my relationship with my father that she insisted I should find a way to speak to him. "It's not that I don't forgive him, I do," I said. "I know now, more than ever, my life was supposed to be like this. It was all supposed to happen this way."

"Well, if you forgive him then why won't you talk to him?"

"Because I'm not sure we know how to have a relationship. He just says stuff that bothers me. And the way I judge him ... well, it doesn't seem fair."

"I just think this will continue to be a block for you until you can have some sort of closure to all of this. That's all."

"Maybe you're right, in fact I'm sure there's some truth to that, but nothing seems to be shifting me in that direction, so I'm not gonna push it. I'd rather just let it happen on its own terms, you know?"

∞

My dad left just before my birthday ended its loop around the sun again. Jupiter had just entered Aquarius, whatever the hell that means, and I received exciting news: my brother Jack was on his way.

When Jack had gotten word I was moving off island, he sprung at the opportunity for some quality sibling time together. He had missed Ben's wedding while out at sea on a Navy ship, so he was due for a trip to the islands anyway.

Jack and Ben in some ways are polar opposites. I have always imagined that I got the best of both their worlds split right down the middle. Jack is perpetually upset about his and Ben's relationship, or lack thereof, really. Ben's forever laughing off my requests for him to email his brother so I don't have to hear him whine anymore. Jack is very sweet, endearing, and just wishes his younger brother would care more about their spotty correspondence. Ben is, well—Ben. He is aloof, and terribly inconsistent with communication, and doesn't really have a good excuse for either, because in real life he is personable, a very good communicator, and in fact gets paid very well for how well he communicates.

Needless to say, I was a little nervous about the two of them *bonding* when I picked Jack up from the airport. "Hey, beautiful," he said while wrapping his arms around me in a big bear hug, kissing my forehead. "It's good to see you." He let go, grinning, yet I could tell he was checking me out like a father might when visiting his little girl at college. "You look good," he said, sounding not so sure, which I disregarded as I paid him the same compliment. He later admitted that he thought I looked a little too skinny.

"Glad you made it safe. How's the fam? What's everyone up to? Tell me everything."

I really hate that my brothers are so spread out. When I indulge in one family's holidays, I miss out on the other's. In fact, Jack had offered me a room in his house at the same time Ben had, and was still giving me a guilt trip about picking Hawaii over Virginia. Not to mention that the kids were growing like weeds and I was just getting shorter, older, and depending on whose calculations, loonier by the second.

My apprehension about the whole visit dissolved within minutes of showing Jack into the house. The kids, of course, were there to welcome him. "Uncle!" Ben was already drinking and was his personable funny self—at his best after a few beers (and about two beers away from his worst). The two of them, who hadn't seen each other since Gma's funeral, jumped right into talking shit, and aside from wedgies and noogies, were right back where they were twenty-five years ago—except now with matching beer bellies.

Ben took time off from work so we could all go surfing. I rearranged my schedule so I wouldn't miss out on any of the fun. I was instantly eight again, and we all fell into our rightful roles. We played golf. We showed Jack all our favorite spots, had margaritas at Cholos, beers at Kona Brewing Company. We spent my birthday at Makapu'u, where Jack crawled out of the water after a good pounding—I got to show them both how it's done, bringing in thirty-one with plenty of shakas.

I showed Lee's picture to Jack and let him be his Casanova-self with her on the phone one night. She'd said that I would need the twin approval, so I decided she would have to win over my brothers. Who was I kidding, though? She was hot, and the few pictures I pulled up for them in her albums, especially the cleavage shots, got a "Nice!"

—yeah, she passed.

Besides, Jack had loved all of my girlfriends, before he even knew they were my girlfriends. (Somehow he didn't get the memo.) He is a charmer; they both are really, but Jack can really lay it on thick. He's more of a schmoozer than Ben. I guess it was about three days in when it was more their similarities than their differences that had Lea and I rolling our eyes at the two of them.

I couldn't help but laugh when Jack asked midweek, in all seriousness, "Are the kids always like this?"

"Yup," I said, chuckling.

I could tell he was concerned. "Were my kids like that?"

"Sometimes," I said, a mild attempt to defend Ben and Lea.

He marinated on that for a few seconds before he sighed. "Well, no family's perfect I guess."

"We'd make great poster children for that campaign," I said, laughing.

"True dat."

∞

I couldn't leave Hawaii before getting a tattoo, or at least that's how I saw it—after the trip I'd had. It wasn't my first tattoo, but inking up my arm was making a much bolder statement than all the others I could conceal rather innocently in a little more than a bikini. In fact, each could be easily forgotten.

Much like the time I got caught stretching in the kitchen at the beach house wearing baggy pajama pants. "Jesus Christ, Kate, what the hell have you done now?" Gma startled me at the entrance to her tirade. I looked down to see what else (besides the belly button ring) she could be freaking out about at the level of where her eyes were fixed.

—*Oh yeah, that.*

"What do you think you are … a slut?" I reminded her that I was over eighteen—it was legal—the shop was legit. Yes, it was clean. No, he wasn't a pervert. She may have even used the words "tramp stamp." I never knew where she came up with these things.

I saw *this* tattoo, thirteen years later—and far more thought-out—as my way of dodging ever having to get a real job again, but Lee burst my bubble when she said that two of her colleagues at the high school had full sleeves. The thought of waking up to an alarm or going to meaningless meetings or sitting in on a parent conference with a delusional mom who had clearly never met her son made me anxious and clammy. It would be impossible, after all *this*, to ignore the physical response I had. I didn't want that life—not now—even though there were so many aspects of teaching I loved.

Standing in front of twenty-five students, sometimes six times a day, was only worth it when I imagined in the car ride home that just one of those one hundred and fifty students had heard a single word I'd said and actually retained something. And I'm not talking about the algebra or geometry here; I'm talking about all the other important anecdotes I fed them between "open your books ..." and "... don't forget your homework." I was one of those teachers I'd loved in high school, whom you could easily get off the subject. Since I thought "life" was a much bigger lesson than the Pythagorean Theorem, I always found opportune moments, "teaching moments," to slip in Hurley-isms that could often lead us on a fifteen-minute tangent—easy. But all the other administrative junk that accumulated more and more got in the way of that glint of passion—each year teaching less and less and testing more and more. I always thought if I stayed in education, I'd create my own damn school where I'd be equally apprehensive and eager to hire teachers just like me.

Ignoring Lee's attempt to get me comfortable with my new tattoo AND a new teaching career, I stepped into the studio ready to do the damn thing. Lee was very practical. She had already obtained a 401(k)—like with stuff in it—and even more absurd, a savings account that she allocated money for each month. I'm sure my flying-by-the-seat-of-my-pants antics made her, at least, mildly concerned. We weren't much of an item yet where her opinion held the weight of a couple who, say, had met face-to-face. Skype wasn't mainstream just yet, and we hadn't even had phone sex. Yet, I had already taken note that her twin, Catherine, was an artist—a cute, frivolous painter—which meant that Lee must appreciate some aspect of the whimsicalness in both of us.

I imagined if we lived in the same state that she would have been here to hold my hand. Instead, I sat for six hot, sweaty hours as I endured the pain—alone. I had designed the concept for the new ink, and the tattoo artist collaborated with me to pull it all together. In the end, I had a bright band of color around my forearm with surf and setting sun, red and yellow plumeria flower (common in leis), a pink orchard (which means grace), a totem pole (Chief Little Owl, that stood in the town of our old beach house), and a dangling rosary for Gma. The tattoo artist had darkened in the white star I had on my opposite wrist for my mom and put a cute little sidekick on the top of my hand beneath my thumb for you know who. Five hundred dollars plus tip later, I left smiling with a swollen, throbbing, bloody arm, gooey with ointment, wrapped in plastic cling wrap.

∞

It's always a good signal that it's time to go when your gracious hosts are walking out the door with you. Ben and Lea had gotten word that their company had big plans for the whole family in Korea the following year. Lea, who's Korean but doesn't speak a lick of it, having been adopted and grown up in Ohio, seemed more thrilled than Ben to have the kids experience the culture that is half their own.

Lea cracked me up; she could easily switch between business and local Hawaiian full of "shoots" and "how's me?" all in the same conversation, clicking between callers. I loved when she got all business on someone. I think it was all the acronyms that got me so turned on, I have to admit, or maybe the flared nostrils—no—probably the strong, stern monologues accompanied by the even more stern hand gestures. (The black-on-black lesbian power suit didn't hurt.) I couldn't understand a syllable between the "computer breach" and the "defense" because everything else sounded like a conservative mom spelling out strings of foreign words. Still it entertained me to no end to watch her pace around the living room with her headset on, talking with her hands, letting people know, left and right, what the fuck was up.

Ben may have been excited about the move for a change of pace, a different backdrop to his motion picture of work and play—heavy on the play—but that's all he gave me. They didn't know when they were leaving, but soon—maybe April—whenever they got the word though they'd pretty much have a month.

Both Lee and Brooke seemed anxious to know when I might be coming home, for clearly separate reasons, but curious all the same. I had started to give hints at the gym that I'd be leaving soon, trying to muster the courage to make my graceful exit.

I'd had an ongoing conversation with Shiva, my yoga instructor, about meditation. Like the kid who insists on sitting up front with her hand fluttering in the teacher's face, I was always eager to share my latest accomplishments: what I was reading, how I was feeling *in the moment*. He pushed me toward the next logical step—a meditation retreat.

"But I don't have any money," I insisted.

"That's fine. You don't need any," he said, flashing that impeccable, sparkly grin. "It's free! On Big Island. It's awesome. I've been there. Maybe I'll go back with you."

And with that went my sole argument. So, that very night, at home, I researched the Vipassana retreat on Big Island. Coincidentally, there was a course scheduled for the following month, and all the *signs* were pointing for me to ante up. (I'd heard about it at least four times, which to me constitutes a *sign*.) I could always cancel. Besides, Shiva had given me the gist, "They serve delicious vegetarian food."

How'd he know he would have me at food?

As I scrolled through the website, I realized that this was way more involved than a cheery guitar accompanied circle of "Kumbaya" with a hearty vegetarian buffet to follow. It seemed Shiva had failed to mention that it was eleven days of complete silence and ten hours a day of sitting meditation, two *minor* components. With this new, clearer, portrait in mind, I was brought back to the small glimpse of Vipassana I'd gotten from one of Oprah's *Soul Series* interviews, where O spoke with Jenny Phillips, and subsequently, two death row inmates who had gone through the course inside their Alabama state prison. Their journey had been documented and later became the film, Phillips produced, *Dhamma Brothers* (which I still haven't seen). And maybe it was that I chose to ignore or had actually forgotten the inmates' words, "It was the hardest thing I've ever done." I mean, for a guy on death row that could be interpreted lots of ways, right?

I was aware my healing out here had all happened outside my element, and I was daunted by the cleanup that topped my *to-do list* back home. I knew deep down that before I could leave, feeling more authentically confident than I'd ever felt before, and maybe just a little big for my britches (they're European sizes), I had to sign up for this course.

Yet, due to its stunning location (I imagine), the course on Big Island was chock full—with a waiting list. It was all good. I swallowed the disappointment well, given that three weeks later, at the time of the reply, the *bigness* for my *britches* had long since deflated.

So, I retreated back to Baltimore as planned. It was March of '09.

∞

I couldn't leave, though, without a farewell pau hana ("happy hour"). My Hatch ohana showered me with an array of beautifully scented, brightly colored leis. All my lunch ladies (those who rarely missed a noon class) presented me with a very thoughtful gift before dumping me, fully clothed, into the swimming pool. My clients each slipped a generously stuffed envelope into my hands when they hugged me off. It is a typical Asian custom to give monetary gifts for good luck to someone who is departing, and I was very grateful for this totally unexpected, typical Asian custom.

My boot camp class all showed up for one last, good, agonizing sweat. Even the two Japanese/American college-aged sisters, who had the bodies of cheerleaders—except not so much *leaders*, just all *cheer*—came. They cracked me up. The first time they dropped in on a class they left after fifteen minutes, the next time they lasted thirty, quiet as two mute mice, no verbal exchanges, just embarrassed smiles as they awkwardly ran in and out of class. The first time, I thought they might have shown up for the wrong class. Had they not read the schedule—boot camp? Sure enough, each successive time they lasted a little bit longer, until finally they became regulars and started in with music requests, groans at the workout posted, all kinds of attitude.

They were at my pau hana along with the rest of the class and some of my other faves. Even the little Korean woman, Grace, my first client—who at sixty-five, with a full head of black hair and flawless skin, barely a crow's foot, had hired me to teach her how to swim—came. She shrieked so loudly in the pool every time I let her go, clawing at my face, until—finally—one magical day she was actually doing it—swimming! She was just as surprised as I was. So surprised, in fact, she simply stopped mid-stroke and began shrieking as her petite and slender frame sank like a cold, iron anchor. By the time I swam over to scoop her up in the four feet of water where she was more than tall enough to *touch*, she was spitting water at me, laughing, asking in her broken English, "You see me?"

It was an amazingly warm farewell, and it was very difficult to leave. But after training the new girl, a fireplug no doubt, a crazy Irish redhead with blue eyes and a face full of freckles and no qualms about texting me a picture of her tits (in case I hadn't heard her when she mentioned she was bi-sexual), I knew they'd be just fine. Plus I was excited to get home and meet Lee, and start over, AGAIN, but this time equipped with a much better arsenal.

I boxed up my new library of books and shipped them off well before packing my bags. I also shipped all my flyers and business cards for Freeterrain, hoping that door hadn't already been sealed shut after the blood and sweat I'd put into it. All in all, I worried less of what the future held, trusting the plan would all play out accordingly, just like it always had.

TWENTY-ONE

OPEN HOUSE

March 3rd, coincidentally the sixth anniversary of Gma's death, I boarded my plane back to Baltimore. With an understanding that everything had happened exactly as it was supposed to, I went home to the middle of my mess with a whole new perspective. I had forgiven both myself and the respective parties. I had stopped pointing fingers and had taken responsibility for my own happiness. *Thank you, Byron Katie.* Sure, some relationships still stunk of vulnerability, some wounds, not quite healed, oozed resentment; yet I had earned the Brownie badge for what to do when it all went down—and I wasn't afraid to use it.

By then, Brooke had decided she didn't like the idea of us living together after all—"it would be too weird." So, the weekend prior to my coming home, she orchestrated a last minute skedaddle. We had exchanged several phone calls and emails about the furniture. "Take it, Brooke, I don't want it." She was willing to pay me for half of what was once divided on the joint card. I saw any offer as a bonus, considering I honestly wanted nothing to do with it. I would later learn that she had shoved all she could muster into a five-by-ten storage unit, which meant it was just Brooke, her wardrobe, and Porter that had moved in with Julie. Either way, when I opened the door to a nearly empty, sad lookin' house, I couldn't help but feel as though I'd been robbed. And by the looks of Lucky Badass, even though she was a witness to the whole shenanigan, she too felt swindled.

I was frustrated Brooke had separated everything before I'd arrived—right down to the T-shirts. I knew there were things unjustly split that probably got "lost in the shuffle," but I guess that was to be expected. I tried to stay put on my Positive Party Train, but it felt like Brooke was throwing rocks on the tracks somehow making the ride anything but smooth.

I'm not sure when it was exactly that I got to say, "Thanks for being such an asshole," with a glowing smile and every bit of sincerity, but the time finally came. And it was as sweet as morning sunshine. Brooke took it like a champ, admitting, yes, she had been an asshole. There was also a shared moment of "thanks for pushing me off the diving board, *ya jerk*." I really needed that.

And, it was true; we had both needed it, and I think we were friends still because of it. Soul mates even (according to one definition from *Eat, Pray, Love*):

"A true soul mate is a mirror, the person who shows you everything that's holding you back, the person who brings you to your own attention so you can change your life. A true soul mate is probably the most important person you'll ever meet, because they tear down your walls and smack you awake. But to live with a soul mate forever? Nah. Too painful. Soul mates, they come into your life just to reveal another layer of yourself to you, and then they leave. And thank god for it." --Richard from Texas

I also can't remember exactly whether it was weeks or just days before Brooke would wake up next to Julie and realize, "What the hell am I doing here?" And like we had installed a revolving door, Brooke arrived with her boxes of clothes, Porter, and her bed (that she and I both had unearthed from the storage space and pitched into the back of my truck).

As she unpacked her things, she stopped mid-carload and asked, in all honesty, "Seriously, what the fuck was I thinking?" And then finally, after all that time spent waiting to hear the words I knew all along, I was fully justified. The conversation took place in the parking lot of our condo, over the roof of her car, with Porter at our waists, back and forth, confused as always. She said, not over emotionally, but rather matter of fact, "You were the best thing that ever happened to me, you know? I was so stupid. I had no clue what I had."

To which, from this vantage point, I could only smile and say, "I know."

∞

I should admit that all the shenanigans were a lot easier to juggle because I had a beautiful woman in New Jersey whom I'd been anxious to meet after three months of, what you might call—cyber courting? I had arrived home on a Tuesday afternoon but wasn't going to meet Lee until Friday evening, in Lambertville, her quaint riverside Jersey town. She had made reservations for us for dinner at Lilly's on the Canal, but we would first meet for drinks at a cozy little fireside wine bar, Left Bank Libations, just a few blocks from her apartment. It was near dark when I arrived, yet the sunset's lingering, squiggly stretches of purples and oranges illuminated the beautiful drive along the Delaware River, which had been enough to perhaps make me reconsider my preconceived notions of Jersey.

I stopped at the Exxon in town to use the restroom and check my hair and makeup before I met her at the bar. It still smelled like winter out, brisk and chilly; nevertheless, I was nervous, uncomfortable, and sweating. I called to tell her I'd arrived, and since she hadn't left her apartment could she grab some quarters for my truck? I didn't know there'd be meters. Plus, that would buy me some time to peruse the wine list and dive face first into a tall glass of pinot noir.

The bar was adorable, a perfect pick; I was impressed already. A few friendly people introduced themselves as I waited for what seemed like eons for Lee to arrive. From what I found out later, she was busy running up and down the stairs taking pictures of herself in the foyer's full length mirror to text Catherine to see if she was appropriately dressed while I was just hanging out, making friends.

This felt like my very first real *first date*, and if you want to get technical, it was as good as blind. You never know, any and all of those photos online could have been doctored. I've heard of crazier. She could have a humpback, bad teeth, a weird gait, eye-watering halitosis—after three months there was still a whole lot at stake here. For all those reasons, I was half-drunk by the time she walked in. I stood up from my bar stool a little wobbly in my heeled boots. We hugged almost desperately and didn't let go, half because we couldn't believe we were finally real, tangible beings, and half because the longer we hugged, the less we'd have to speak—at least that's what I was thinking.

She had straightened her long chestnut hair. While we sat there, it dawned on me that I had hinted once that I liked it that way. Her eyes were, in fact, green and stunning, sparkling in the candlelight, peeking out from behind a touch of mascara, the only makeup she wore, and really the only makeup she'd ever need. Her skin was flawless, her nose and cheeks, dusted with tiny, cute freckles. Her smile revealed beautiful un-Photoshopped teeth, and her fit, petite frame thankfully did not have any surprise appendages.

I Think I'll Make It

I ordered Lee a glass of wine rather hastily, hoping the sooner she caught up to my faint slur the better. I could tell she was nervous; she refused to make eye contact and was talking into her lap with a sort of gangster New York accent I was sure she typically reserved for the basketball court. I lifted her chin and looked her in the eyes, just to—one more time—make sure she was real. But before I could say anything, she blurted out, "Don't kiss me yet. I'm not ready." I laughed, assuring her that wasn't my style. She hadn't even gotten her wine. What kind of suitor did she take me for? Besides, I was happy just sitting there and talking with a real person, rather than typing my innermost thoughts in one of our lengthy messages. I think she was about three or four gulps into her glass when she interrupted me, spilling out, "Okay, now you can kiss me."

When we left the bar for dinner, I bid my new friends farewell, fairly confident—from the looks of this tiny town and the way things were going with Lee—I'd see them again. Lee grabbed my hand, leading me, smiling out the door. Then she tucked herself right under my arm while we walked the short distance to Lilly's. There we had a beautiful candlelit dinner, and Lee insisted on interrupting more conversation with kisses than I felt comfortable with. I politely mentioned that I wasn't a big fan of PDA, but with three months' worth of catching up to act on, she acknowledged what I'd said, and then politely ignored it. I was embarrassed when we paid the bill and our waitress sent us off with, "I'm so happy you two feel so open."

I thought that may have been a nice way of saying, "You're lucky I'm bi-curious because I may have barfed on anyone else making out like that." Needless to say, Lee broke all rules of what she said she would absolutely *not* do on the first night. And things went so well that I stayed the whole weekend.

I fell in love with Lambertville, the budding spring all along the tow path, the ducks and geese flirting—all puffed up—in their showy scene. The big rock Wing Dam was the perfect place for our first picnic lunch while the river went roaring by. I also enjoyed the community of artists, the eccentrics, and foodies, and athletes intermingling, and the little antique shops and boutiques. And just across the river was New Hope, a Pennsylvania town bursting with rainbows and biker bars garnishing a strip permanently set up for a Gay Pride Parade.

New Hope had just as much charm, and definitely as much character, with its leather clad bikers and big husky Harleys barking down the same lane as pink, blinged-out Vespas and handsome boys in high heels. When Lee led me, in hand, down New Hope's main drag to Farley's bookstore, I knew things with us looked really promising. We spent almost an hour in there, our lattés getting cold, picking up books and turning to our favorite pages.

After stacks of several others, Lee picked up a book of poetry from Rumi, opened it and read aloud one of his exquisite poems. Looking up from the page, she suggested, "How about you, me, Rumi, a bottle of wine, some cheese and fruit—our next picnic lunch?"

And that's how I came to own a copy of the enchanting lil' *Pocket Rumi*.

∞

I sent her off to work Monday morning. Then I scooted out of town and headed back down I-95 elated. I sang with the wind in my face, coasting above the speed limit, for no other reason than to keep up with my heartbeat—skipping through the meadows. We had talked through all my apprehensions of starting anything resembling a relationship while I was in the midst of all sorts of life-changing madness. As of that moment, I had no job. I barely had two pennies to rub together. There was a possibility I was going to foreclose on my house, and my ex-girlfriend, whom I still couldn't help but feel a little emotional around, may or may not be living in my house.

Lee was very patient. When I told her I would absolutely *not* meet her parents until I had secured a better job other than what I imagined would be bartender, she laughed it off. "In my family if you *have* a job, that's all that matters. No one will judge you. Two of my brothers and Catherine, for that matter, have no clue yet what the future holds. None of us do, really." That did make me feel better; three out of seven *is* almost fifty percent. But Lee's oldest sibling was only a year or two older than me. I had six years on the baby of the family, which I know, in the grand scheme is nothing, but I had sort of hoped to be more put together by this stage in the game.

Like I used to, she earned her claim of old soul, and suddenly I took on young at heart. She didn't even get some of the references I made. "Oh yeah, you weren't born yet," became the running joke. Yet, I was the stubborn one on just about everything. It was evident I was still deeply scarred, and even though her friends teased me for being an old, prowling cougar, Lee was often the one driving some sense into me.

When she didn't call me during the day, I'd get all worked up, or when we'd speak at night for only a few minutes before she went off to grade papers, I'd get pissy. I was used to women dragging me around in their fist like their woobie (blankie). I had grown accustomed to being doted over and kept on a short chain. And even with all my enlightenment, a part of me wasn't used to doing all *this* without all *that*. Many of our first skirmishes were of me, or should I say my ego, battling for attention. "I just don't understand why you don't call me or even text me during the day."

"I'm teaching," she pleaded.

"Planning period—lunch?" I snapped.

"I'm planning or eating."

"Fine—what about when I talk to you at night and all we talk about is the mundane and then you have to go."

"I dunno'; I'm tired, and I have so much work to do. I'm reading books and planning lessons. It's hard for me to exhaust any more energy than I already have to."

"Fine," I said, sulking.

"Fine, what?"

"I have to go."

And here I thought I was past all this. I knew I was being childish. I knew everything I was saying as it spewed from my lips was ridiculous, but I had only ever known one kind of love, eros. I had never known grown-up love, mature love, love that could wait till the weekend when we'd be able to see each other again and give each other our undivided attention.

Instead, I had doubts and built walls and even talked to Brooke about my reservations as she shared with me her drama with Julie and the prospects of her new crush. With all guards down, she and I established some sort of friendship. As odd as it seemed, it was kind of nice. In one email to Brooke, I said, "I have never adored and hated someone so close to me ever ... it's kinda special, really."

∞

Brooke and I had exhausted every option for what to do with the house. We sought help from the government as Obama was passing bills left and right for homeowners in his housing plan. As it turns out, though, we weren't eligible for any of those programs because we had continued to pay our mortgage. Even though we were going broke doing so; some months I might as well have been putting the mortgage on a credit card. And all we got was, "Sorry, ma'am, we can't help you." Through the advice of a good lawyer and a stiff suggestion from a real estate agent, we did what many Americans had already done. We stopped paying.

We put the house on the market and crossed our fingers that it would sell quickly under the terms of a short sale. We had no equity; we just wanted out. The house had been appraised at $40,000 less than what we had bought it for just shy of three years earlier, which I guess was about the going rate of what many people lost, less even, but it was still hard not to fall into that comfy place of self-pity with the rest of the depressed lot of the country. Our first open house was in April, no more than a month after I had returned home.

TWENTY-TWO

FOR THE LOVE

Because the plan is bigger than you are and because life likes to keep you on your toes, dancing, I walked into the restaurant where I used to work after almost two years of self-discovery to ask for my job back, feeling like it was just par for the course. The Metropolitan, though, was a great place for someone like me, who had just dropped a little weight from a shrinking ego, to ease back into the world of food and beverage hospitality. Not only did everyone receive me with open arms and a warm welcome, I was pleased to see that most of the faces of the quirky employees and customers were comfortably the same. And the new eccentric additions had already eased themselves into their rightful bitchy habits and routines; hence, it wasn't long before I felt like I had never left.

After Hawaii, my Buddha-esque three times a day had fizzled to more like three minutes a day. Perhaps it was the sirens and smoke stacks of Baltimore that left me a little less inspired. And there were other fumbling excuses; it was like I was gaining all the weight back I'd lost, a yo-yo diet of sorts—for seekers.

Yet, in retrospect, there's really no better place to practice patience than in a restaurant. Believe you me, if you ever want your prejudices and your biases highlighted, because you think you may have graduated from prejudice and bias; go get a job waiting tables. Oh, how difficult it is to be Zen when people are rearranging the dining room, seating themselves and barking orders because apparently their momma never taught them manners. Your innermost thoughts are battled back, beating against that Zen umbrella, which has its flimsy tendency to flip inside out in the high wind of absurdity. I mindfully pep-talked my way through each shift, finding patience in places I never knew existed. And much to my bewilderment, I discovered teachers in the unlikeliest of people and circumstances every day. I learned that *me* (the good guy) getting all worked up for nothing was just my own dense ego responding to theirs (the bad guy(s)).

Thankfully, the Metropolitan is as close to Baltimore's Federal Hill will ever get to a *Cheers*, and our neighborhood regulars made coming to work feel as though I was walking into an old friend's living room. If it wasn't for them, I think I may have turned a table up on the laps of some of my loathsome favorites, only after offering them a hot coffee and one of our heaping desserts, of course.

∞

I still had my gratitude journal, and sometimes, I would have to play catch up (five times however many days I missed). I think thirty grateful things at one time was the lengthiest stretch. I was grateful for the little things—things I was continually aware of, even at home where my Zen was constantly compromised. But I was also grateful for the big stuff, like say, my finest moments in unanswered prayers: for not being squished, in eighth grade that one time, in despair, I lay in the middle of the road; for being ignored all those times I wished "I could just die," or for not letting other people fall ill each time I wished they would just go away!; for not letting all those "forevers" I asked for, actually be forever; for my *Real World* tape not being accepted (at nineteen, God that would have been awful). I never tire thinking of all the blessings that have been bestowed upon me.

When I did make time to meditate, I couldn't help but judge it inferior—rarely feeling like it had before. Thoughts about the house, a job, where I would live, what I was going to do financially took turns flicking the inner walls of my head and the backs of my defenseless little eyeballs. I didn't feel the same energy in my hands and warmth on my skin; any connection at all seemed faint and distant. I blamed it on the lack of nature in my condo's planned community, the rest-assured lengthy debates the developers spent on the planting of each tree. It was nice and all, but nothing about it said *nature*.

One time stands out, though—not quite meditation triumph, yet good energy must have been somewhere in the vicinity. I sat out back on our patio in one of the wicker chairs I had dragged to the edge, scooting it into a sliver of sunshine. I sat up tall with my feet flat on the concrete slab, trying to ignore the hacking start of the air conditioner just feet away. It wasn't my favorite place to meditate. I was often interrupted by our crazy neighbor walking her dogs, hollering, "Why don't you just come to the pool with me if you're trying to get some sun?"—a disturbing invitation from a walking cancer campaign ad. With loose, wrinkled, leathery skin hanging from her gaunt frame and a long cigarette with drooping ashes dangling from her lips, she'd laugh herself into a coughing fit every time she spoke. And even with the lack of wind, her conversations always rattled on at length.

So, I sat out back, hoping she wouldn't show up, falling into a trance with the slight rustling of the trees. Then, all of a sudden, I felt a flutter in front of my face. I opened my eyes and was startled by a very real, tiny hummingbird staring back at me, nose to beak. I flinched at first, justly nervous. (I'm not particularly fond of birds quite so near pecking-out-my-corneas range.) Yet, I worried any small movement would frighten her off. I stiffened like a corpse. What if she was trying to tell me something? She hung out with me for only three good blinks or so, my eyes as wide as watermelons in between—they were quick blinks though, considering my brain could hardly make sense of the tiny little creature with two blurs for wings—yet she hung out long enough for me to recognize her.

Well I'll be damned, Synchronicity had followed me home.

∞

I spent my days reading, writing, and working out, and I spent my evenings hustling for whatever shifts were available at the Metropolitan. I left my weekends free to bounce up to New Jersey, or for Lee to come down to Baltimore to drag me through the Inner Harbor, one more time.

Thankfully, Lee was patient and practiced her own mindfulness, because I'm not sure how she put up with me in those first few months. While sitting across from her at dinner, or facing each other standing on the Bridge Street Bridge, or looking into each other's eyes while we lay sprawled out on the bed, I would try to chase her away with all the uncertainties that utterly engulfed me. I didn't know where I wanted to live, what I wanted to do, how I wanted to do it. Hawaii had taught me anything was possible if I was brave enough to create it. Even Freeterrain, which had gone mostly untouched since I'd gotten home, was evidence that "if you can dream it, you can do it." That whole platform had been manifested from one tiny spark of imagination. Even if the follow-through somehow still needed a little work, it was enough proof it was possible—and that's all that mattered.

I wanted to be back out in nature where I felt so alive. British Columbia, California, Colorado, somewhere where I could feel the buzz of life in its own habitat again, find my rhythm. Sure, Lambertville had the river and the endless trails which helped, but I didn't live in Lambertville, and every Monday morning when I left, the pit in my stomach reminded me as much. (Yet, showing up with a U-Haul was not an option. Nope, not this time. I swore I wouldn't make that mistake again.) Besides, the Metropolitan was great for the time being, even if I wasn't officially back on the schedule yet.

I had very little money, and all I earned I tossed out the window each month to my good friends at Visa, MasterCard, and American Express. What had originally been manageable at three percent now skyrocketed to twenty-plus percent once word got out that we had stopped paying our mortgage. This ship was beginning to sink in a cataclysmal, *Titanic*-like fashion, and while I was busy grasping and clinging to whatever I could hold onto, I made every effort to save Lee from the horror of watching the whole thing plunge into the abyss—a hopeless popsicle.

∞

I enjoyed Lee; I really did. And what was growing between us, I couldn't stop even if I wanted to. I know; I tried. I wasn't intentionally being an asshole. I was just offering a voice of reason because—someone had to. It was really no time to begin a relationship, no matter which way you sliced it. She argued otherwise, perhaps since here we were, indeed, beginning a relationship.

Even after a couple of years of soul-searching, to have my honest self reflected back in a brand new set of eyes was painfully difficult. I saw vividly what I knew she couldn't help but *not*, and it killed me. So I pushed every little button Lee revealed as tender, and just so she couldn't say I didn't warn her, I'd constantly hang my flaws out on the line to flap loudly in the breeze.

"I'm OCD. I'm not a big fan of cat hair everywhere. I very rarely believe that I'm wrong. I'm a stubborn perfectionist. I like things done a certain way. I don't do bugs or rodents or trash. I've been guilty of frivolous spending and acting impulsively, and I can't say that I won't do it again. I'm a hopeless dreamer. If you shook my savings account it would rattle a little and then echo back the three coins tumbling around inside, and I don't envision a dramatic maturation in the foreseeable future. I have a four-year rule before I will even entertain the idea of marriage, and since marriage requires a savings account, those years might as well be measured in decades. I've always dreamed of being a mom and having three kids. Oh, and by the way, yesterday I decided to go vegan."

My rants were all punctuated, of course, with that "so, there you have it—if none of this happens to work for you, the sooner you let me know the better" attitude, which I'm sure never went unnoticed.

She wasn't perfect either, but she was patient. She was kind and knew when I was airing out the dirty laundry to just let me do it. Maybe it was in those first three months of emails that she saw enough potential in me that she would just wait out the storm. Don't get me wrong though, she was no pushover. When I pressed the right buttons enough, she came after me. When I told her I was moving to Colorado if I could find a job, she fumed at my nonchalant excuses favoring a long-distance relationship. She stood up for herself, and each time she did, I fell harder for her—and her grit.

"We're *already* in a long-distance relationship. What's a few more states?" I said, egging her on.

"A few more states is a plane ride instead of a road trip. There's a big, *expensive* difference between Baltimore and Boulder. The difference is seeing each other every weekend or once a month, at best. I just wish you would have thought of all this *before* you began this relationship. You're not going. And, it's final. So stop talking about it; you're really starting to piss me off!"

When I'd giggle at her adorable arguments, she'd get even more irritated. I couldn't help it; I loved it when she got all *Miss Haggarty* on me—assertive and teacher-like. Don't get me wrong, I was still going to Colorado if it worked out. I mean, there were still *signs* to be considered and all, but not even one measly hint thus far. So I dropped it for the time being; no need to get her all worked up just yet for nothing—even if it was ridiculously cute.

I guess in the back of my head I was fine keeping things über casual until I figured stuff out. I knew she and I had a great connection, and I trusted that it would either work out or it wouldn't. I had learned that trying to control anything, especially the reciprocated love of another human being, was both foolish and futile, so I went back to the old adage, "If you love her, let her go." Plus, she was still in those awful mid-twenties where life, at any moment, could flip her on her back and have her pinned, leaving her helpless to do anything but change and then slip out the back, hoping to go unnoticed. I didn't trust it. I'd seen it too many times before.

∞

She did, however, come with her own conspicuous set of *signs* I suppose it was impossible to ignore. Neither of us will ever be able to make sense of how it all came to be. New Jersey—Hawaii? I know MySpace is magical, but really? How she says she almost didn't send that email, because she thought I was out of her league. She would often look at me, in bewilderment, and say, "Where did you come from?"

And I'd always answer with the same, "You manifested me."

Despite our initial failings, we were exactly what the other was looking for. Honesty stunk up the place like pungent incense, and Trust whirled around gracefully, free, in her own simple dance. We built our foundation around the basics, and as it turns out, that's all we really needed. No drama, no magnificent fights lusting for long passionate makeups, no intense resistance to the key phrase "I'm sorry," no games.

I did enjoy the short road trip between us though. It was my first long-distance relationship, one that I knew at any point earlier I would have been too immature to handle, but here and now, it was a welcome holiday. We had our independence all week and each weekend felt like a well-deserved vacation. Maybe that's why things worked out so nicely. Come Friday, we were so excited to see each other, it may have been just enough time for her to forget all the warnings I'd woven through the passage of the previous weekend. When I quieted my inhibitions, things fell into place naturally and rather effortlessly. It was keeping them at bay that became its own balancing act.

The thing I loved most about Lee was her independence. How she lived alone, in a town where she knew very few people, getting along just fine. I loved that she had established a routine all on her own without the help of familiar faces orbiting around her— something I had never done. Sure, she was younger, yet she taught me so much about autonomy in the real world. After all, I had done most of my growing up in never-never land where responsibility had limits and consequences died quickly, forgotten at sea.

TWENTY-THREE

SOUL FOOD

T he River Poets Writer's Workshop was the first writing group I ever belonged to. After having been lavished with generous compliments at the Full Moon Café poetry reading, sponsored by the River Poets, I had been invited to join the group of at least twenty longtime writers. We'd meet every first Saturday at the Lambertville Library and read our poetry for the discussion and critique of the group. I loved it. I could tell they didn't quite know what genre to put some of my writing in, spoken word was not necessarily a part of their collective lexicon, but they welcomed me just the same with warm smiles and kind critiques. It meant the world to me to be considered a writer among writers.

It was those meetings and my lack of enthusiasm for Baltimore that most often led me to living out of a laundry basket (my preferred luggage), driving back and forth to Jersey. On those journeys, Pema Chodron, Wayne Dyer, Louise Hay or Deepak Chopra sat right alongside me, talking me through my newest set of suffocating stresses and reminding me of the wonderful landscape laid out ahead. Even Eckhart Tolle made an encore appearance. And each time I listened, I would pocket something new, find another gem to squirrel away to get me through the latest season of tur-moil.

As I had learned before, making up stories about *tomorrow* when I hadn't yet dealt with *today* was not only a waste of time, but to put it plainly, stupid. So, I did just what I'd learned to do before. I put one foot in front of the other and kept on truckin'— one day at a time. And it was in that stride that Lee and I comfort-ably fell in together, which not only made things with us possible, in many ways, made it easy.

∞

I went back to work at Federal Hill Fitness where they welcomed me with even more enthusiasm after all the experience I'd gained. I told the owner of the gym, my good friend, Andrea, that I could now teach almost everything except yoga and Pilates. It wasn't that I couldn't teach those classes, it was maybe more that I shouldn't; so I made sure to specify, anything else, but *not* those two.

I don't know if I wasn't clear enough. Maybe I didn't enunci-ate. (Gma did always say that I mumbled, never mind that she was deaf as a doorpost.) Or perhaps Andrea had heard exactly what she wanted to hear. (I've also been accused of that a time or two.) All I know is that in the *welcome our new personal trainer* email sent to the entire staff two weeks later, Andrea not only highlighted my strengths in both yoga and Pilates, she referred to them as my *fo-cus*. And before I knew it, I was back on the schedule teaching, of all things, Yogalates.

Perhaps it's because I have a habit of accepting whatever the universe offers me or maybe it's the slight crush I've always had on Andrea—this would not be the first (or the last) time she sold me, and I willingly bought, a single, used shoe—or it could have been because I *was* willing to be flexible, and literally so that I learned to teach both yoga and Pilates in a matter of days from the revered experts at P90X and YouTube.

I had steady shifts at the restaurant and picked up more and more whenever I could. It was about that time, too, that I began to work on my new website. I needed a business page to forward to schools so I could start presenting my talks. Brooke asked, "Don't you think you should write your book *before* you start speaking at schools?" That was one way to look at it, but I couldn't wrap my brain around writing an entire manuscript while only chunks of time were being offered in smaller and smaller increments; hence why poetry became my surefire creative outlet.

∞

I gained more and more confidence on the microphone with each performance. Every time I stood onstage in the sooty shadows with that naked spotlight on my face, I felt more certain and further invigorated in my pursuits. I just needed to put it all together when I could finally get a minute, I'd grumbled to Lee. My poems all justly started taking on the same theme: "Make something of yourself." Originally it was for the sake of motivating youngsters, yet every time I recited the lines, I couldn't help but invest in the prayer myself, hoping the heavens would heed each syllable I spit.

I began networking with new writers and was invited to speak as a *featured* poet on a few surprising occasions. I kept thinking, "About when should I tell them I'm not actually a poet?" No one seemed to notice I was just playing the part. All they cared about, I assume, was my passion evident in my message, and I was thrilled to oblige.

I was often the only white girl on the mike, sometimes the only white person in the building, but nobody appeared bothered, and *I* certainly didn't care. In Hawaii, the poetry slams were diverse and colorful; in Baltimore, if there *was* a dress code, I didn't get the memo. I just kept showing up.

Be Free Fridays was one of my favorite nights in Baltimore, at the Eubie Blake Jazz Center on Howard. Love the Poet had three simple rules: "Respect the mike, respect the mike, respect the mike." The room was always filled with warmth and respect for creativity, for passion, for God *and* his people. Even after nights of almost five hours of waning poetry, I still left buzzing, hungry to scribble something down.

I loved the audience participation at Be Free. When people heard something they liked, they made noise. When they felt what the poet said, they made more noise yet. When the poet blew their mind, leaving them nothing to do but retire, they threw pens at his feet, sometimes papers, sometimes a cell phone would skirt across the floor, whatever they could get their hands on to let him know they were finished … through … done. People got to their feet, stomping around sometimes, cheering and hollering. Poets would have to repeat their last few lines because no one could hear over the outbursts. It was a family, one in which I never doubted that I belonged.

∞

For one performance I did at Rutgers University, on the brochure our witty host, who'd initially invited me, had written "she ain't white" next to my name before making the hundred or so copies for the event. I had to ask a friend backstage if it was for real, leaning over her lap to compare my brochure to hers. When she looked at her sheet and fell out laughing, I kind of figured. His introduction of me, though I can't remember his exact words, was also priceless. I think he cracked himself—and the audience—up with something like, "This white bread ain't no small wonder," as he invited me onto the stage.

I always did love my gospel, and boy did those nights get to feelin' like the Holy Spirit was *up in here*. Some of the poets would weave perfectly into their pieces their gratitude to God for all their blessings, their courage, their strength. I certainly was no stranger to that. They would thank God for granting them peace and joy and love. I joined right on in with the communal "amen." Each performance, whether it was the energy, lyrics, music, or passion, something would resonate, a spark would ignite. I began to realize that I was meant to be sitting in that audience just as much as I was meant to be onstage—finding God now through witnesses was profoundly moving. I'd walk out of each event feeling lifted, perhaps even carried out in His hands.

That night, at Rutgers, they loved my church piece and the others. I fit right in—with God and everybody—not a difference among us could have squeezed in between the mercy and the joy. The standing ovation felt heart-thumping incredible. I bowed to a sea of wide smiles. If only every moment could hold this much love. Lee and I made up two-thirds of the white people present in the theater that night. We hadn't noticed until we stood in line discussing the faint possibility of finding something vegan hidden in the deep soul food buffet.

I drooled over Lee's plate, up until she licked her spoon after polishing off her pile of macaroni and cheese. Instead, I ate a few sprigs of raw broccoli, carrots, and cauliflower, and a smushed energy bar I had shoved in my bag for emergencies. I was fine though, really. No room for complaints, my soul was stuffed on gobs of grace and goodness.

TWENTY-FOUR

DEM BRITCHES

This whole Vipassana thing wasn't really my idea, again. Submerging myself into a silent, ten-day think tank, now, after all this *real life* seemed way more absurd than before. I blamed Oprah. Because Shiva wasn't around, and really if it wasn't for me listening to that *Dhamma Brothers Soul Series* interview again, I wouldn't have felt as though I'd been dared.

Looking back though, I suppose I could have remained deferentially in the dark—the smelly, damp, dungeonous dark. *It does have its quirky comforts.* But something told me I'd learned too much, I'd experienced too much already to turn back now. I knew one thing: if ignorance is bliss and enlightenment is bliss, it's all that questioning in between that seems to be the issue.

It was in the midst of the house going on the market, creditors calling, and threats coming in the mail that I researched local Vipassana chapters. I figured my departure would no more further complicate the situation nor lessen my entanglement, so my excuses, one by one, fell from beneath me. Plus there was something like a Nike ad playing in my head, for months, nagging me, "Just Do It."

Turns out I had missed the deadline for the Maryland retreat by days. Afraid I might lose this breeze of audacity—again—I applied for the *soonest* and *closest*, Virginia, for its upcoming retreat. And with the click of "Submit," I succumbed to a slight nervous panic. The faint possibility I'd signed my life away to a cult lingered in the stiff silence as I stared at the yellow, suddenly creepy smiley face that floated under the "Thank you for your application" on the screen.

∞

In the weeks that passed from my acceptance email to *go-time*, I joked about my trip to "Jesus Camp" and prepared for my dip out of society. In all seriousness, Vipassana has absolutely nothing to do with Jesus, yet sarcasm is my coping mechanism of choice in all matters like this—striking multiple chords of anxiety. I got shifts covered at the restaurant; I picked up shifts to make up for the impending deficit of funds. I paid bills, assigned Brooke to cat duty, and purposely avoided any literature or media on Vipassana altogether. I'm hardly one of those people who map out their itinerary or study the guidebook before they travel. I much prefer rolling with the punches—even if that periodically means getting punched.

I said my goodbyes to a small few and set up away messages on my computer networks. My Facebook status (I'd since graduated from MySpace) alluded to a camping trip, boasting about the mountains and "no access to a computer or cell phone for two weeks," offering the appearance of *confidently unattached*—so not the reality. And only Lee had an emergency number and address if, in dire circumstances, I needed to be contacted—or, in case I happened to show up missing after a couple weeks—just saying.

Brooke was no help. Her banter was playful and funny, but when I got tripped up answering the series of questions she fired at me, ones that I hadn't thought to ask myself, her sarcasm started to peel my fingers—one by one—from the fun-loving, free-spirit monkey bars from which I'd been contentedly swinging. She was convinced it was a cult and that I'd be sure to come home with, at best, a shaved head, "and God knows what else!"

That was according to her—*if* I came home.

I told two of my aunts and my brother, Jack, that I was leaving for a yoga retreat. I'm already a lesbian, so I was nervous a meditation retreat might totally put them over the edge. I should say in their defense, for Roman Catholic and Republican, they have always been incredibly supportive of me. I'm sure it's my issue that I insist on protecting them, mostly because I know they still worry if I'll ever turn out normal.

I packed and unpacked my bag three or four times in an effort to appear less high maintenance. (I had flashbacks of my last camping trip—those stupid yurts—how cold and traumatizing Camp Timberline was.) With a dress code that suggested simple, modest, and comfortable, and emphasized a minimal distraction to others, I went for the blacked-out workout attire that made up a decent portion of my wardrobe. I counted out the days on my hands, how many outfits I'd need, and sifted my bag of excess items. I never do this, by the way.

Sometimes when you Mapquest the directions minutes before you drive off, you fail. This just so happened to be one of those special *sometimes*. The assumed two-hour drive was really more like four and a half. In a panic that I wouldn't make it before registration ended, I emailed the center to warn them of my late departure. There was a short sub-conscious debate regarding the creation of a more colorful story—a flat tire, saving a roadside turtle, feeding the hungry—rather than admit my own stupidity. Yet honesty seemed like, you know, the *healthy alternative* for Day One at Jesus Camp.

KAT HURLEY

In the car—about an hour in—I realized, in the most mindful and compassionate way I was capable, another reason why I'm a hopeless idiot. Since I'd packed at the last minute, it seemed I forgot more than a few very important items from that neatly penned un-checked checklist. I assessed that I had only one sheet and a pillow, and no covers, no sleeping bag, no top sheet, no towel. I figured I'd stop when I passed a store. Unfortunately, my selection in the boondocks was limited to either Walmart or Sheetz—a super-sized, mega-mart gas station that carries everything under the sun, except sheets—one item I could have really used at that point.

Without proper signage in the boonies, I got lost. *So much for Walmart.* Now with further urgency, the needle on the dash bounced toward 80 mph. I drove aggressively, passing people on the right and the left, not slowing down even to appease my conscience, which was steadily aware of my ridiculous road rage—in route to Jesus Camp—and laughing at me. I struggled to join the fun and get over my self-inflicted hour-long detour, when startlingly, the skies opened up, and rain that would piss off a dinosaur began pounding against my windshield. *Is that hail? Great! This is awesome. Camping in the pouring rain—perfect.*

Then as quickly as it started, it stopped—*clearly, the Universe needs a hobby.* With scattering clouds and the sun, obviously in on the hoax, gleaming through proudly, I still felt really sorry for myself, for no other reason now than *just 'cause.* At that moment, from behind the parting pines, the most magnificent rainbow dashed in and painted itself across my rearview mirror. A rainbow like those I hadn't seen since Hawaii: big, bold, beautiful, confident, majestic—my poetic opposition at this point. I smiled at the realization; it was looking like I wasn't late after all—fashionably right on time for all to play out accordingly. *I get it, already.* Wayne Dyer played in my head like a broken record, "There is no such thing as coincidences."

I arrived at my destination in both relief and disbelief I had made it this far. I called Lee for one last quick goodbye, feeling chirpy and brave, and foolish and reluctant all in the same. "All right, I'm here. Yes, I finally found it. I'll call you in eleven days, okay, sweetie? Wish me luck!"

"You're gonna do great. I'm already so proud of you. Call me as soon as you can. I adore you."

She so could tell.

With two tightly gripped hands on the wheel, I crept my way up the long drive. As it was, single-family ranchers, fallen wooden fences, and large, open, unkempt lots made up the community that surrounded the Virginia Jaycee Camp. The crunching gravel beneath my tires seemed so poignant for this road less traveled. With a deep, apprehensive sigh, and a long press of the *power* on my cell phone, I cut myself off from the free world. Chest tight, I was alone in a way I had never known.

I pulled into the unpaved lot at the end of the long, doubt-ridden drive. There was an enormous pig near the edge of the fence, grunting for attention from the women standing by. I smiled, thrilled I'd have a friend—*Wilbur*, of course. With no bellman greeting me at my car door to welcome me, take my bags and guide me faithfully—*Right this way, ma'am. Lovely day isn't it?*— and not even a camp counselor to coddle me along, I left all my belongings in the car. Just in case.

I took a stab at the small, white cinder-block building, thinking it might be the place to start. I could have tripped over the tiny *registration* sign as I neared the screen door. There were men and women loafing around outside, some talking, some already off in contemplation. A little disorganized if you ask me, but I got the idea I should leave all judgment at the door. At the registration table, clearly marked *registration*, I apologized as I explained I'd gotten lost. "You're not late," the woman seated before me said with a warm smile.

Yup—it's a cult.

She handed me a packet of papers, including a couple to fill out. I recognized the Code of Conduct from the online application (must be reiterated for good reason); I diligently reread and signed on the dotted line. I pondered over the section where it asked about mental health, past and present, and family history. *Do they really want to know ALL my business?* Was I on medication? *No.* Was I seeing a therapist? No. But I was definitely here for a reason. *Weren't we all?*

In the Family History/Traumatic Events section, it seemed unnecessary to write that my father had killed my mother when I was five—like gratuitous information for such an occasion, yet I saw no need to lie if they were asking. I wrote it out—funny—it seemed like someone else's story on paper. I added that I no longer had communication with my father—the short version. I described present family life with my brothers, aunts, uncles, and cousins as healthy, and painted a rosy picture of how things had all turned out. My life looked paradoxically simple, yet woefully uncomfortable cramped into a four by four square.

God knows if they even read these things.

I returned my paperwork and was given a dorm number. Mary, as it stated on her name tag, instructed me to find my dorm, pick out a bunk and claim it with my belongings. I saw people handing in valuables in the plastic bags being provided. I skipped that line, aware any discreet escape would be foiled otherwise.

Back in the truck, I crawled my way up the gravel to the Beaver Den marked *3*, all eyes peeled for any excuse to peace the fuck out. I had never attended sleep-away camp, so now at thirty-one, this dusty, spider web-ridden, musky cabin reminded me of that old TV show *M*A*S*H* (a reference my girlfriend will likely not get), and my OCD already tweaked. Thankfully, the cabin was empty—I needed a moment to take it all in.

It was a long and narrow space, six bunks to a side; the one-ply plastic mattresses had more stains on them than I cared to investigate. With army precision, I laid out my one sheet, ensuring it covered each corner of the mattress—the one I determined the lesser of the unclaimed evils. I folded the thin barrier in half. *I'll just taco myself inside at night.* I placed my bag out at the foot of the bed, opened it up and shuffled things around a little—*there, settled.*

∞

Turns out Wilbur had roommates. Two horses stood along the fence when I returned from the parking lot behind the mess hall. I was pleased with the personality they gave the place. Since I'd arrived, I had been trying to ignore the sad-looking, murky, half-empty swimming pool and the disheveled chain-link fence and the rusted playground equipment. A true portrait of tranquility, really.

I bet the Hawaii course has nothing on this place.

A black woman's Southern drawl and big belly laugh echoing off the mountain called my attention away from my smelly, fickle new friends. I'd been so impressed with the diversity of people I'd seen thus far. I have to admit I was a little nervous I'd be silently bonding with a bunch of Hare Krishnas for the duration. Not that I have an issue with Hare Krishnas. In fact, I know not one thing about Hare Krishnas except for maybe what I'd witnessed that night on top of Mount Makakilo. My guess, though, is that they'd inherently find an eleven-day silent retreat a walk in the park—and that would just *really* irritate the ohm out of me.

"Is this your first time?" she asked (time being *tahm* where she's from), giving me a signal to join her and the other women at the table. I couldn't help but wonder how inmates might first greet each other. Two of the three women at the table were new; the Southern black woman was from North Carolina, and there was a Caucasian woman with a Czech-sounding accent. The other of the three, an Indian woman, lived near me, in Baltimore; she had attended the Maryland course last year. And why someone thought asking her to compare the two seemed like a good idea, don't ask me. "A lot nicer than this—bigger, cleaner," she said.

Happy now?

Brooding—on the inside at least—I only partially participated in the chit-chat about what we might expect and what we'd previously heard. My mantra, *I'm exactly where I am supposed to be*, was already quavering. They grilled the Indian woman for more clues, and I forgot I was sort of upset when we shared our skepticism about making it through.

The dinner bell rang.

Hooray! My anxiety can almost always be diminished with food. They had the mess hall set up like the land of Oz, with giant curtains clothes-pinned together, dangling from the ceiling to separate the kitchen from the dining room. I was excited to see what might emerge from behind the phantom curtains. I'd heard utensils clanking against pots and pans when I'd arrived and smelled something worldly and exotic seeping in from behind the white wall of fabric.

I sat by my friend at dinner, whose name I still didn't know— the Southern black woman I just couldn't get enough of. She, like me, was worried about the "not being able to eat after midday" rule. She, a little heavier set, and I, just a big eater, were eyeing the room for snacks we might be able to confiscate. "Well, at least there're some raisins and seeds over there. I'm thinkin' I can make a meal outta' that," she said in her endearing Southern twang.

It wasn't until dinner that we realized we were all in the same cabin: me, my Southern friend, and the Czech lady. That comforted me. Not like we could talk to each other or anything, but it lowered the percentage of possible weirdoes to bunk with considerably.

After dinner, a volunteer stepped forward to welcome us. It was a stretch to hear her stuttered, vague overview. Thankfully she smiled a lot between the "ums," and she wore an apron (definitely someone to thank for our delicious first meal), so even though I could barely understand a word, I liked her anyway. My nerves settled a bit, looking around, digesting the masses that appeared "normal"—women outnumbering the men: forty to fifteen. There was a peaceful air in the room, a *familiar* positive energy. It was evident; we were all here to become better people.

The volunteer pulled out an old boom box and placed it on the table. She slid a matte white tape in, mispressed at least four buttons, twirled the giant knob for a dramatic volume adjustment, and a crackly deep voice was finally audible, reverberating through the speakers. The voice offered a terrifically succinct summary, laying out a basic itinerary, for which I was very grateful. We recited the five precepts that I'd already signed off on twice now. We all agreed to abstain from killing—seemed a far place to travel if I had murder on the mind, but I'll buy it. No stealing, no sex, no telling lies, and abstain from all intoxicants—fair enough. The "old students," as they call them (those brave enough to return), recited three more: no eating after midday, no sensual entertainment or body decoration, no high or luxurious beds.

From what I'd witnessed, ain't nobody with a high or luxurious bed. And what's sensual entertainment? Clearly, something fun I'd been missing if they were swearing it off. We were dismissed to our cabins. The curtain was closed between the men's and the women's side of the hall, and we were herded out through the door into the "female area" where we were to stay, between the markers, from now until Day Ten.

∞

Back in our cabin, we were finally able to size up our dealt hand of housemates. Everyone was speaking quickly and far too much, anxious it was their last word. Nervous laughter broke up the small-talk about shower schedules, cabin operations and routines. I sat this one out for a change. It is rare times like these that I'm crap as an operations and routines kinda gal. Instead, I calculated the idiosyncrasies of each roommate as they fiddled through their belongings, digging out of their bags items I never thought to pack.

Mary Poppins was just across the cabin from me. She plucked more and more out of her duffel. My eyes widened with each new prize. The methodical placement of each object bragged of experience. I overheard it was her fifth time here.

It was in the room that I finally got some of their names. It's no wonder I fell in love with my girl from North Carolina. With a name like Sherba, I just adored that she reminded me of a tangy waffle cone. My Czech friend was Inga, and there was a mild-mannered soft-spoken Mirriam from Poland. I shuffled through my things, only because everyone else was. More worried that I hadn't brought enough, I missed a few more names—not that I would have been able to use them.

At the meeting, they had offered items (sheets, towels, blankets, flashlights, and such) we may have forgotten, but I was too stubborn to admit that I'd been so absentminded. Plus I was nervous about how they'd been washed and by whom—only *modestly* particular. I deemed my extra pillow case my towel and decided to suck it up—*I'm roughing it.*

The bell rang, interrupting the chit-chat. We awkwardly wished each other well, grabbed our jackets, pillows, and water bottles; some of the super-cautious snagged their flashlights, and single file, we rolled out to our first meditation.

We stood in a very serious silence just outside the doors of the meditation hall, all eyes averted down or at the doorway. No eyes meeting, no expressions shared. I studied mannerisms, postures, outfits, hairdos, laugh lines, dissecting all that I could to figure out the ins and outs of my new silent confidants. They called us in one at a time, moments apart—*guess there's a real method to this.* In the hall, I removed my shoes following those called before me. I held my fancy meditation pillow—which I'd borrowed from Lee—tightly between the fingers of one hand, acting casual with one hand free. Others dug through the provided pillows, meditation chairs, and fluffy foam cutouts like it was a shoppers giveaway.

The meditation room was an open, bland space with curtains drawn to keep out further light and noise. Our teacher sat in the front of the room on a platform, wearing a shawl over her light flowy clothes—*at least she's dressed the part.* She sat cross-legged with perfect posture, her hands at her knees, eyes closed, an effort-less smile, breathing calmly, exuding peace in her presence. A stunning black woman, with short hair to the scalp—*lucky*, I've always wished I could wear my hair like that and *not* frighten small children. I followed the majority lead while names were still being called, stacks of pillows, for some, still being situated. I positioned my pillow dead center of my mat, sat down, crossed my legs and shut my eyes.

Long, deep, natural breaths came freely as I slid into charac-ter—immediately consumed, I was spared the reality: this was the first of the 60,000 minutes ahead.

After the last few names were called and the rustling in the room settled, our teacher, Victoria, pushed the magic button on the stereo and the same deep voice belted through the speakers, this time in a bizarre crackly chant. *Whoa, whoa, whoa.* I fought not to peek. With fluttering lids, I squeezed my eyes as tightly as they would go, inadvertently scrunching my whole face. No one got up and glided out like my inner voice suggested, not even a rustle in their seat. So I, too, went with the program, reluctantly.

I had heard peaceful chants before, quiet in a low resonance. This was loud and a far cry from peaceful, said to be in the native tongue of Gautama Buddha. S.N. Goenka, an unpolished guru whose throat needed more clearing than a hurricane-swept town, elongated vowels at random and enunciated syllables in an awkward rhythm, making it difficult to buy into and even more difficult to concentrate. All skepticism aside, I was just not particularly enamored by the display.

Following the chant, we were given instruction. I squirmed to stay comfortable. First my back, then my knees, then feet, all took turns fighting for attention. My singular pillow already felt like cement, yet I was far too stubborn to create a love seat out of the provided foam cutouts. The old students sat on tiny wooden benches for God's sake. Moments before we were released for our break, Goenka covered our code of nobility, and we pledged our vow of silence. He closed in a short chant, resembling the first. The old students answered back something discrete I couldn't make out. And off we went, to the bathrooms—in silence.

I took note that the men's cabins were close, making bathroom breaks *shockingly* convenient. We ladies had to walk down a path, over a bridge, through the rusted jungle gym and out toward the parking lot to get to our closest restrooms—to wait in a long, silent line. We broke for about ten minutes, just long enough for the observations to ensue and the ladies' room line to diminish. Learning character traits and idiosyncratic details seemed a great way to pass the time. Talking to myself (in my head, but seemingly noisier than usual) had already commenced—ages ago, if you add the grueling drive—so any hesitation in that department was long out the window. The chime of the bell let us know it was time to return. Not an official clock, so we meandered back casually. Off with the shoes, back to our pillows; this time we got comfortable for the first of our nightly discourses—a prerecorded video, circa 1991, featuring Goenka with glimpses of his wife at his side.

He was just as unpolished on screen as he was on audio, clearing his throat, wiping his brow, sitting slumped in his seat. A pudgy guy, from Burma, with an accent and dialect boasting the cutest little sayings—"nothing doing, nothing doing." His silver hair swept to the side was rooted high enough away to see his squinty, deep-set eyes. The lines on his forehead seemed to be placed, just so, for effect. His big cheeks and prominent jowls made his smiles and big belly laughs that much more endearing. He sort of reminded me of my grandpa, Mert—you know, the Indian version.

His wife, sitting to his left, only shown in momentary takes, had the same cheeks and jowls, yet she never smiled. Not even at his cute little jokes. So she'd either heard them a thousand times or was just not really all that amused by him. Her giant rimmed eyeglasses made her dark, deep-set eyes pop out near the lenses, accentuating her blinking. It was the long blinking too, like she wasn't in a rush to get back to the moment. And then the yawning totally sealed it for me—she was bored to tears.

The hour-long DVD was very informative. "This technique will allow you to develop insight through the observation of bodily sensations, discovering the reality of the impermanence of suffering, and egoless nature of our mental-physical structure." It was nice to put a face to the crackly voice and learn more about what it was that I'd signed up for. I could already see myself looking forward to each evening's discourse. Goenka ended with, "take rest, take rest," after reminding us what time we would be up and at 'em in the morning. He and his wife chanted their way out of the room and that was it—end scene. Victoria dismissed us, and in single file silence, we made our way to our shoes and out the door.

I was thrilled to see stars—stars Baltimore would never dream of entertaining and even stars Hawaii rarely got clear enough for. They reminded me of being little at our beach house. Every so often, Gma would let my brothers take a rock to the streetlight near the deck just so we could better see the stars. There we were mesmerized by the moon and loved to be misguided by Gma's poor attempts at astronomy. We'd drag Grandpa's telescope out to the dark, splintery deck, only to be disappointed by the blurs we could never truly make out. And no one knew how to operate that damn telescope except for Grandpa, who would rather sit in his chair and watch the back-to-back news, pondering the last few blocks of the Post's daily crossword than help us figure it out again.

I will never forget the night full of falling sanguine stars that swooped up my grandpa, Mert. I was fifteen and frustrated one night (like most), having lost a battle at home. I walked outside behind the shed to smoke a cigarette, and much to my surprise, a meteor shower rained down overhead. I think I stopped counting at around twelve shooting stars, but I continued to watch, allowing myself to be mesmerized by the depth and complexity of the universe. It was August 11, 1993, ten years to the day after my mom's death, and all I could do was stand there, disgruntled, complaining about life's inequities, seeking solace in her presence. The crying and yelling and punching of trees that I was no stranger to, were stifled by my own wonderment of the world, of heaven.

After enough time had passed that my whereabouts were questioned when I returned home, I sunk back into my fifteen-year-old melancholy and forgot about the whole tremendous display. It wasn't until the next day, when I was sitting on the floor in Whitney's room, sniffling-crying, having just received the call that my grandpa died, that I thought about that star shower in all its splendor. I imagined my mom had somehow flown down on the tail of a meteor to scoop him up and take him on home.

My Gma later confirmed the connection. Her take was that he had died of an "honest to goodness" broken heart. She said in a solemn voice with her hand cupping her chin, her brow lifted, all matter-of-fact-like, "He never got over losing your mother, you know. It just killed him inside each day—end of story—no ifs, ands, or buts about it."

I walked the whole way back to Beaver Den *3*, head cocked, hoping to find Gma's dipper, smiling all the way to the door. Inside, with teeth brushed, I taco-ed myself into bed and passed out like I'd swirled my way through several vodka martinis. (Not that I'm much of a liquor girl, but that's how I imagine someone, perhaps a tad classier, passing out—all corpselike.)

The thought of 4:00 a.m. rattled me—in fact, I'd only ever seen 4:00 a.m. when at 3:00 a.m. I was still making poor choices—so I hadn't even gotten into pajamas. Not that I had formal pajamas to get into, but shedding my sports bra might have been nice. Instead, in sweat pants, long T, sweatshirt, and my rice-paper-thin sheet, I was out by 9:15.

Pau.

TWENTY-FIVE

SIT STILL, THIS IS GONNA HURT

W hy people were given alarm clocks when the bell was to chime at 4:00 a.m. was beyond me. Sure enough, at 3:50 a.m., the most annoying noise I'd ever heard came blaring through the cabin like a siren accompanying a careening truck through an intersection. It was those same people who had scrambled for the flashlight rentals that now had alarms going off at unnecessary times and ridiculous volumes. I will say that I ultimately slept through the early morning mayhem, yet I took a good minute—a tooth-pulling, treadmill kinda minute—to get ferociously perturbed in the most Zen way I knew how.

I, on the other hand, waited for the second chime of the bell at 4:20 a.m. With plenty of time to brush my teeth, wash my face and go, I was all set—*this isn't prom, people.* Like Goenka said, we're all supposed to be "so intensely focused on ourselves, we don't notice each other" anyway—spoken like a true inhuman.

From 4:30 a.m. to 6:30 a.m. we meditated with no instruction following the simple technique that was laid out for us the night before. "Focus on your breath, the breath from your nostrils that touches just above your lips, the triangle from your nose down to the points on either side of your lips. Focus on the sensations." I shuffled from knees to a cross-legged position and struggled to maintain a posture that didn't hurt something. My *focus* was more on my back that ached and my feet that kept falling asleep. It was evident a little practice before I'd arrived may have been prudent. Here at meditators *boot camp*, where tears should only ever fall as sweat, I was committed—"no pain, no gain."

Even with eyes shut, I noticed the moment Victoria entered the room. (According to my calculations, it was about 6:15 a.m. when she sauntered in.) Quiet as a mouse, it wasn't her movement that called my attention; it was her essential oils diffusing the musty air that I picked up instantly. With newfound heightened senses, I heard everything, even the soft *click* of the button on the CD player. Goenka blasted through the speakers in his usual chant. The awkward rhythm teased that it would soon be over "mukti—dukhon—se—hoya" and then continued with staggered repetition, keeping us guessing with each word.

I'm in a lot of pain, and I'm starving, so if we could just get this moving ...

Finally, the recognizable phrase I'd been furrowing my brow to manifest was sung. We responded, "sadhu, sadhu, sadhu," and then Goenka and his wife trailed off a bit more. (The "sadhu, sadhu" response means, "well said, well said." So, while we're *pretty* sure what he said is probably great, most of us—that is, those who don't speak Hindi—really have no idea.) I assumed this was hardly the mindfulness one would expect *here* as I mentally pushed Goenka and his wife out the door. Yet with a grumbling stomach and legs cramped and asleep, wanting to rush him through his chant seemed only natural. It had been two hours for Lord's sake.

The bell for breakfast was like a little piece of heaven. Echoing on the crisp mountain air, it rang a few times to call us to the kitchen. I spared no hesitation, botching attempts at cool and subtle as I briskly made my way to the hall. The stars were just beginning to hide as the moon held on with one bold planet welcoming the sun as it rose. "Good morning, beautiful," I said under my breath, smiling. I don't think I've ever seen her look so proud.

Walking into the dining hall, the smells greeted me as if I'd survived a famine. Oatmeal and stewed cinnamon prunes suddenly bred the excitement of a gluttonous Sunday brunch. I went up for seconds and thirds, despite the eyes I could feel on my back. With only fruit in the evening, I ate like a bear, treating each meal as my last. Goenka reminded us repeatedly to eat only what we needed to sustain ourselves—mindful eating, "less is more," he said. I found it a little difficult to take such advice from a seemingly happy, cute, and content, fairly round fellow. Enlightened or not.

∞

Our schedule after breakfast included seven more group meditations, broken up by bathroom breaks, lunch, teacher meeting time, tea, and our evening discourse. Our breaks were spent walking, stretching, resting—watching. Come day three, my talking to myself, I was afraid, had reached proportions beyond my control. Indeed, I was of unsound mind, mad as a March hare, nutty as a fruitcake. Hence, the only way to manage sanity was to imagine I was an embedded reporter, like Lisa Ling, here on a mission. I was to take careful mental notes and not miss a beat.

I blamed my mental breakdown on the incessant breathing. For three days and thirty hours of mediation, all we did was breathe. Breathe and focus on the "heat, cold, itching, pulsing, vibrating, pressure, tension, pain," only in that little, bitty triangle just below the nostrils and above the lip. Each set of instructions was the same, a spun-out, broken record. I began to feel that perhaps I was being shortchanged. If it weren't for the discourses at night promising that something was actually working, I may have thought Goenka was "full of bologna," as Gma would say.

During the ten hours a day we endured the sitting meditation, I was in so much pain I was certain my knees would splice through the flesh. Instead of stacking on more pillows and building greater thrones, as I saw others doing, I stuck stubbornly to my single pillow that felt like cold concrete each time I sat. Amidst the throws of pain that had become unbearable, I heard a voice, almost a faint whisper, "This is the pain you've caused others."

Great. I knew this was coming.

I cried silently with the pain. I had energy whirling all around me. I felt waves before they mentioned waves; I saw light before they mentioned light, but the pain was just unreal. "Sankharas," Goenka called them. Sankharas are the root of the pain. Negative energy planted in our bodies over the years was now coming up "like surgery with no anesthesia," he so graphically put it, "the operation into the unconscious has begun, and some of the pus hidden there has started to come out of the wound."

During teacher meeting time, I crawled up to the cushion at Victoria's feet to ask her if I should be in so much pain. "Is it true that, based upon your past, you could experience more pain than others?"

"Yes. It's possible."

Shit.

Not one for many words, she was kind but didn't seem to veer too far from the script. "You *are* allowed to adjust though," she said, smiling.

"I can?"

"Yes. It's not until Day five when you will be asked to remain still."

"Oh, okay. That's good to know." I smiled in relief. "Thank you." Hands in prayer, I bowed politely like I'd seen others do.

I wouldn't though. Even with her permission, I wouldn't budge. If I set a goal to run ten miles, I'd run ten miles. With toes bleeding and heels blistered, I'd finish like one of those fool-headed runner freaks. And I'm not even a runner—just extremely fool-headed.

Everyone was in their meditation shawls, cozy. I was sweatin' like a lying-cheat in church, trembling with my trespasses. I saw people sitting peacefully, smiling. I clenched my teeth and tightened my jaw. My muscles burned, my bones ached and my body stiffened—nothing "equanimous" about me. I was certain I had missed the lesson on "learning how to observe sensations without reacting, examining objectively, without identification."

Day five was the worst. In a zone, or in pain, or half asleep, I don't know which. Nevertheless I missed the bathroom break to get up and stretch. So after sitting for our regular two-hour afternoon meditation, Goenka, in his chant-ready voice announced that we would be sitting for a whole 'nother two hours—"this time no movement." *Wait! What? How did I miss the break? I can't do this. I ... I... I haven't been moving all along!*

"We will start from the top of our head."

Great. Just great. The top of our head.

We started scanning. I resumed panicking. I scanned the top of my head.

Fine—it's there.

"Focus on the right side of your face. Scan from the top of your head, slowly downward. Give attention to everything, your eyebrow, your lashes, your eye—"

Tears from just my right eye began to fall. Silent, detached tears fell on cue. We'd only just begun.

We scanned down from our nose and ears, farther to our lips and chin. When we got to our neck, my throat closed and my muscles tightened. My mind immediately scrambled for *my story*; in pain, any trigger was enough to dredge up old haunts. I even held back tears to let the clouds swell before the inevitable rain. Yet for some reason, nothing happened. The story never came, the replay; the images, the sounds—my father's ghostlike hands, her fighting his fierce grip, the scream—vanished.

It's just a story ...

I smiled at the space, welcoming the tender peace.

And just like that, it was gone—the peace bit, I mean—not one pinch of it around to save me from what was still to come. I couldn't take the pain. Pain I associated with giving birth. Pain I could only imagine, like a wartime amputation. I thought about "Baby Jessica" in that well and her poor little legs that had fallen asleep. Pins and needles must have felt like knives as they pulled her from the depths. Goenka's words became a backdrop.

"Next is your ego." The voice, not my own, was stern and un-relenting.

It was the same voice that had threatened with "the pain I caused others" who was now going for the jugular with the *ego*. I'd spent all year reading about the ego and had learned that mine was good and hardheaded and had been with me a long while. It was what gave me my swagger; my lil' bit of gangster; my confidence, false though it may be; my excuses for everything manipulative and slightly unwholesome, even my holier-than-thou Buddha nature. It was the little devil on my shoulder I'd high-five when we triumphed as teammates, and the same fool I could never seem to flick off when we were baited as rivals. I was scared. I had to shi-shi. *I'm not going to make it.* I fell into a zone. My body chose *flight*. We were making our way down the scan and *fight* apparently wasn't working, so *flight* it was. A few seconds of what you might call peace—numb was probably more like it—lapsed. We got down to the toes, and I was in an tolerable place, *we're almost there, I can do this.* My concept of time was gone. I was definitely numb.

"Now, we will go back up, scanning bottom to top."

Fight! Fight! Fight!

There went my chi. I began to sob. Sniffling loudly this time. Losing it. The pain had reached proportions I knew were doing damage, later confirmed by the popped blood vessels behind both knees. Still, I didn't move. I knew, somewhere, somehow I deserved this. All the lies I ever told swirled around in my head. I felt like the chubby kid in *Goonies* when he admitted to all the chocolate he'd eaten—the cheating, the stealing. Clearly no one else here shared a past like mine. They were all floating through poppies, having their toes tickled by fairy dust, while I fought a war with an army of one. I was down to my tank top. Against the rules, but I didn't care. I was sweating like I was being questioned, like the wrath was yet to come. I zoned out again.

I begged now. *What can I do?* With energy *hot* all around me, I figured this was as good a time as any for answers. *Just tell me what to do, and I'll do it.* I had found faith and was ready to trust whatever was in store for me. I was willing to follow. I just needed the lead. *What can I do?*

"Play the lotto," the voice said, monotone, seemingly bored. I felt like I just shook a frickin' Magic 8 Ball. *Really? That's it? Play the lotto?* I smiled though not convinced I was amused.

I found when I went to the pain it dissipated. When I drove into it, it went numb. I honed in on every ounce of my pain, channeling my sniffles into concentrated breaths. The force was so thick around me. I was alone in this cocoon, battling to get my wings. Suffocating when I thought about the tight room, peaceful when I could get beyond my concept of time and space.

Eckhart Tolle: "This too shall pass."

We were back at the top of the head. With anticipation, the pain returned. Goenka uttered the last phrasing of his chant. We all responded; I managed a whimpering, "Sadhu, sadhu, sadhu." I pulled my limp legs out from underneath me, folded my forehead to my knees and cried—like a toddler—nose running onto my pants crying.

The lunch bell rang.

The room was almost empty before I felt the circulation begin to fizzle back into my legs. With pins and needles, I struggled to stand and take a few steps toward the door. Limping, wiping my nose, unashamed of how I must look, I headed toward the door where I'd left my shoes. I opened the curtain to step out, and my senses were completely overwhelmed. Everything was new: the sky, the trees, the birds, the breeze. I was completely taken aback. I took three steps to the bench in front of me and collapsed, head folded into my hands weeping. *Thank you, thank you, thank you.* Thank you for the birds and the trees. Thank you for the breeze and not getting upset when I didn't notice any and all of this beauty. Thank you to the sun and the stars and the moon and all that I take for granted, every day. Thank you. Thank you, for you.

It was only recently that I had gotten comfortable with the idea of talking to God. I like how some refer to Grace or the Divine instead. I guess *God* can just seem so played out, cliché even, having lost its meaning through centuries of misrepresentation. Nevertheless, I was talking, which reminded me, Elizabeth Gilbert didn't seem so "God-y" anymore. I had gained my own conviction. I had earned my wings, and the funny thing is, I recognized them. They were mine all along. I just kept pushing them to the back of my closet, never the right style, or right season.

Here I stood, hardly a Victoria's Secret goddess, but a snot-dripping, red-nosed, watery-eyed angel. I had surrendered. I had given my all, and for the cause of the greater good. I was here to shed who I was and become the shepherd of thine peace I so wished to be. As I begged on the beaches of Hawaii, legs folded three times a day, "Lead me to the way, I shall follow." It seems all that begging led me straight to Virginia Jaycee Camp among bugs and mold and dirt and bunk beds smelling of musty thirteen-year-old boys' feet.

I had to wash my clothes in a sink with bar soap and hang them on the line to dry because I had sweated through everything I'd brought with me. Here, my ribbed Hanes white cotton tank shared a line with someone's black lace thongs. (And I was worried about coming off as too high-maintenance.)

I had to listen to snoring that sounded like rumbling thunder, stomping feet that matched elephant hooves and musical glutes that could have sat first chair with the trumpets in the middle school band—after all the vegetarian fiber they'd been feeding us. It was penance through patience, and ultimately, learning more about my own faults while meticulously pinpointing *theirs*.

I had watched people in their routines talking to themselves, eating their food slowly and systematically. I presumed they might be going nuts. I had talked to the two horses on campus and the one lone fat pig, Wilbur—who got hauled away at week's end (by the way, *not* cool)—and wondered, instead, if it were me that was really going nuts. I had dropped to my knees to watch an ant carry her giant load—completely entertained, smiling at her bravado. I collected acorns and pine cones because they reminded me of Gma. I talked to my mom every night while staring at her bright star amid the sea of envious tiny sparkles, thanking her for keeping me safe. They were both here with me at camp; I could feel it. I had the most vivid dream of Gma reaching out for me.

I was so close.

After lunch, I did my best to shuffle back to the meditation hall, even though I was certain I couldn't go on. Neither my legs nor my exhausted mind or aching heart had recovered. I had eaten more than my allotted portion in the dining hall without regret. I was working, man, no denying. *Their* three leaves of greens and cup of tea could sustain running through poppies. I needed at least three piled plates to stay charged on the front line.

Goenka began, "Start again, start again."

Yeah, yeah.

According to Goenka, there are two forms of suffering: craving and aversion. Here we had come to rid ourselves of these two forms, and all I seemed to do was perfect mine. I craved that they'd ring the bell to dismiss us for lunch or tea, and I had aversions to every negative sensation bestowed upon me. (Something told me I wasn't going to podium in this event.) I made it through two more meditations on Day five, only by the grace of God, I swear. I was torn and tattered, and by the end of the evening discourse, I was relieved to hear, "Although this process is unpleasant, this is the only way to remove the impurities. It would be wise to understand that what seems to be a problem is actually a sign of success in meditation, an indication that in fact the technique has started to work." I didn't trust a word of it. Yet, I was too spent to begin dwelling on it for now. I went to bed still vibrating from the energy of the day—turbulent, vivid dreams accompanied me in a deep sleep.

Even when going to sleep at 9:30 p.m., 4:15 a.m. still comes awful early. Thankfully, the alarm clocks got the boot after the second day. My bunkmates woke up with the first bell to wash up and get ready. I waited for the late, second bell, now at 4:25 a.m., swooshed some mouthwash and rolled. It was still dark out. I was certain that the animals that witnessed our morning crawl to the meditation hall with one annoyed eye open were curious as to what the hell we could possibly be doing at this hour. Even the bugs were still sleeping, aside from the crickets that had been chanting their mantras religiously all night long.

TWENTY-SIX

GET YOUR OHM ON

D ay six seemed to start off on a much better note. My body had recouped a bit, and my "monkey mind" was stoked that I was on the downward side to this bell curve. It was Day six, my *Zip Pity Doo Da* day, my finally *I've got poppies* day. I remembered my mission: embedded reporter. We had been asked not, among other things, to write here, which made me crave it. Instead, I spouted off sentences and phrasing in my head, giggling at my own simple sarcasm and cunning wit. I imagined how it would all look, how it would all go down. I saw myself sending the complete story all the way to *O Magazine.* Because let's face it—in the depths of all my pain and suffering, I couldn't help but think *this is all Oprah's fault.*

I could see Oprah inviting me on her show, after all these years of it just not working out. She would announce me in her "Kat Hurlaaaaaaaay!!" kinda way, and I would walk onstage, holding back tears because everything was culminating all at once, finally. How it should have been all along. Oprah giving me that nurturing hug, the one that touches spirits and feeds souls. The one that says, "You've earned it. I anoint you." And then offers me a makeover.

I was meditating, can't you tell? Empty mind. Look, I was just happy to be halfway comfortable without battling my inner and outer being, so let me have my fantasy—*sheesh.*

So, it was just me and Oprah. We talked about my book that was in the works, and we talked about the irony of being neighbors in Hawaii, and how she really was my long lost homegirl, but I could call her "Auntie." She laughed at my jokes, and I was poetically articulate and well spoken, naturally.

∞

Day seven took a definite downturn—it was my *Zip Pity Doo Da's* gone flat and *poppies are all wilted* day. On the brighter note, I had my sankharas in check, but three more days here seemed like a life sentence. And I had a new issue. That whole vibrating thing was making me have to shi-shi—in a urinary-tract, intense, not quite burning, yet painfully uncomfortable, fashion. I squirmed around in my seat and was the first one running out the door, racing to the bathroom. I couldn't explain anything to anybody, so instead I looked like a twerp darting out seconds after the "sadhu, sadhu." At least I was out in front so no one could see me holding my crotch like an anxious kindergartner with soggy Underoos.

I hated not being able to talk. I felt like a brass New Yorker, bumping into people with no apology or waking up next to someone with no "good morning." It was hardly the Southern charm and hospitality I so enjoy extending. And it was distracting, worrying that people might think I was just plain rude as I selfishly operated about the joint. Plus I would have liked to explain why I was running out of the room so impolitely, because without an apology I just looked like one of those annoying kids who always have to be line leader.

So I had to shi-shi and I tried to convince myself, *this too shall pass*, but the truth was the only way it will pass was in my pants if I weren't careful. I limited my tea intake to offer some relief, and still nothing. I danced and squirmed on my pillow the last five or ten minutes of each sit, only to fight back accidents on my way to the loo. *I gotta do more kegels*, I reminded myself as I booked it down the yard.

By Day eight, my tingles all over were really prominent. I'd now dreamt my way through *O Mag* and vigilantly concocted all the other things I would accomplish this year. I had written and illustrated an entire children's book, all in my head, of course—titled, "Karma Kamille"—featuring a little girl who is innately mindful and enjoys *simply* sitting under her tree with all her friends in nature. So, while not really meditating with these intense vibrations and waves, I figured I was just multitasking.

∞

I finally quieted my mind so well that I fell asleep. It was embarrassing startling myself awake each time I teetered toward falling forward—like every day of psych class in high school. I decided to go out for fresh air. It wasn't recommended to meditate outside. In fact, I think the wording was closer to "not allowed," but it was my favorite, so I politely ignored the *subtle* suggestion. I parked myself in a chair near the bathroom—just in case—tucked to the side, out of clear sight, so I wouldn't get in trouble.

I'd already been scolded twice since being here. The first time was for my tank top, after I'd been asked respectfully not to show too much skin. To which I replied, rather vehemently, "Well, if you'd just turn on the air conditioning—some of us are really fighting in here." I was confused … *Aren't their eyes supposed to be closed anyway?* And once for my stretching that eked a little too close to a standing bow pose, where they reminded me I'd be distracting the campers. Again: *They're supposed to be SO intensely focused on themselves*... which I didn't say. Instead I apologized because she was probably right, although she couldn't really blame me for trying to unwind the pretzel I'd begun to resemble as we had now sat for over seventy hours.

In my chair, by the toilet, I sat. Breeze feeling delicious, bugs sounding delightful, the frisky fragrance of flowers dancing on the tip of my nose, and the vibrations came. I could scan my body all the way through with one breath. Up and down, in and out, or side to side. I could pull the energy in and then blow it back out like the hot air of a balloon, extending to each cell through the far reaches of my body. I would have a free flow for a few minutes, and then a blockage would come up—*sankhara*. I'd go to the center of the pain for a few minutes, and breathe it out. Like a masseuse working out a knot, I could feel it dissolve, and then the free flow vibrations would return. I must say it *was* pretty awesome.

Only problem—my delicious chair in the delightful breeze by the toilet I wouldn't have to sprint to had a small bug problem— not so awesome. I ignored the first bite and then the second. By the third, I was convinced it was bad karma that I'd come out here in the first place. I didn't budge. I was raw bait. A sitting duck. A vibrating mosquito hotspot. I sat, stubbornly, receiving what I was due. I deserved it.

∞

I returned to the meditation hall for our next sit looking like I'd contracted chicken pox. I didn't scratch—I refused. I sat obediently in my designated spot. By now, I'd traded my pillow for one of those tiny wooden benches, because yes, it had been proven, I *am* a masochist. Meanwhile, I hadn't been able to talk to anyone about the feelings I'd been having during meditation. I truly had no clue whether I was doing any of it right. Victoria's ambiguous answers to my questions left me frustrated, so I stopped asking. Besides teacher meeting time, the hour after lunch, had been reduced to my precious nap-time each day. I had become so fatigued through meditation that naps were necessary to recharge the battalion.

Plus the discourses in the evening better answered my questions as Goenka seemed more honest about all that can go on throughout the course. "Dhamma (law of liberation) teaches us to accept the bitter truth of suffering, but it also shows you a way out. For this reason it is a path of optimism, combined with realism and 'workism'—each person has to work to liberate herself." I thought Goenka's past was a little closer to mine than those sharing pillows with me. "Committing suicide will not help; it will only create fresh misery." I howled laughing at his comic relief at eve's end. Others appeared to be a little less amused.

I bet they just didn't get it.

Day eight or nine—they started to run together toward the end—I had my vibration thing working, my scans going and my sankharas fizzling, when I scanned all the way down to my seat and stopped for a second. *Well isn't this convenient—no batteries.* Sex hadn't crossed my mind one iota. Not before my arduous five-hour drive to the mountain, my doubtful stroll up the drive, nor my timid steps through the registration door. It definitely hadn't crossed my mind when I'd arrived at my bunk only to be thrown back by the scent of pre-pubescent boys. And, it certainly hadn't crossed my mind when I was in all that pain or when I hung out with Oprah. But here. Now. With intense vibrations in between my legs. Sex. Yes—definitely sex.

Guilt ridden, I shamed myself back into meditating. *Empty mind.* Goenka was constantly in my head, "Suppressing defilements does not eliminate them."

Damn.

I went back to my scans chastely, too embarrassed for vibrations, still egocentric enough to imagine I'd been caught blushing. So now my scans felt more like waves of pressure. I could even control the intensity of the pressure. I made passes from left to right and up and down. Still not sure if any of this was right, but I was almost positive this *was* what I was supposed to do. It felt right. Well—mostly.

I had this immense pressure all of a sudden between my legs. This was definitely different; this was not sexy—not cute. This was like I'm pinching some sort of nerve or something. *Ummm ... I'll give a leg, and a busted capillary, but*—I shifted just slightly, not to break the rules; yeah, this was really uncomfortable and really no fun. *I mean sacrificing the vagege seems like a whole 'nother course entirely.* I shifted a little more, but to no avail. It was almost like a cramp or something but deep and very near all my essentials. For once, I didn't have to shi-shi. This *too* was not passing. *Craving, Craving! Aversion, Aversion!*

The bell rang.

Oh, thank God.

I thought I was gonna pop or something.

So the pressure on the vagege seemed to come and go those last few days. But worse—between the stone-cold pillow, the rock-hard bench, and the half-ply recycled toilet paper they had around this joint—I was certain I'd given myself hemorrhoids. Sure, I'd come here to lose ego and vanity and all that good stuff, *but ain't enough pride gone to ask a camp counselor for some Tucks.*

I'm just keepin' it real, folks.

I'd never had hemorrhoids before, but I'm almost positive this is what the commercials describe. And yet I pressed on. No itching. No wiggling. Just me and my vagege pressure and my swollen anal sphincter. I was a hot ticket. I let go. Again.

Come night's end, I was a zombie. I really enjoyed the discourses, and it seemed that everyone else was finally getting the jokes. I think I may have been on the fast-track program for this whole gig here. I could overhear the Q & A with Victoria in the evening, and people were just starting to ask questions that I had, like day two. I'm not trying to toot my own horn, but on day ten when we were finally allowed to talk and actually describe what we had been enduring, people were like, "Wow, man, that sounds intense!"

Um, yeah. You think?

Others had some really good stories about hallucinations and vivid dreams, but no one seemed to understand the depths of pain I had visited. I proudly showed off my war wounds, proving my veteran status.

∞

Smiles were as wide as jack-o-lanterns. Laughter was loud with giddy fits. We could finally talk! I felt like I was on drugs—not a first for this trip. I swear had I known about this meditation thing in college, I could have saved several clusters of brain cells. Of course, I would have had to exchange *life of the party* and innumerable dramatic meltdowns for a more patient, calm, and loving existence.

Nahhh. No regrets, right? Our experiences shape us— "everything happens for a reason."

Throughout my stay, I had tried to remain invisible. In silence, my vibrant and friendly personality, which I most often exude to effectively gain the affection of others, was extinguished. I was disappointed when I realized, about day three, that all that personality was just another extension of my ego. And here I had thought all along that I was just really charming. In silence, talking to my-self, with everything magnified a hundredfold, it was obvious I was really an *attention seeker*. With that insight (although now that I think about it, it wasn't all that profound), I had searched for an-onymity. No eye contact, no Baltimore "hon," not even so much as a smile.

Yet, somehow, I still managed to attract an unnecessary amount of attention. Women—some of whom I hadn't even no-ticed throughout—approached me, admitting how they'd cataloged me the entire course: "You're so strong." "You must work out." "You have such good posture." "You're such a warrior ... not get-ting up for breaks."

Yeah—breaks are for sissies.

Oh, and the food: "Girl, you can eat!" "I've never seen some-one your size put away so much food." One girl even called me "Groceries."

Seriously, you have no idea.

So much for slipping under the radar.

We shared stories and laughs and anecdotes. We shared our backgrounds, glimpses of our family lives, and reasons for coming here. We all felt like we knew each other in so many ways, all the ways we had made up entirely in our heads, but brethren just the same. People exchanged emails and Facebook pages in the general feeling of connectedness—hoping to make the goodbyes a little less awkward—promising to write.

Pralina, the old Indian woman and "Vipassana regular," told me she does a lot of exercise like me, but her husband says she should "exercise her mind more than her body." There was Tim-my, who introduced herself from Transylvania, which until then, I thought was a fictional place; Emily, who was only seventeen and without a doubt exponentially more grounded than me; and Swayze, who said her inner voice started to sound like Goenka's.

The short, older woman I watched all week chasing crickets was from Russia. The stuck-up girl I had been sure I wouldn't like was a really nice lady named Colleen from New Finland, Canada. One woman, sporting dreadlocks, whom I'd barely noticed all week, was from Poland; she had done some work in the White House as an art conservationist. And my girl, Sherba, was all smiles and laughs, bending over heaving and sighing like she'd just run a race.

We made it. I wanted a tattoo. Like the *Ironman* finishers get. Those who endure that insane bike, swim, run, a comparison I could readily make given my background in sports. Though the blood, sweat, and tears of this trip made those I had endured on the court or the field seem like picking daisies at T-ball tryouts. I bet, though, a hundred hours on a bike could give you some mega vagege pressure and some serious hemorrhoids.

∞

The whole air on the campus had changed. People unearthed their cell phones and began packing their things. Voices, both male and female, could be heard coming from every stretch of the yard. We still had a discourse that evening and a meditation in the morning, but as far as we were concerned—we had made it. I fetched my keys and walked down to the lot where my *getaway* truck had been sitting patiently on standby. The *real world* seemed vastly unfamiliar.

My cell phone was warm like a burnt, dry biscuit from baking in the glove box all week. I powered it on to make a call. Vaguely familiar voices from several awaiting messages helped connect me with life again. I made one call to Lee.

"Hello?"

"I made it!" Lee on the other end almost seemed foreign; I almost seemed foreign. Even my outside voice was unusual—the tone, the pitch. "I'm coming home tomorrow. I made it."

Tomorrow came, and the morning meditation was a walk in the park. "No sensation is eternal. Therefore one should not have preferences or prejudices toward any sensation. When a gross, unpleasant sensation arises, one observes it without becoming depressed. When a subtle, pleasant sensation arises, one accepts it, even enjoys it without becoming elated or attached to it. In every case one understands the impermanent nature of all sensations; then one can smile when they arise and when they pass away." He left us with, "May all beings be happy, be peaceful, be liberated!"

I sat attentively, exuding gratitude to Goenka, his moody wife, Victoria, my pillow mates, Sherba, and all the staff who had made operating in my agonizing, yet enlightening little bubble, possible. I floated through breakfast, still grinning from ear to ear. I said my goodbyes and thank-you's and rushed off, feeling a little guilty for not having offered to help clean up.

All guilt was forgotten with the start of my engine. I reached for the nearest pen to scribble notes, jotting down everything I could remember. I didn't want to miss a moment as it all seemed so surreal already. I left the way I came in, yet lighter having lost the *timid*. Bouncing around with the loose gravel, I feverishly wrote, dialed the cell, and navigated. I headed south. I was in the mountains, so south seemed appropriate. Two hours and almost two identical phone calls later.

" ... and then I heard this voice, and it said, 'play the lotto.' Can you believe that? Play the lotto? I totally thought it was a joke.

Wait a sec, hold on." I saw signs for Tennessee. *Holy shit, where the hell am I?*

Note to self: Maryland is NORTH of Southern Virginia, even when in the mountains.

I lost it! I lost every bit of chi that I had stapled to me. Every bit that I had Scotch taped to myself. Gone. Flying out the windows with my tears and faint sniffles. I felt like I did when I used to get lost in Kmart—panicky—hot—mind racing. Then I could just go sit in the car until someone found me, even if that *someone* was the police that one time. Here I was left to pull it together on my own. Ain't happening. Clearly, NOT liberated.

"All I wanna do is go home!" I wailed into the phone, looking for sympathy. What did I get? Laughter. Howling laughter. What did I do? *Click.*

I wallowed in my own sorrow, listening to the phone ring again and again from the caller, who was supposed to be my supportive girlfriend—who by now had probably realized the error in her callous response to my *well-justified* meltdown. I let her think about what she had done while I wallowed. *I knew I should have helped clean up.*

After a good fifteen minutes of sulking, I, too, started laughing. Not willingly at first, but it came anyway. Although adding an extra four hours to my already four-hour trip was no real laughing matter, I laughed at the irony. I laughed at the possibilities. I laughed at myself for thinking I wouldn't be immediately faced with adversity. I laughed for thinking I could walk on water leaving Virginia's Camp Jaycee. I laughed because Buddha said, "The highest welfare is the ability to keep the balance of one's mind in spite of the vicissitudes, the ups and downs, of life. One may face pleasant or painful situations, victory or defeat, profit or loss, good name or bad name; everyone is bound to encounter all these. But can one smile in every situation, a real smile from the heart? If one has this equanimity at the deepest level within, one has true happiness."

I laughed, because albeit shakily, equanimity was coming along.

TWENTY-SEVEN

GIVE ME A REASON

Less than thirty days after I returned from Vipassana, the months of living in my house, a sparsely staged show-room, were over. Showing after showing, quite often un-announced, finally amounted to a sale that met our conditions. Brooke and I spoke constantly—all business—negotiating what documents needed to be signed and sent, where and when. Tension between us had risen and fallen with the tides of "Yes, we have a buyer! Damn, they backed out. Keep your fingers crossed, we just got another one. Shit—that one walked, too."

In a short sale, the buyer is essentially "helping you out." I mean, it can be a win/win situation in the long run, but it certainly doesn't feel that way while you (the seller) are bent over backward, begging for anyone to throw you a frickin' bone. Brooke was for-tunate to miss the worst of it; she had found her own apartment and had made her lasting exit, leaving me cursing, packing a truckload of residual junk when it came time for the final curtain call.

All was forgiven, however, that early October day when at last we signed the hundreds of papers releasing our debt and deed. We were clueless as to what repercussions might follow us out the door, but on that day, we walked out with a pair of half-moon grins, not once looking over our shoulders.

Porter was there too, in the car, for me to kiss after I hugged Brooke in relief, happy to have stuck it out amicably. He looked as confused as ever about where he might be headed next but was just as content to see the same familiar faces somewhere along for the ride.

Lucky Badass had already moved in with Lee and her cat, Bella, creating even more of a colossal cat-hair shag carpet, but other options were scant, believe me, I tried. I itched just thinking about the likely fur-nadoes. Nevertheless, Lee and Bella seemed pleased as punch with the new bitchy entertainment.

I packed my meager things into storage and moved into Whitney and Dana's finished basement to ride out the wave of financial insecurity. I lived out of my suitcase, tucked back and hidden in the corner of the curtained-off storage space. My modern futon style bed folded into a couch with just one click. So with the sheets and blankets removed and the curtain closed, I did my best shuffling things out of sight to keep my existence to a minimum. In fact, I endeavored on making my presence as covert as possible, but in their tight and narrow Baltimore row home, my attempts were futile at best.

The truth was, I needed them, and I hated that. It changed things somehow, even when we pretended it hadn't. They were kind and generous to share their space, their meals when I was around, and their groceries on occasion; but no matter what the accommodations, nothing distorted the fact that I had few options. I had been offered other rooms from friends or family, yet Whitney and Dana lived just blocks from both of my jobs, therefore it made the most sense. Plus, we were *besties*; we could do this, right?

Whitney spoiled me by doing my laundry every so often, folding each piece precisely, stacking them in neat little piles like they do at J Crew. Dana and I spent cold, rainy afternoons, between clients, watching the Sundance Channel, sprawled out on opposing couches, drifting in and out of sleep. When we were hell-bent on being productive, Dana pored over the daily deals on the Internet, perched on her chair in the dining room while I cussed at the new website software I couldn't operate from the couch in the living room. Whit and I eventually had to plan lunch dates just to rope one another in. Our opposite schedules left us chirping hello and goodbye often in the same breath.

I worked nights, and at 2:00 a.m., would attempt to sneak past Parker (their senile, fourteen-year-old Jack Russell), barking her fool head off like I was some sort of relentless robber. She'd charge down the wood floor hallway toward me with nails clicking—like scurrying mice in stilettos—sliding to a stop and then jumping and twirling and back peddling in a barking frenzy like she'd never seen me a day before in her life.

And even the few times Parker somehow slept through my entrance, I'd still manage to cause a fuss. In every effort to be quiet, I would inevitably knock over an umbrella, trip on a cord, or set off the alarm—cussing under my breath the whole way.

If I was hungry or thirsty or, more likely, had leftovers for the fridge—*I was totally screwed.* I'd tiptoe into the kitchen where, just beyond, the girls (and the furry *vicious* one) lay sleeping in their bedroom, a paper-thin, frosted glass door between us, not more than six steps away. Any noise seemed to be amplified tenfold; the crackling of the spinach bag, the jostling of the coconut water, even the light from the fridge seemed obnoxiously loud. And heaven forbid I had the door open for more than five seconds (I'd somehow get distracted and forget every time). That *too smart for its own good*, overgrown, stainless steel tattletale would start beeping at me, until frantically, I shut it the *hell up*. By this time, I could usually hear Whit snickering from the bedroom, considering I must have sounded like a drunk, dancing bull in a china shop. But the awful part was that I was really trying—not to mention stone sober.

I spent a lot of my weekends in Jersey with Lee just to get out of the girls' hair. Things with Lee and I had lightened up dramatically with what felt like an unburdened new beginning. Future still seemed far off as we both had so much work of our own to accomplish, yet we were content to let each other have her dream, even if mine was always a little loftier.

On the rare occasion when Lee made the trip down to stay with all of us, I'd try to impress upon her how best to remain invisible, which only seemed to backfire in some way or another. Our messes were double, our noises were double, and our space occupied and hot air exhaled was, despite our best efforts, double. Lee felt about as comfortable as a cactus coming down, and I didn't blame her. Not by any fault of the girls, mind you, just my emitted, heightened anxiety of the whole situation.

∞

It didn't help that I had fallen back into a slight depression during all this. I felt needy and helpless, driving in a snowstorm with broken wipers. I'd sit on the floor in my basement bedroom and spread all my bills out on the carpet next to stacks of cash that I'd earned from the restaurant. I called consolidation companies and financial help lines, feeling more frustrated and depleted when I ended the calls than when I'd started. Even with glimpses of solace during my half hour of meditation each day—"everything happens for a reason"—I still couldn't ignore the familiarity of the underlying ache that held on like a life-sucking leech.

As time passed in beats and measures, the chords played in a heavy minor, and the song, always muted, dragged on. My poetry got a little darker, my seasonal depression felt a little colder and hung on a little longer, my enthusiasm all around took dips and dives between the "it's all goods," and I hovered around *just all right* for a few months at least. In that time, I forged ahead, hoping progress would release the poison I stood weakened by. I worked on my new site, I began penning some of the pages that would eventually make their way into this book, and I was granted an unexpected "way out" that I'd previously been too proud to consider.

I summoned my mantra: "Just tell me what to do"—but this time, it fell on deaf ears, a hollow shell, only breeze and rolling tide echoing back dispersed emptiness. I had indeed been "playing the lotto"—*could it really be that literal?*—but, to no avail. Yet, when my lawyer uttered the words "fresh start," I was struck by the enticing notion of bona fide freedom—that I actually had a *chance*. I would do anything. I was ashamed to have to go this route, but I had finally admitted that I was in way over my head, and other options looked both bleak and barren.

Yes, it was my mess, but it wasn't *all* my mess, and for that reason I think Lee was quick to support the use of my one *get out of jail free card*. It had taken me months to admit to her all that was going on, maybe just as long for me to admit it to myself, but with uncooperative credit-card companies with whom I'd never missed a payment, more guilt dropped with each embarrassing, harassing phone call.

My lawyer was kind and supportive through the ugly process that is personal bankruptcy. It made the piles of paperwork Brooke and I had completed for our short sale look like a breezy recycle bin at a slow business office. Filing for Chapter 7 was another job entirely. Pay stubs and taxes and credit-card slips and the online credit course and letters of documentation; thank God I had no assets.

This is not the copout for the lazy, folks, let me tell you. No ma'am; you have to be put together, intelligent, organized, resilient, and able to come up with $1,329 cash for either a cashier's check or a money order to legally wave the white flag of financial surrender.

It would have been easier just to have a baby and wait for the check to come in the mail—just sayin'.

The whole process took five grueling months of me wondering whether I'd be granted the pardon or not. When the early April morning of my hearing finally came, I was suited up and ready for whatever the judge had in store for me. I had done all that I could. The rest was out of my hands.

∞

Traffic court is fancier than this place was. And there were just as many of us here as there generally were defending red-light-camera violations and speeding tickets, except this place was set up with a few informal conference rooms, not your typical *Judge Judy* set. The long line of us was split up into four rooms, depending on where your name fell on one of the lists taped to the drab wall. The judge in each room sat behind a wide table and microphone, with court officials on either side. My lawyer, Frank, with wads of manila folders bursting with papers tucked under his arm, kept racing from one room to the next, apologizing to me, and I'm sure his other clients, as he tried to serve us all at the same time.

Without Frank at my arm, I sat in the room, tall, crossed-legged, uncomfortable, in the middle row but off to the side, observant of others, feeling a little out of place. I wondered about the company I kept: their backgrounds, their education, their families, our differences, our likely commonalities. I worried they could see through me—a phony—a spoiled, selfish, college-schooled kid who needed her Uncle Sam to bail her out of her own mess. I knew, deep down, that's not who I was—I had tried everything—but I could only imagine what they must have been thinking. My own insecurities sat next to me where Frank, and all his folders, should have been.

There was nothing private about each case. The judge called the faceless names off his list and then fired questions like it was everyone's business in the room to hear what had brought each person to the table. There were sad stories and repeat offenders; there were slumlord complaints and countless job losses.

When it was my turn, I responded to the judge's questions honestly and concisely. When asked, "What got you to this point?" My best, succinct answer was, "divorce" (rabbit ears included).

The judge smirked and got kind of smart when he asked, "Why does everyone put divorce in quotes (again, the rabbit ears)?" I wish I had the court reporter's personal cell, because if I did, I'd call her and ask exactly what I said that day as I'm sure she remembers it better. In fact, she has probably given her own recounting at, say happy hours, family gatherings, and Sunday night pool with the girls, but since I don't have her number, I'll tell you it went something like this: "Well, Your Honor, I'm not exactly sure why everyone else does it, but for me, I do it because I'm a lesbian and the court would rather not recognize my relationship as a 'marriage' (rabbit ears!)."

"Eh hem—right." He adjusted in his seat, nodding. "That'll be it, Miss Hurley, thank you."

∞

It was about that time I could feel the girls getting the itch to have their place free of my scattered accoutrements. Whit had dropped a hint or two, and despite me getting all misty-eyed because she had said it before I'd gotten the chance to say it myself, I agreed whole-heartedly. I too wanted my own space to breathe.

In response to a craigslist apartment ad, I walked up to the door and chimed the bell of an old brownstone house that had been split up into apartments. I could picture myself there already, sipping a buttery chard on the white marble front stoop, smiling at all the pedestrians passing me on my block, wide with towering trees, smelling the light fragrance of blooming flowers from neighboring homes that had window boxes boasting "proud keeper." The loud buzz of the door and the voice over the intercom of Jenn, the chick trying to rent her place, startled me out of my daydream. "Come in."

I opened the first of two massive doors, inviting myself in through the second just as I was greeted at the entrance. Jenn welcomed me into her tidy studio, cluttered only with books and creatively hung kitchen utensils in an attempt to manage space. She showed her place, furnished and lived in, because she and her boyfriend were breaking the lease and needed someone in as soon as possible to avoid the extra charges. She was a med student at Hopkins who would be doing her residency in Boston and needed someone almost right away, *check*.

I saw cathedral ceilings, huge front windows, wooden floors, an old marble fireplace, and a large enough floor plan for my meager belongings. I saw character, charm, creativity—future.

I stayed only a few minutes, barely stepping all the way inside, and just long enough to be polite. I didn't tour, I mean, what was there to tour really? It was a studio. Later, Jenn admitted that she thought I was completely uninterested. Yet, I'd seen enough. I'd seen potential. I left before the next person could arrive; Jenn said she had showings all afternoon. I didn't want it to be awkward, you know, telling them the place was already taken.

I smiled, walking down the sidewalk, confident, plucking at the numbers on my keypad, dialing the management company, the same company whose property manager, Eric, had shown me two other places earlier that day. One the size of a mini-camper, where the seven-foot ceiling gave the illusion that I should duck about the place. I also took note of its *kitchen for one* that could be operated entirely by a slight ninety-degree rotation to reach its mini-stove, mini-sink, and mini-fridge, just like that.

Our second stop had been a place they had not yet been given the opportunity to clean, or my suggestion, fumigate. It flaunted scattered piles of dirty clothes and dusty clumps of hair weaves strewn about all over the floor, not to mention the rank smell. I'm not sure what kind of goggles he thought I wore to see past my repugnance to its true potential.

I was frightened by the prospects in my price range. I'd even started to think the mini-camper wouldn't be so bad after all (good posture is totally overrated anyway). So at the sight of this diamond in the rough, just $50 more than the first two crap-holes, I wasted no time. "Hey, Eric, it's Kat. I just toured Jenn's apartment on Eager Street. I'll take it."

∞

Imagine a large, open living room of a nineteenth century affluent row home; enclose it with a wall and a door, add a narrow kitchen about six feet deep, a squatty full bath, and only so much as a coat closet. That was my new place. I called it my shoebox, and I loved it—mostly because it was my very own—my very first space all to myself. I could come and go as I pleased, be as loud or as peaceful as I wanted. I could even leave a dish in the sink without an ounce of guilt—except that I wouldn't—but indeed I could. I could also clean the whole puny thing in about five minutes, right down to the scrubbing of the tub, the toilet, *and* the tiles. And at $625 a month, not only could I afford it, I could also begin dropping a few coins into that lonely, dejected savings account I'd be surprised the bank hadn't already closed, assuming sheer lack of interest (pun intended).

I dug my futon out of storage and set it up near the giant curtainless windows. I wanted the light of the day to greet me each morning and get me moving—no more excuses to coddle me back into a lazy sleep. I also brought the desk that I never used from the condo, but looking at it inspired productivity, which I thought was key. I took my surfboard out of its travel bag and stood it proudly in the corner to remind me of my second home, Hawaii (never mind that the closest surf was two and a half hours away).

I brought my mom's wrought-iron baker's rack that had been in the kitchen of our condo, but after much deliberation decided to leave the china cabinet in storage, fearing it might not survive another couple of moves. I did make sure to grab Gma's old antique rocking chair though, and the large envelope of saved letters she and Mom had written back and forth while my mom studied in Italy that I'd been meaning to read. (Each thin, crispy page smelled just like our house in Manor Club.) No room for a couch or TV, which suited me fine. I had chests that created some sort of storage and shelves filled with books; just looking at them pleased me to no end. My coffee table did some moonlighting as a candlelit shrine when I'd sit up on one of my many cushions for daily meditation—my mom and Gma, both settled on the mantel, watching over me.

I lived in Mount Vernon, the artsy-fartsy district of Baltimore, where queers and artists alike run around footloose and fancy-free. It's where being a vegan isn't scoffed at and is probably considered trendy, like lopsided hair, tight jeans, and desperate attempts at being hipster. They all made me smile: the queens; the drama; the dreadlocked, musty-smelling intellectuals, as I strolled up and down my new little hood, dropping into politically charged coffee shops and incense-blanketed natural food stores, just checking things out.

I loved to scope out places to sit and write and feed off the energy of the quirky crowd. At this point, with financial freedom in my sails, I felt like I could write anywhere, without worry, without a debt to unpaid time. I sought after the finesse it takes to carve out time for your craft, which was no small feat. The story had been writing itself, I just needed the time to put it to the page. As I took the first steps into my new, empty apartment, I remember thinking: "This is where I will write my book."

And the more I said it, the more I believed it possible.

∞

Between the gym, the restaurant, Jersey and Baltimore, I began to live the lessons I'd learned in Hawaii, and on that stone-cold cushion I sweated my way through at Jesus Camp. There was nothing perfect about it, but there was a practice. A daily practice—every day, almost every moment, I kept pace, fueled on, I'll admit, sometimes the sputtering fumes of passion. Dr. Martin Luther King Jr. put it best: "If you can't fly then run, if you can't run then walk, if you can't walk then crawl, but whatever you do you have to keep moving forward."

And there *were* days when I crawled, believe you me. In some ways, I felt like a dying patient who'd been given a new lease on life. I would be foolish *not* to feel blessed by even a bug bite. Besides, I never doubted that I should live this life for the both of us, Mom and I, that is. I mean, if I could somehow manifest the love that she encompassed and match it with my own—what couldn't we accomplish?

I suppose if it weren't for stifling fear and insuperable roadblocks I might have already been there, but then again, if it weren't for those crippling things, what would I have conquered? I truly believe that one can only attain glimpses of enlightenment when they themselves have come to know deep, dubious darkness. Befriending the night is the most sincere way to greet the morning and its harbored mysteries.

If you ask, you shall receive. Sometimes, not in so many words, perhaps instead, a distant path cleared of thorns, but when God gives you a reason, son, you better be ready to step up to the gosh dern plate.

Come hell or high water, as Gma would say.

∞

At thirty-three, I would have hardly imagined a shoebox would mean so much to me. A few years ago, I may have seen it as a prison, perhaps my own personal cell. But now, I walk in each time grinning like I've come home to an old friend. Countless shades of gratitude color my world: for my independence, my solitude, for the good energy that greets me back, "you're welcome."

A few years ago, I imagined I'd be refinancing my condo by now, or even better, upgrading to a single-family home. I anticipated that I'd be married and thinking about starting the family I've always wanted—checking off the items on my meticulous five-year plan. I may have gathered that things would be amazing in my relationship, and the four of us, Porter, Lucky and all, would be ready to take on the world, strong-backed by the confidence of our own bliss.

It's true, I wanted the fairy tale. I always have. I wanted a white picket fence. I wanted a wraparound porch with rocking chairs worn by warm bodies and seasonal weather. I wanted a big family a few years after my big, fat, gay wedding. I wanted comfortable simplicity—very comfortable, cushy simplicity.

All of which included me being successful by, at least, thirty. Because unlike my eight-year-old ideals to marry a rich man and become a housewife, being a lesbian meant that I was to assume the responsibility of breadwinning. Well, we both were. But in my attempts at being the provider, I would've always liked, ideally speaking, for the winning bread to come from my basket.

Funny how you find yourself happy despite all those plans broken, all those devices strewn all over the floor, stepped on, forgotten. In fact, shit-grinning happy is where I found myself, surprisingly. These days doing nothing at all amazing, just letting things happen as they do, and not investing time far beyond the moment at hand. Letting life push me in the direction it has denoted, because let's be honest, there's still plenty of time for fairy tales.

I have finally learned to let go of the concept of time that used to chase me into hysteria. A great lesson I've picked up along the way is embracing the love and tranquility in *trust*, and opening your arms up to possibility, as opportunities are available all for the taking, but only when you allow yourself to stretch your arms wide and welcome them in.

As you know, this didn't happen overnight—this *shit-grinning* stuff—this love of self and endearing relationship with life. This was a fight or really more like a beat-down. This brawl went into several rounds, and despite the odds stacked against me, I came out triumphant—well, me and my homegirl, Synchronicity, that is.

I have no idea what the future will hold, but I honestly believe it will land me right where I belong. I can now confidently say that I'm doing my part, finally.

I played the damn lotto—all just by taking my chances.

∞

"Whether you believe you can do a thing or not, you are right." —Henry Ford

ACKNOWLEDGEMENTS

Since this story has been writing itself for as long as I can remember, it would be nearly impossible to thank all the people who by some act of generosity no matter how small have played a pivotal role in giving me the confidence and courage to tell it. Instead, I will focus on those who played particularly important roles over the years, but please know that I am deeply grateful to all those whom I've crossed paths with that made a difference.

First and foremost, I must thank my two Catherines, the two most amazing angels a girl could have ever asked for. I cherish every moment that I was blessed with each of you on this planet, even if I had a funny way of showing it then. You will forever be my guiding light, my biggest heroes, and the true source of all my passion.

To my entire family, especially Ben and Jack, Mary and Paul, Chris and Jeanne, Joe and Jean, and all the extended family that over the years have helped raise me in one way or another. I am forever grateful for all that you've done and continue to do to support me. Thank you, also, for the freedom you've granted me in letting me tell my version of our story.

To my Hawaiian family who took me in and gave me the time and the space to set out on this incredible journey, I love you all dearly: Ben, Lea, Hilton, Gavin, and of course, Michelle and Sheila, Suki—the parrot—and the pups. Also Steph, Denise, Katy Browne, and all my ohana at the Hatch, thank you for all the aloha!

To two incredible besties, Whit and Dana, who opened up their quaint home and allowed me to, despite my best efforts, disrupt its entire flow. I can't say enough for your patience, your generosity, and the duly critical comic relief.

Some big shoutouts go to my extended brothers and sisters: Jennette, Marie, Matt, John, Liz, Eric, Chris, Dillon, and Danielle. I love you all. To the Fields, the Gannons and the Garaytas: Christmas would be so boring without you. To my ladies: Whit, Jess, Brie, and Kate—I'd do it all over again. To Tina and Thad, Anne and Marshall, and Kathy and John, for all the hugs, the sleepovers, and the snacks. To my new family, Mr. and Mrs. Haggarty, and their entire crew, thank you for your amazing support. To all my peeps at the Metropolitan, Federal Hill Fitness and Two Boots, thank you for supporting my dreams.

To all my Kickstarter backers, especially: Catherine Haggarty, Andrea Sommer, Gina Baracelli, Marian Lee, Eric White, David Wilkerson and Marie Thoma, Bruce Dorsey, Kara Ieva, Karen Blood, Tom and Laurie Field, Jim and Margaret Haggarty, Mary and Paul Stea, Jack and Jill Hurley, Ben and Lea Hurley, William Hurley, Cindi A. Small, Tom Patrick, Katherine Nilbrink, Laura Motley, Mark Sullivan, Keith Laysoya, Janet and Matt Napora, Christina Garayta Sommer, Deva Mecredy, Dan and Molly Field, Dan Kosh, and last but not least Libby and Aaron Shadis. I can't thank you enough for your generosity and support. All of this couldn't have happened without you.

To all of the people who appeared in the pages of this book. Thank you for letting me tell my version of our intermingled story. Your early reads and permissions were a true blessing.

To my dear editor, Holly Franko of My Word!, thank you for being the first person in publishing to believe in this book. Your

ACKNOWLEDGEMENTS

kind critique, honest feedback, and sideline cheerleading were exactly what I needed to see *I Think I'll Make It* through to completion. Not to mention, the synchronicity of our meeting; to Anne Connell, I am also very grateful.

And thank you to my other angel, my fiancée, Elisa Haggarty. If it weren't for your unbelievable patience, unending support, and incredible belief in me, even when there was nothin' but a dream, none of this would be possible. You are the most perfect answer to my every prayer, even when you're grouchy. I adore you. Thank you for knowing just how to love me.

Kat Hurley is excited to be back in the U.S. after a year spent perpetually lost in Southeast Asia, where she was amazed to find
enough quiet to write *I think I'll Make It*. Beyond toiling over
words, Kat is incessantly plotting her next endeavor. In 2014, she
will hit the stage to empower youth, tackle that triathlon she's been
talking about for years, and maybe even marry the beautiful woman who has stood by her the whole time. Kat lives in Brooklyn
with her fiancée. She can be spied online at *kathurley.com*,
ithinkillmakeit.com, and her newest project, *gratitudeisthenewsexy*
.com.

22486705R00185

Made in the USA
Charleston, SC
22 September 2013